THE

POWER

OF

EMOTIONS

AT

WORK

Also by Karla McLaren

The Language of Emotions:
What Your Feelings Are Trying to Tell You

Embracing Anxiety:
How to Access the Genius of This Vital Emotion

The Dynamic Emotional Integration® Workbook

The Art of Empathy:
A Complete Guide to Life's Most Essential Skill

Escaping Utopia: Growing Up in a Cult, Getting Out,
and Starting Over (with Janja Lalich)

Karla McLaren, M.Ed.

THE
POWER
OF
EMOTIONS
AT
WORK

Accessing the Vital Intelligence
in Your Workplace

sounds true
BOULDER, COLORADO

Sounds True
Boulder, CO 80306

Published 2021

Cover design by Jennifer Miles
Book design by Linsey Dodaro

 The wood used to produce this book is from Forest Stewardship Council (FSC)
certified forests, recycled materials, or controlled wood.

Printed in the United States of America

BK05950

Library of Congress Cataloging-in-Publication Data

Names: McLaren, Karla, author.
Title: The power of emotions at work : accessing the vital intelligence in
    your workplace / Karla McLaren.
Description: Boulder, CO : Sounds True, 2021. | Includes bibliographical
    references and index.
Identifiers: LCCN 2020050936 (print) | LCCN 2020050937 (ebook) | ISBN
    9781683645443 (paperback) | ISBN 9781683645450 (ebook)
Subjects: LCSH: Emotions in the workplace.
Classification: LCC HF5549.E39 M35 2021 (print) | LCC HF5549.E39 (ebook)
    | DDC 650.101/9--dc23
LC record available at https://lccn.loc.gov/2020050936
LC ebook record available at https://lccn.loc.gov/2020050937

10 9 8 7 6 5 4 3 2 1

CONTENTS

Part 2: Building Your Unique Healthy Workplace

GLOSSARY OF TERMS

This book explores the vital emotional labor and empathic labor that occurs in the workplace every day, yet is usually undervalued, ignored, or even suppressed. To make this labor visible, beneficial, and workable for everyone, I rely upon research concepts and terms I developed to daylight these essential yet unmapped areas of workplace intelligence and behavior.

BANANA TIME: Informal break-time rituals that are developed and led by workers themselves.

DEVIL'S FLOORPLAN: The disastrous open-plan office.

DYNAMIC EMOTIONAL INTEGRATION®: My educational and consulting process that helps people develop emotional skills and awareness, healthy empathy, and emotionally respectful mindfulness practices.

EMOTIONAL DYNAMICS AT WORK®: My workplace consulting process, which focuses on emotions, empathy, communication, and the social and emotional well-being of workplace communities.

EMOTIONAL LABOR: Sociologist Arlie Hochschild's concept of the paid work you do to display or suppress specific emotions and emotional responses in the context of your job.

EMOTIONALLY WELL-REGULATED SOCIAL STRUCTURES: My nine-part model explores vital features and agreements that create healthy, supportive, and workable social environments for people, their emotions, and their relationships.

EMOTION PROFESSIONALS: People whose work depends primarily on the gifts and skills in one or more emotions, such as grief for hospice workers, or focused anxiety for air traffic controllers.

EMOTION WORK: Sociologist Arlie Hochschild's concept of the work you do outside of your paid position to manage your own emotions or the emotions of others to sustain your relationships and the smooth flow of everyday life.

EMPATHIC DESIGN: A design process that focuses on end users' needs and emotions, and employs multiple tryouts and redesigns until the end product meets those needs.

EMPATHY: A social and emotional skill that helps you feel and understand the emotions, circumstances, intentions, thoughts, and needs of others, such that you can offer sensitive, perceptive, and appropriate communication and support.

EMPATHY WORK: My conceptualization of an extensive and multilayered form of emotion work that involves an understanding of emotions, empathy, relationships, social structures, and large-group social skills.

FIKA: The Swedish tradition of friendly and relaxing coffee (or tea) breaks that involve sweets and socialization (or sweets and private time).

GOSSIP NETWORKS: In contrast to formal information networks that exist to support the formal power structure, these are essential informal networks that contain extensive social, emotional, and empathic information about the complex inner workings of a workplace or a group. We work to make these networks ethical, supportive, and empathic.

KEYSTONES: Workers who perform (usually unpaid) emotion work or empathy work to fill in the social and emotional gaps in an emotionally unregulated workplace. I focus on four types of Keystones, but of course, these are not the only ones:

- **Agitators:** Workers who act out unwelcome emotions in an emotionally repressive or empathically unskilled workplace community.
- **Ambassadors:** Workers who take on the (usually unpaid) task of welcoming and training new people in a workplace where there are no effective onboarding processes.
- **Connectors:** Workers who develop and maintain relationships throughout the entire workplace structure. Connectors are especially valuable in large bureaucracies, workplaces that have expanded quickly, or workplaces that are fragmented by artificial or hierarchical divisions between people.
- **Peacemakers:** Workers who do emotion work and empathy work to smooth out troubled relationships between disconnected or conflicting departments and/or individuals.

LARGE-GROUP SOCIAL SKILLS: Our ability to understand, navigate, relate, and work successfully within large and interconnected groups such as extended families, schools, committees, workplaces, and organizations.

OSHA: The Occupational Safety and Health Administration in the US, which was founded in 1971 to protect workers (and whistleblowers) from unsafe or hazardous working conditions. However, OSHA does not protect self-employed or contract workers, which is a big concern for gig workers (for example, more than 4 million contractors in the US drive and work without workplace safety protections for immensely wealthy companies such as Uber, Lyft, Instacart, and DoorDash).

REPAIR STATIONS: Sociologist Erving Goffman's concept of protected backstage areas where people can be real and honest about what they're facing, or where they can rest and get away from the frontstage demands of their lives or their jobs. Repair stations in the workplace can be physical spaces such as break rooms or smoking balconies, or they can be social spaces such as intentional communication practices or trusting relationships.

SELF-DETERMINATION THEORY: This theory by Edward Deci and Richard Ryan focuses on motivation, human development, and well-being, and identifies three requirements for healthy and lasting internal motivation:

- **Competence:** The ability to interact skillfully and effectively in your environment.
- **Autonomy:** The ability to make choices, regulate yourself, and make decisions about your own life.
- **Relatedness:** The presence of healthy relationships and a sense of closeness, belonging, and love.

THEORY X: Management professor Douglas McGregor's two-part model of worker motivation. Theory X views people as unwilling workers who have to be coerced or ordered to work via rewards and punishments; their motivation has to come from the outside or they won't perform. Contrasted with Theory Y, below.

THEORY Y: In McGregor's model of worker motivation, Theory Y views people as willing workers whose motivation is natural and internal, and who require trust and a healthy social atmosphere in order to do their best work. McGregor proposed that Theory Y was a more humane, logical, and profitable way to treat workers and to run businesses than Theory X.

TOXIC POSITIVITY BIAS: A dangerously mistaken belief that the allegedly positive emotions are the only emotions that should be felt or shared in the workplace. This bias causes extensive suffering as people suppress all forbidden emotions, lose their emotional awareness and skills, and become unable to address serious problems that *require* the gifts, skills, and genius in the forbidden emotions.

UNINTENTIONAL COMMUNITY: A group of people who are thrown together haphazardly without dependable communication processes, emotional skills, empathy skills, or clear models for relationships or conflict. Sadly, most workplaces are unintentional communities.

WORKERS OF THE WORLD (WoW): Members of my Dynamic Emotional Integration licensee community who gathered together to offer support and ideas during the writing of this book.

PREFACE

I was so excited to write this book about the vital intelligence of emotions: how they help us do our best work, how they help us understand ourselves and others, and how (if we learn how to harness their power and genius) they can contribute to the health and success of every workplace. Certainly, I was aware of the many serious troubles in the workplace, but I was so happy to have the freedom to share my vision of a healthy new workplace and explore the ideas I've gathered in the many decades I've spent studying and consulting in the workplace. I was in a type of utopian mindset as I began to write this book, but then the Covid-19 pandemic began — and the extensive troubles in the workplace became all too clear to everyone.

Disasters will do that; they'll uncover what's true about relationships, families, groups, workplaces, governments, nature, and the world. Though they're shocking and painful, disasters can tell us what's true. If we pay attention, we can rebuild after disasters with a new awareness of our problems and a new dedication to recovery and healing, to the protection of nature and all living things, and to the soul of the world.

So, I've paid attention, and I'm still paying attention. In this troubled winter of 2020, I'm writing about the workplace as so many workplaces and schools have been shut down and many of us have been sent home. Here in the US, where Covid-19 continues to spread and take a devastating toll, we don't yet have a clear idea about when indoor gatherings will be safe again; we may be working (and schooling) from home for a while to come. As an author and developer of online courses, I already work mostly from my home office, so the transition to working at home has not been too difficult for me. But for the people who have been sent home to work remotely, or those who were sent home because there *is* no work, the move away from the physical workplace has been a blessing, a curse, and everything in between. As we go about work, we're all learning about closeness and safety, about what's important, and about how to live, work, and survive in a pandemic.

I've been thinking back to another pandemic: the 1918 flu pandemic that eventually infected more than 500 million people worldwide (50 million souls were lost).[1] That pandemic showed us where our healthcare approaches and defenses were least effective; we saw the holes in the system. After that worldwide catastrophe, we understood more about disease transmission, public health, infection control, and our healthcare systems. We learned so much from that excruciating public health disaster, yet much of that knowledge was not available to the public when Covid-19 first appeared. We all needed to relearn, quickly, how to live and function in the presence of a highly infectious disease. We're still learning.

I've also been thinking back to the workplace conditions people faced in 1918. This was before the Great Depression in the US, and we had basically no workplace protections: no minimum wage, no worker's rights, no retirement benefits for most workers, no unemployment benefits, no social security, no job security, no protections for child workers, and no Occupational Safety and Health Administration (OSHA). The US workplace was an unprotected environment that could be dangerous or even fatal.

OSHA

The Occupational Safety and Health Administration in the US, which was founded in 1971 to protect workers (and whistleblowers) from unsafe or hazardous working conditions. However, OSHA does not protect self-employed or contract workers, which is a big concern for gig workers (for example, more than 4 million contractors in the US drive and work without workplace safety protections for immensely wealthy companies such as Uber, Lyft, Instacart, and DoorDash).

For instance, just 7 years earlier in New York City, the horrific 1911 Triangle Shirtwaist Factory fire killed 146 garment workers (and injured another 78), because the factory's owners regularly locked their workers inside the building to prevent theft and unauthorized break time.[2] The fire started in a pile of discarded fabric on the factory floor and might have been extinguished quickly, but the building had no fire extinguishers, no sprinkler system, no alarms, and no way for workers to exit the building quickly. It was and still is the deadliest single occupational disaster in US history.

But New Yorkers and people across the world learned from that catastrophe; fire safety and workplace safety were suddenly taken very seriously indeed. Investigations and regulatory committees sprung up to address the glaring dangers that many other factory workers faced, and the Triangle disaster helped to solidify the rise of workplace safety measures and the International Ladies' Garment Workers' Union (among other workers' groups). We learned from that tragedy, and much of that learning can still be seen in our workplace safety practices today.

The Covid-19 pandemic is also having a kind of Triangle factory effect, in that the many workplace problems we're now seeing so clearly — for remote workers, gig workers, and the people we now call "essential workers" — are showing us where long-standing and workplace-wide problems have been smoldering.

For many remote workers, comfort and freedom have been startling new additions to their workdays, and many are now realizing how unnecessary most workplace rules and meetings have been. Comfort and freedom are improving people's work output and mental health in most cases (however, loneliness is a big issue), and many meetings, we're all learning, could have been done by email (though too many emails are a big issue now too). For many people without work, even with the anxieties and dangers unemployment brings, there is also a sense of having their lives and their time back. No one is flourishing, really; we're all dealing with loss, upheaval, anxiety, and uncertainty, but many of us have the time now to be able to consider the meaning and value of our work in our lives.

Our essential workers (such as medical workers, home health aides, public transit workers, grocery and retail workers, agricultural workers, etc.) have learned a different lesson, however. As they've been working outside the relative safety of their homes, many have realized with a shock of betrayal and despair how little their employers actually care for them.

Here in California, which instituted shelter-in-place in mid-March while our federal government tripped over itself, I watched as the people at my local grocery stores worked without gloves, hand sanitizer, or masks, and without appropriate distancing regulations at their checkout counters. They were exposed to sometimes hundreds of customers and suppliers each day, some masked, some not, but their employers didn't provide them with any protections at all. A few weeks in, I saw workers wearing many different types of masks at our local big-chain grocery store, which suggested that the chain itself (a multibillion-dollar corporation) hadn't supplied anything, and that some of the workers were beginning to protect themselves if they could.

Finally, the grocery and drug stores in our area got serious and installed plexiglass shields at the checkout counters, marked 6-foot distancing measures on the floor, and began limiting the number of customers who could be in the store at any given time. Workers started wearing masks and gloves, hand sanitizer became available, carts were being sanitized between customers, and worker health and safety started to be taken seriously. But it was too late for many workers who had already contracted Covid-19 because they had been forced to work in public during a pandemic in unsafe conditions without any protection at all, for weeks on end.

It's the same for essential workers of all kinds: Unprotected transit drivers all over the country (and the world) have also contracted this virus. Workers in agriculture and food processing plants (many of whom are Hispanic/Latinx[3], Asian, and African American) have been particularly hard-hit, but were forced to go back to work anyway. In our local police force here in Sonoma County, eight officers contracted Covid-19 in March 2020, and one young detective died. These essential workers weren't protected by their workplaces in the early days of the pandemic; many still aren't being protected now.

But it's not as if any of us knew how to do this; we didn't remember the lessons of the 1918 pandemic. Grocery stores and transit systems didn't have pandemic-protection plans in their workplace manuals (hopefully, they do now); no one knew we'd have to shut down parks and beaches because people kept turning them into dangerously crowded mosh pits; and for goodness sake, most of us didn't even know how to wash our hands properly (hopefully, we do now). We've learned our lessons the hard way, and when the next pandemic hits (which is likely, due to the many ways that global climate change has destabilized our environment), we'll have some skills and ideas ready — individually, as a community, in our workplaces, and across the world.

However, there's one workplace that should have protected their workers immediately but didn't: the healthcare workplace. Though the healthcare industry is a leader in infection control, many essential healthcare workers were placed in dangerous situations without protective equipment early on — *not* because there weren't enough masks and gloves at the time, but because many hospitals and medical centers were bizarrely trying to downplay the pandemic or control costs on the backs of their workers. Nurses and doctors across the country were threatened or suspended for asking for masks or for wearing them.[4] Many medical professionals contracted Covid-19, and too many died; they're still dying.

In-home support services (IHSS) workers, who care for people on disability here in my county, were classified as essential workers, but only in late March did they receive 5 masks, 20 pairs of gloves, and a ziplock bag of 10 disinfectant wipes. They received nothing else until late May, and nothing else after that.[5] This low-wage work is done primarily by women and requires lots of travel (often by public transit) and close contact with multiple vulnerable clients in homes where social distancing isn't possible. But it wasn't until our service workers' union got involved that my county thought to offer IHSS workers any protective gear at all. IHSS workers in other counties didn't even receive that much, if anything.[6]

Usually, low-wage workers are the worst treated and the least protected in any occupation, but high-wage earners in the healthcare industry weren't protected either. Some of the doctors and nurses who were threatened or suspended for taking precautions or wearing (or even asking for) protective gear had multiple graduate degrees and were paid $50 or more per hour — yet they were just as unprotected as the $12 per hour IHSS workers who provide close physical care in the homes of ill, disabled, and elderly people. Healthcare is a deeply troubled and troubling field, and this pandemic is exposing many of the everyday worker abuses that plague our healthcare system.

On the other end of the spectrum, some business owners reduced or refused their own salaries so that they could continue to pay their workers during the pandemic, and many business owners figured out ways to protect their workers even before any standards were in place. We've seen the best and the worst of the workplace at the same time, and we're all learning so much about what's important, who and what is essential, and how our workplaces treat and define us.

Do Our Workplaces Value Us?

This disaster has opened our eyes and led us to ask the hard questions: Are we cared for as workers? Or are we replaceable cogs in an uncaring machine? Is our health and safety considered essential? Or do our employers have to be forced and publicly shamed into treating us with even a minimum of respect? Does our workplace deserve our time and dedication? Or have we been throwing good effort into bad businesses for no reason? And does our government care about any of it?

In this upside-down time, many previously hidden aspects of our daily lives have become visible, and we're now able to see ourselves, our families, our communities, our environment, our governments, and our workplaces with new eyes. We've become aware of the unequal toll that this disease is wreaking in the Indigenous, Hispanic/Latinx, African American, elder, disabled, institutionalized, and impoverished communities here in the US, and how Asian people are being blamed or attacked because of racist remarks about China by our government.[7] In late May 2020, the horrifying murder of George Floyd and the equally horrifying murders of Ahmaud Arbery and Breonna Taylor (and too many others) brought the undeniable facts of White supremacy and unchecked police brutality out into the open. In response, protesters all over the world gathered in public spaces, even though the pandemic and police brutality were rampant, to grieve, mourn, rage, and demand revolutionary changes to a deeply abusive and broken system. Though voter suppression, especially for African American and Hispanic/Latinx voters, is a continual form of corruption in the US, I and many others worked to ensure that voters were registered and could make their voices heard in the crucial 2020 election.

As many states and counties here in the US close down after reopening haphazardly, we're seeing how low-wage and essential workers are being endangered by customers who don't respect safety regulations because they confuse self-absorbed recklessness with freedom. In August, a push to open schools treated the health and safety of teachers and students as less important than getting back to "normal," whatever that is. We're seeing the ruthlessness that lives inside the modern workplace, in capitalism, and in our world economies; this pandemic is daylighting what was swept under the rug before. My hope is that we who are fortunate enough to survive this pandemic, physically and financially, can look at what had been hidden with clear eyes, and rebuild our world to be more just, more empathic, more functional, and more equitable for everyone.

I'm hoping that we can learn from this disaster, and that we can come together to confront and change the inequalities, injustices, structural problems, and abuses that have been uncovered by this pandemic. We're *all* essential workers and essential citizens because — as we've seen so clearly — the workplace, our economy, and our society cannot survive without us. We all deserve to be treated as valued equals, and we all deserve to work in safe, humane, and respectful workplaces in a just and healthy world.

This book is my contribution toward building a new and better world where responsible, safe, supportive, inclusive, emotionally healthy, and equality-based workplaces are available to everyone.

The Great Migration

What does an emotionally healthy and functional workplace look like, and how does it work? What do humans need to feel safe and respected in the workplace, to develop and maintain their motivation, and to be able to do their work (and work together) effectively? How can emotions contribute their vital intelligence to our workplaces, and how can we create a place for healthy empathy? And most importantly, how can the workplace support all of these crucial aspects when so many workplaces hinder or even erase them?

These questions are vital in this time of upheaval and disaster (and in any time, really), because even if we're working from home, we *live* at work. If we work full time, we may spend more time at work (and getting to and from work) than we do in any other area of our lives, except sleeping. Most of us spend more time at work than we spend with our families or our mates! Our work relationships and work environments take up the lion's share of our time, our energy, and our lives, but sadly, the workplace as an entity hasn't realized this yet. The world of the workplace hasn't learned how to create or maintain a healthy social and emotional environment for us.

In this book, we'll focus on ways to create and sustain workplaces that support human emotions, human beings, and human groups. However, just as New Yorkers had to study the many problems that led to the Triangle fire of 1911 (so that they could prevent future catastrophes), we need to study the many problems that led to the dysfunctional workplaces that most of us are enduring today. There's so much social and emotional trouble in the modern workplace, and while many of us knew this before the pandemic started, it's now obvious to everyone. However, nothing we've been doing or are doing is alleviating it much.

We've got workplace fix-it books and employee engagement processes in the thousands, management training programs and workplace consultants and coaches everywhere you look, and endless corporate mindfulness and emotional skills trainings — yet the workplace as a whole continues to be a troubled and uncomfortable place that most of us want to get away from. Workers, managers, consultants, and executives know about these troubles, our emotions know about them, comedians and endless television shows and movies show us these troubles, but the workplace as an entity is still mostly ignorant about how to create a healthy social and emotional environment for human beings. And the research tells a story of wide-scale suffering caused by the social and emotional ignorance that has been allowed to exist in the workplace.

I'm going to share some research here that may shock you (or not), because it clearly shows that the workplace is a social and emotional disaster area; it's a five-alarm fire. This research, which I've gathered across countries and across time, doesn't point to problems with individual types of workers or industries; it points to widespread and fundamental problems at the very center of our workplace model. Or perhaps I should say at the *foundation* of our workplace model, because these problems stem from a terrible decision that segregated us from ourselves and undermined our workplaces: We fooled ourselves into believing that emotions had no value at work.

We wrongly thought of emotional skills as "soft skills" and kicked the emotions out of our factories, our offices, our workplaces, our boardrooms, and our working lives (or we *thought* we did) — and in so doing, we created an inhumane and emotionally unlivable environment that doesn't truly work for anyone.

For instance, most of us are trying to find better jobs, even when we're already employed. A 2017 research study of 17,000 workers in 19 US occupations discovered that the vast majority of employed people (71% of them) were looking for other jobs because their workplace social and emotional environment was uncomfortable or even abusive.

In that study, 81% of workers reported that job stress was negatively affecting their home lives; more than 8 out of 10 workers were struggling at home because of social and emotional trouble at work. Another 63% of workers preferred to work alone due to hostile or unproductive work relationships; they were isolating themselves and essentially checking out because their social and emotional environment was so poorly managed. And fully 79% of workers were distracted by emotional turmoil in the workplace and had a hard time focusing on their work because of it.[1]

In each of these examples, emotions are *clearly* active in the workplace, but because the workplace as a whole does not value emotional understanding or emotional skills, most workers are miserable (and miserably unprotected).

In another US study on employee silence from 2003, 85% of upper-level workers reported that they avoided sharing crucial workplace problems with their managers because they didn't trust what would happen if they did.[2] Many had already learned the hard way that they would be punished, branded as troublemakers or whiners, or that nothing would be done about the problems they identified. Workplace abuse and bullying is also a daily reality for nearly 30% of US workers, and I've included supportive resources on page 249 if you're dealing with abuse at work.[3] (As a human resources [HR] administrator, I want you to know that there are laws against being forced to work in a hostile environment. US workers should contact their local labor board or labor commissioner if their manager or HR department will not protect them from bullying or abuse.)

Worldwide, the situation tends to be worse, though there are a few wealthy or socialist countries (such as Scandinavia) that provide better work environments (at least in mid-wage to high-wage jobs) than the US does. But even accounting for these few bright spots, over 85% of people worldwide are working in emotionally unhealthy and/or demoralizing workplaces, and only 32% of workers throughout the world say that they have good jobs.[4]

If you remember the way grades work in school, you'll likely recall that missing 50% of the questions on a test or doing only half of an assignment would earn you a failing grade of an F. Studies of the workplace continually show that on all measures of employee engagement, employee voice, mental health, and emotional health, the workplace as a whole is not even achieving a failing 50% performance level. The workplace would have to work very hard to raise its grade to a pathetic and unacceptable F.

If you're a worker, these astonishingly bad percentages may not surprise you, because we've all had (or have) to deal with the 63% to 85% of workplaces that are socially and emotionally miserable places to be. But if you're a manager or business owner, these numbers may shock you because you can clearly see productivity, stability, and profits draining away. Some research suggests that miserable workplaces drain hundreds of *billions* of dollars from the US economy alone, every single year.[5]

Whether you're a worker, a manager, or a business owner, you may be concerned about whether the workplace itself — as it's set up now — is sustainable at all. I share this concern, because this workplace-wide situation is unprofitable and unacceptable. This book is my contribution to workers, managers, and business owners everywhere who have always deserved better than the workplace has given us.

My Intentions for This Book

Throughout this book, I'll focus on what we can do — emotionally, socially, and communally — to build a workplace model that actually *works*. However, this book isn't just for troubled workplaces; it's also for the 15% to 37% of workplaces that are livable and healthy already, because people in healthy workplaces are usually open to new ideas and more effective ways of doing things.

This book won't contain endless lists of percentages, but I did choose the studies I refer to in this book with care; they don't focus on "checked out" or disengaged employees and how to make them behave. These studies are more serious than that, and they don't blame the victims of miserable workplaces for their normal human responses to misery. The studies I chose focus on our collective mental and emotional health and the damage that unhealthy workplaces inflict on all of us.

The widespread failures of the workplace can't be fixed by focusing on workers alone, or by instituting employee engagement parties, individual coaching, mindfulness trainings, emotion-management trainings, ping-pong tables in the break room, open-plan offices, a kicky new vision statement, or gluten-free snack wagons. These failures are a direct result of kicking the emotions out of the workplace (though, as we all know, they never, ever left) and the only solution is to welcome them back consciously, intentionally, and skillfully.

Most of us have been fed the absurd idea that the workplace is a rare setting where emotions are unwelcome, illogical, unprofitable, or even unprofessional. We've also been taught that people can and should be treated as emotionless cogs in a machine, as numbers in a spreadsheet, or as consumers and cheerleaders of corporate vision statements. And tragically, many managers have been taught to interfere with workers' emotions (and their rights to privacy and dignity) by putting them through coaching or counseling instead of listening closely to what their emotional responses are saying about their workplace environment. We haven't been taught how to make the workplace a healthy social and emotional environment where each of us can do our best work in an atmosphere of respect, professionalism, kindness, laughter, and community.

You and I — we *are* the workplace, and most of us essentially live at work. But because our emotions have been banished or treated disrespectfully, the workplace as an entity has become an unlivable environment for human beings, with almost no concept of what humans need or how to create healthy social and emotional social structures. The workplace as an entity has failed us emotionally, socially, financially, and in every other way — but it never needed to fail, and it doesn't need to continue failing now.

This may sound utopian, but in reality, there's no profit in the way we've set up our workplaces. We can overturn this disastrously failed model and make the workplace a worthwhile place for us to spend our time and our lives.[6] As I noted, 15% to 37% of workplaces have already figured out ways to create healthy and livable environments. It's not impossible or even difficult; it's just unusual in the tragically emotion-avoidant world of the workplace.

Removing emotions from the workplace (or blaming individuals for their natural emotional responses to unhealthy workplaces) was a wildly irrational idea that never worked anyway. Emotions are everywhere in the workplace — they never left because they cannot leave — they're essential to every aspect of thinking, acting, and working. Emotions are inseparable from human beings and human groups. As such, the work we'll do in this book won't involve some sort of heavy emotional lifting, where we force-fully push emotions back into the workplace. Instead, we'll learn how to identify and support the emotions that are already there — in you, in your colleagues, and in your workplace community.

This approach will require learning some new concepts, but it's actually much easier and more effective than what we're doing now, considering the widespread misery and failure the workplace has created for all of us. Welcoming emotions back into the workplace means welcoming our full humanity back, and that's exactly where we want to start.

Emotions Are Vital Aspects of Thinking, Acting, and Working

People once believed that emotions were the opposite of rationality, or that they were lower than or inferior to our allegedly logical processes. But decades of research on emotions and the brain have overturned those outdated beliefs, and we understand now that emotions are indispensable parts of rationality, logic, and consciousness itself. In fact, emotions contain their own internal logic, and they help us orient ourselves successfully within our social environments. Emotions help us attach meaning to data, they help us understand ourselves and others, and they help us identify problems and opportunities. Emotions don't get in the way of rationality; they *lead* the way, because they're vital to everything we think and everything we do. Emotions aren't the problem; they're *pointing* to the problem, and they're trying to bring us the precise intelligence and energy we need to deal with the problem.

In this book, we'll learn how to listen to emotions (yours and everyone else's) as uniquely intelligent carriers of information, and how to build healthy and well-regulated social and emotional environments at work — not by ignoring or silencing emotions (you can't), but by listening to them closely, learning their language, and creating a communal set of social and emotional skills that everyone can rely on. This work is not difficult at all, but it's unusual in an environment that wrongly treats emotions as soft, irrational, or unprofessional — and wrongly blames individuals for their normal and necessary responses to profoundly unhealthy workplace environments.

The serious problems we've baked into the workplace don't come from any specific management style or ideology, so I won't focus on managers or leaders as if they're uniquely powerful or uniquely to blame. These problems also aren't limited to specific occupations or income brackets (though low-wage work is often dehumanizing and hazardous); these are long-term, widespread problems based on a failed workplace model and an outdated social and emotional approach that does not support (or in many cases, even comprehend) human behavior, human relationships, and human needs.

This book is the result of decades of exploration and study into how the workplace got to be so unworkable, plus decades of experience in how to access the existing genius in people's emotional responses (in surprisingly simple ways, once you understand how emotions and empathy work). With the help of the power in our emotions, we can create emotionally well-regulated and worthwhile places for all of us to earn our living and spend our lives.

In my work, I help people learn how to work *empathically* with emotions. By that, I mean listening to emotions, working directly with them, and understanding their purpose so that we can access their astonishing intelligence. Many people see empathy as only a person-to-person activity where we feel for and with other people, but I view empathy in a larger context than that. I also see empathy as our capacity to feel for and with everything alive (people, animals, nature) — and also with everything conceptual (ideas, emotions, the arts, the sciences, and everything else). I see empathy as our capacity to engage and relate — not just to people, but to anything. Accordingly, my work relies upon our innate empathic capacity to relate directly with the genius and power inside emotions.

EMPATHY

A social and emotional skill that helps you feel and understand the emotions, circumstances, intentions, thoughts, and needs of others, such that you can offer sensitive, perceptive, and appropriate communication and support.

Emotions are crucial to everything we do and to every aspect of our work; therefore, we'll learn how to listen to emotions, work with them empathically, and respect their intelligence. And in so doing, we'll build a better workplace — and a better world — from the ground up.

Dreaming of Work and Loving Business

This may sound weird, but I love work and I love thinking about, creating, and running businesses. I dream of new businesses in the way some people dream of vacations. I love to imagine designing the physical space and the workflows, developing environmentally sound manufacturing and distribution plans, creating unique and interesting jobs for people I respect (and treat well), and designing logos, websites, marketing plans, and ad copy — all in my head. It's fun!

In the real world, I currently run four interconnected businesses and employ people throughout the US, Canada, Europe, and India.[7] I offer business consulting for individuals and companies, I'm certified as a Human Resources Administrator and a Career Development Facilitator, and I've been working continuously since I was 11 years old, when my father hired me as an administrative assistant for his home office (he was a traveling insurance adjuster).

You might think that starting my work life at home, with a boss who cared about my welfare and trusted my intelligence and abilities, would have set me up beautifully for the working world. But in fact, it made me an outsider who continually wondered: Why are most workplaces so inefficient? Why are people being stopped from doing their best work? Why do training programs treat workers like backward children? Why don't people trust each other? Why are ridiculous rules and wasteful workflows being allowed and even supported? Why are slackers being protected and rewarded? Why does this person know so much more than their boss? Why does that person get to break the rules? Why doesn't anyone see that this person is always picking up the slack? Why won't anyone speak directly about obvious problems? Why doesn't everyone go to HR with their issues — or why is the HR department so ineffectual? Why is the workplace so noisy, uncomfortable, miserable, dirty, and/or ugly? And so on, into infinity.

I prefer to run my own businesses because I don't have time for the waste, unnecessary conflict, and demoralizing nonsense that so many workplaces generate and tolerate.[8] And for the longest time, I thought that maybe it was just me — maybe I was seeing unusually dysfunctional workplaces because I only worked in specific occupations, or because I had unnecessarily high standards or something. I thought I was a strange outlier, until I began consulting in workplaces. I hadn't intended to become a workplace consultant, but as my Dynamic Emotional Integration work became better known, people would ask me to consult them about emotional and empathic issues in their workplaces.

I was pretty shocked by the social and emotional turmoil and burnout I saw, even in good companies with well-meaning managers, so I knew that I needed more information. I went back to school and majored in the sociology of work and occupations in order to understand the history of the workplace and became certified as a Career Development Facilitator in order to help people find work that was best suited to them.

But I still had questions about why the modern workplace was so emotionally and socially harmful, so I focused my attention on the HR department, which is where people go for help when their workplace environment is troubled or abusive, right? I thought so, but whenever I suggested that troubled workers or managers go to their HR department, they told me that HR was no help at all. Why?

I needed to know more about the failures of HR, so I became certified as an HR administrator. I hoped to learn how to bring social and emotional support to the workplace, but that wasn't what my HR education was about. I thought

I'd find the solution workers needed, but what I found was the *problem*: HR departments aren't built for workers, they're built for organizations.

In my 2-year HR certificate program, I didn't learn about the social and emotional care of individuals or groups. There was only one beginner's course in psychology, no training about emotions, and no training about how social groups form or manage themselves. HR administration students at the bachelor's or master's level may receive that training, but most of my training was in the paralegal work that HR departments do: hiring and firing, benefits administration, labor law, workplace safety and protection from abuse, payroll, and sick leave or family leave administration. These are all vital tasks, but they don't focus on the social or emotional condition of the workplace.

Most HR professionals are in the paralegal and administrative role of overseeing the organization as a whole; their focus is not on individual workers, so they often have a conflict of interest. For instance, if an owner or manager (or high-performing department) is abusive toward workers, some HR departments will protect the people in power. This is deeply troubling, because in most workplaces, the only people who are available to help workers deal with everyday social and emotional difficulties in the workplace are HR professionals who may not be trained or (in many cases) fully available to do that work. In addition, the workplace itself is not an emotionally healthy or emotionally aware entity, so even if HR administrators were willing and able to support workers, they might have a difficult time doing so.

I'm glad that I got my HR education and certification, because even though it was a failure in one sense, it helped me deepen my understanding of workplace-wide troubles. In research on workplace mental health, employee attrition, absenteeism, stress, and conflict, many people reported that the HR department was the *last* place they would go with their workplace difficulties.[9] Most workers don't feel safe reporting to someone within the organization, and in many cases, the HR department is so focused on administrative work that there's no time to help workers deal with social and emotional issues. And in some organizations, the HR department is disempowered; even if they were trained to help, they aren't able to do so, and as a result, workplace social and emotional health suffers. This is why I focus on helping workplace communities develop healthy social structures for everyone; the HR department cannot be held responsible for the mental health of the entire community, and it's not fair to ask them to be. Each person in a workplace community needs to be involved in building and sustaining a healthy working and living environment, and this book is full of tools and models to help each of us do that.

This work is crucial, because research on workplace mental health goes even further than what I (and probably you) suspected: The workplace is failing us overwhelmingly. It's affecting our individual and collective health in deeply detrimental ways, and some studies suggest that unhealthy workplaces are causing the unnecessary deaths of more than 120,000 workers *per year* in the US alone — not due to construction accidents, fires, or workplace disasters, but due to workplace-created emotional stressors that affect our peace, our home lives, our sleep, and our mental health.[10] And though this information is alarming, my hope is that it will help you realize that no, you're not unusual in finding most workplaces pretty awful. Your impressions and the numbers agree: Most workplaces *are* pretty awful.

But they absolutely do not have to be.

I have jokingly called my workplace consultation process "emotional OSHA," which refers to the Occupational Safety and Health Administration here in the US. OSHA regulates hazardous workplace activities (such as using toxic solvents, running heavy machinery, and other dangerous tasks) so that workers don't get injured. But as we've all experienced, poorly regulated emotional environments can be just as hazardous to workers and organizations as poorly regulated physical environments are, if not more so. The widespread misery that has been allowed to exist in the workplace has led to a tragic loss of motivation, peace, mental health, job security, organizational profitability, and even people's very lives. Considering all of that, we could say that my concept of emotional OSHA isn't a joke at all.

It will take work, but we *can* bring emotional safety and health to the workplace; in fact, we must. The endangering conditions of the workplace are not natural phenomena; we humans created this failed workplace model, and we support it with our presence and our consent — even if we don't mean to. Business magazines and business gurus support this failed workplace model when they artificially separate emotions from logic, and business and managerial programs at universities all over the world support this same foundational error. Workplace consultants and workplace "fix it" books in the thousands support it when they don't challenge this glaring emotional error. Workplace mindfulness and emotional intelligence trainings support it by assuming that emotional responses need to be calmed down or managed individually rather than treated as the priceless information they are. Employee assistance programs, even though they're supposed to help, often support it by treating emotions as private problems instead of clear signals about the social environment. Human resources professionals and career development counselors support it. Reality TV shows about businesses, restaurants, art, music, modeling, and fashion not only support it, but with their focus on cutthroat or emotionally violent competition where there is only one winner, they make the workplace model more toxic and soul-killing than anything needs to be.

We're supporting a failed model that endangers all of us (not to mention our businesses), but it's important to know that a model is not a living thing. It has no life or power, except what we give to it. This absurdly failed model hasn't earned our time, our energy, or our presence — and it owes us mountains of cash for all of the damage it has done and is doing to each one of us. Our emotionally incompetent workplace model is a worldwide failure that needs to be overturned. We all deserve better, and so do our businesses.

Building a Healthy Workplace with the Help of Emotions

So, how do we move from this tragically failed model — which is all that many of us have ever known — to one that respects and supports us, and helps us do our best work in a healthy, emotionally well-regulated, and functional environment?

The answer lives in our workplace communities and in our emotional responses to the workplace as it is. The answer is in our workplaces already. It's staring us right in the face. And luckily, we don't have to do anything special to welcome emotions into the workplace (or even to make room for them), because emotions are and always have been in the workplace.

They're in the responses people have to workplace abuses and injustice; they're in disengaged workers; they're in the 71% of workers seeking other jobs while on the job; they're in the 85% of workers who rightly avoid communicating upward about serious problems; they're in low-wage workers who learn how to survive in hellscapes like call centers, fast-food restaurants, gig work, and robot-like warehouse jobs; they're in living-wage workers who tolerate unhealthy workplaces because they can't afford to leave their health insurance behind; and they're in high-wage workers who may have to bow down to their superiors, exploit and monetize their own passion, and compete with their colleagues to be seen as winners (and whose experiences of workplace abuse may not be taken seriously because they make so much money and therefore have no right to complain).

We can also see the emotions in our responses to workplace successes; in our healthy working relationships; in the ways we gather together to solve problems; in the ways empathic workers and leaders empower everyone around them; in the ways our colleagues support us when we're struggling; in the ways businesses step up in times of loss; in the ways we create open communication and humane workflows; in the ways we teach each other; in the benefits, support, flexibility, and living wages we provide for our workers; in our honesty and transparency about business difficulties or financial losses; and in the laughter we share on great days and rotten days.

Emotions are everywhere in the workplace because emotions are a central feature of human nature. They aren't removable, and in fact, trying to remove them is a huge part of what created the failed workplace model we have today.

All of the things we need to create healthy, efficient, and worthwhile workplaces are there already, and though our current workplace model is inhumane, most of us were never fooled by it, and our emotions certainly weren't fooled by it either. They've been reacting and responding appropriately to the trouble all along. The keys and the tools we need to rebuild our workplace model are already there.

Emotions aren't the problem and they never were the problem; emotions *point to* the problem. Our emotions help us understand the world, respond to the situations we find ourselves in, and figure out how best to respond. Our job is not to suppress emotions, manage them, blame individuals for having them, distract ourselves from them, throw techniques or meditation practices on top of them, or spew them all over the place. Our job is to learn to listen to emotions, respect them, work directly with them, and access their irreplaceable information so that we can build healthy social structures that work — whether we're working from home, in a business with three workers, or in an organization with thousands of workers. We all deserve to work in healthy social and emotional environments, and we're all a vital part of building and sustaining them.

So, let's do that; let's get to work.

But Let's Break Some Rules First

Before we start, I want you to know that this book breaks some rules (okay, a lot of rules). Talking about the genius and power inside emotions (instead of teaching people to merely tolerate or manage them) is the first rule I'm breaking, but it's not the only one. Most business books are written for executives, managers, and leaders who have the power to make (or enforce) changes in the workplace. In this book, I'm addressing *everyone* who works — workers, managers, part-timers, self-employed people, business owners, outside consultants, human resources professionals, executives, board members, and investors — and while I suggest ways to improve the social and emotional atmosphere in organizations, I know that not everyone who reads this book will have the authority to make these improvements.

But even if you do have that authority, *you shouldn't use it*! Nearly all workplace cultural change initiatives come from owners, executives, managers, or outside consultants, which means that workers themselves usually have little to no (formal) say about what happens to them. These enforced changes reliably create conflict and trouble or require large amounts of maintenance. My argument is that the only respectful way to make social and emotional changes in a workplace (or in any social group) is to involve everyone and to give them the information, autonomy, choice, and support they need to implement those changes themselves — *if* those changes make sense to them. Workers *must* have choices about what happens to them; they're not puppets or cogs in a machine, and their relationships and culture belong to them. Change that's enforced upon people's social and emotional culture is disruptive, certainly, but it can also speak to an unequal power dynamic and a lack of trust, empathy, or respect for the value and genius that lives in the cultures that workers have already built.

Culture is not a machine that you can weld new gadgets onto, and it's not a computer you can reboot; culture is the living, breathing heart of a community and it requires respect and care. The heart of a community beats with the emotional and empathic lifeblood of each person in it; it's not something to fool around with, and it's not something that can or should change quickly. Management and organizational expert Edgar Schein, who's known as the founder of the study of corporate culture, says that true cultural change in an organization may take 5 to 15 years if it's done correctly.[11] But it's rarely done correctly, because the workplace ignorantly threw emotions — the heart of culture — out the window.

So, this book does not share yet another workplace-change process that owners and managers (or I) can enforce from the top down or from the outside in. It's also not a book that invites you to develop an inner-peace practice or an internally generated sense of "passion" to protect yourself from demotivating, dehumanizing, or abusive working environments. This book helps you learn how to identify, understand, and access the power of emotions and discover the emotional intelligence and empathic skills that already exist within you, in your colleagues, and in your entire workplace community.

This work is not something that any of us can do alone, and it's not something that can be forced upon us. Because, even if workers are struggling or in conflict, and even if there's chaos and burnout, there's also an existing emotional genius in every workplace community that has been ignored almost completely (or has been intentionally suppressed). I want us to uncover that genius — no matter where you work or how much power you have — and I want us to enter into the deeply troubled world of the workplace and fix this failed model by relying upon the power and genius in our emotions. This is work I've been doing for the past 4 decades, and I'm very glad to welcome you to it.

I'm writing this book for everyone who works, and I'm offering this information with the expectation that workers will be equal participants in any changes that occur — and that everyone will have a choice about whether they want to adopt any of the ideas I share in this book. Therefore, if someone with authority brings this book to you and tries to enforce any part of it from the top down or the outside in, I want you to show them this page. We've had hundreds of years of emotionally incompetent workplace approaches pushed at us, and the workplace has only gotten worse. The modern workplace is on fire, and we need to put the fire out and create intelligent approaches to the extensive troubles the workplace has created for all of us. It's high time to respect the dignity, intelligence, empathy, and emotional awareness that's alive in every person who's learned how to survive in the dehumanizing and often endangering world of work. Considering the wildly unsustainable state of the modern workplace, it's imperative that we do so.

As we explore the power of emotions at work, we'll respect the innate emotional brilliance that lives inside every worker and every workplace culture.

Welcome to you and to your emotions. I'm glad you're here.

◆◆◆

An introduction before we proceed: I'm happy to introduce you to an international group of licensed Dynamic Emotional Integration professionals (DEI for short). These DEI professionals met with me every quarter or so as I was writing this book to explore emotions in the workplace, to argue and laugh, and to console each other about some of the most terrible jobs we've had. I called us the Workers of the World (WoW for short), and I'll share their insights throughout this book. One of the first insights that we all gained (with a thud of despair) is that most of us have never worked in a truly healthy workplace, and that most of us have not experienced true autonomy, dignity, or choice in any of our jobs unless we ran our own businesses. The entire WoW crew and I hope that this book can change that.

PART 1

Getting to Work on the Situation

1

Five Foundational Models to Help You Access the Power of Emotions

What does an emotionally healthy and functional workplace look like, and how does it work? What do humans need to feel safe and respected in the workplace, to develop and maintain their motivation, and to be able to do their work effectively? What information do emotions hold, how do they come into play at work, and how do we create a place for healthy empathy? Most importantly, how can the workplace support all of these crucial aspects, since so many workplaces hinder or even erase them?

In this chapter, we'll explore these questions and learn about five models that can help you identify your own emotional skills and the emotional, social, and empathic condition of your current workplace. In the next chapter, we'll observe these models in action, and in part 2, we'll delve more deeply into specific workplace situations, ideas, and tools.

First, let's look at what it means to be emotionally aware and skillful.

Model 1: Identifying Emotional Awareness and Emotional Skills

Your emotions are fundamental aspects of your cognition, your ability to understand yourself and others, and your ability to engage and communicate. Emotions help you attach meaning to incoming data, and each emotion performs a unique and vital function. Though emotional awareness and emotional skills have historically been treated as "soft," unimportant, or unwanted in the workplace, they are, in fact, essential to everything you do. Your emotional awareness and skills — and the awareness and skills of your colleagues — determine the social and emotional health of your workplace.

Emotional Awareness means that you can feel and identify emotions in yourself and others; it's a vital part of self-awareness, other-awareness, and empathy. Luckily, you can increase your emotional awareness (and your ability to regulate your emotions) by simply increasing your emotional vocabulary. Researcher Lisa Feldman Barrett and her colleagues have found that increasing your emotional "granularity" (the richness of your emotional vocabulary) can increase your emotional regulation skills all by itself.[1]

Identifying your emotions with granularity can also help you calm and soothe yourself. When you can understand that you're feeling anxiety or anger, for instance (and not some mysterious sensation), you may realize that your increased activation does not mean that you're in danger, and that you have many options for how to respond.[2] I've included a rich Emotional Vocabulary List in the appendix to help you develop greater emotional granularity and greater emotional awareness.

Emotional Skills refers to your ability to work with emotions in yourself and others: to identify emotions with accuracy (your vocabulary is vital), to listen to their unique messages (see model 4 in this chapter), to engage with emotions empathically, and to support emotional awareness in yourself and others.

Your emotional skills are a vital part of your social skills and empathy. Your emotions are not merely individual responses; they're intimately involved with and responsive to your relationships and your social and emotional environment (which is why miserable workplaces can be so harmful to your mental health). The emotional quality of your relationships and social structures can support (or hinder) your ability to work with your own emotions, so let's explore how an emotionally well-regulated social structure can support mental and emotional health in you and everyone around you.

Model 2: Developing Emotionally Well-Regulated Social Structures

Each of us is unique and our needs vary, but over the decades, I've identified key features that emotionally healthy relationships, workplaces, and social structures share. As we build a framework for emotional awareness in the workplace, let's explore my model of emotionally well-regulated workplaces, relationships, and social structures.

Your interior emotional awareness and emotional skills are a vital part of your health and well-being, but one of the most important supports for your emotional health is to be a part of emotionally well-regulated relationships and social structures. The devastating toll that the workplace takes on our lives and its own financial health is directly related to its deeply unhealthy emotional environment that may treat people and their emotions without much skill, empathy, or even a passing understanding of human nature.

Well-regulated social structures create healthy environments for people and their emotions, and they help individuals and relationships flourish. These social structures can be partner relationships, family groups, work environments, therapeutic relationships, or support groups, and though the setup of each social structure will be unique and based on the needs of the individuals within them, there are broad similarities.

Here are nine aspects that emotionally well-regulated social structures share. These aspects should be present and available to anyone and everyone in the social structure, regardless of position, seniority, or power:

1. Emotions are spoken of openly, and people have workable emotional vocabularies.
2. Mistakes and conflicts are addressed without avoidance, hostility, or blaming.
3. You can be honest about mistakes and difficult conflicts without being blamed or shunned.

4. Your emotions and sensitivities are noticed and respected.
5. You notice and respect the emotions and sensitivities of others.
6. Your emotional awareness and skills are openly requested and respected.
7. You openly request and respect the emotional awareness and skills of others.
8. You and others feel safe enough and supported enough to speak the truth even if it might destabilize relationships or processes.
9. The social structure welcomes you, nourishes you, and revitalizes you.

If you have one or more of these emotionally well-regulated relationships or structures in your life already, congratulations! Your social structure is your ecosystem, and its health directly affects your health and well-being. If your relationships and social structures are healthy, supportive, respectful, and revitalizing, then your life and your work will feel, if not exactly easy, then at least doable, hopeful, and worthwhile.

But if the social structures in your life are draining, unsupportive, emotionally destabilizing, or filled with conflict (as everyone in our Workers of the World meetings discovered in their work histories), then your life and your work will be much harder than they need to be and your emotions will react accordingly. For instance, you may find yourself disengaging or feeling frustrated, fed up, sad, angry, depressed, and so on. You may find that you're losing your motivation, seeking distractions and comfort anywhere you can find them, heading toward burnout, and planning your escape. As you *should*.

All of these healthy emotional responses to unhealthy social structures are necessary, and it's completely natural for you and your emotions to essentially go on strike when your social conditions are unsupportive or abusive. In fact, I'd be deeply concerned about you (and your emotions) if you *didn't* react and protest. Your emotional reactions to unhealthy situations not only protect your mental and emotional health, but they can help you identify problems and understand exactly what's wrong. In addition, each of your emotional reactions can inform you in a unique way, because each of your emotions contains a specific type of intelligence that helps you understand your world.

For instance, if a social structure or relationship tires you out and depresses you, you're likely not receiving the support you need to function. If you're frustrated or angered, the relationship or structure is likely disrespecting your emotions, sensitivities, and values (or the values of others). If you're hyped up and anxious most of the time, the structure or relationship is probably loading you up with too many tasks and not enough support. And so forth. Each of your emotional responses means something different and important, and all of your responses are necessary and valid. In an emotionally well-regulated social structure, you and everyone around you would know this; therefore, you and your emotions would be noticed, respected, and valued.

We'll explore the intelligence and messages in emotions in model 4, but first, let's look at a topic that most workplaces are either interested in or sort of obsessed with: how to motivate and engage their workers. As you'll see, something crucial is missing from this topic.

Model 3: Understanding Where Motivation Really Comes From

There's a troubling idea at the foundation of our failed workplace model that dovetails with the decision to remove emotions from the workplace: the idea of motivating employees so that they'll want to work. The concept of employee motivation (many people are calling it *engagement* these days) is everywhere, even though the research is pretty clear: You cannot motivate people — not really, and not for long. You can only *demotivate* them. Nevertheless, motivating and engaging workers is a national and international pastime that leads to all sorts of time-wasting and money-wasting attempts to manipulate or coerce people into wanting to work. And what's strange is that we've known about what actually motivates people for more than 70 years.

In the 1950s, Massachusetts Institute of Technology management professor Douglas McGregor proposed two theories of worker motivation: Theory X and Theory Y.

Theory X viewed people as unwilling workers who had to be convinced, coerced, and commanded to work with rewards or punishments; their motivation had to come from the outside or they wouldn't work.

Theory Y, on the other hand, viewed people as willing workers whose motivation was internal, and who required trust and a healthy social atmosphere in order to do their best work. This healthy atmosphere didn't *make* Theory Y workers work; instead, it provided a stable foundation for them so that their natural motivation could arise. McGregor proposed that Theory Y was a more humane, logical, and profitable way to treat workers and to run businesses.

McGregor had been a student of psychology professor Abraham Maslow, who was renowned for organizing human needs and motivations into a simple pyramid hierarchy with biological needs (food, warmth, and physical life) at the base and self-actualization (morality, creativity, and wholeness) at the peak. Though Maslow's pyramid is famous, it has long been challenged for not being based on research. It was a great model to start the conversation, but we understand more about human needs and motivation now than we did in Maslow's time. Research on attachment, in particular, has shown that warm, loving, and empathic human connection is the first requirement for babies to develop properly, and that warm connection, love, and belonging continues to be a first requirement throughout our lifespan.[3] In fact, no aspect of Maslow's pyramid can exist without connection, love, and belonging as a first requirement.

McGregor's Theory X and Theory Y have also been challenged, because there are situations in which people may need some form of outside motivation. Tedious and repetitive work may require external Theory X prompts such as higher per-piece rates based on speed, contests, prizes, and bonuses for beating deadlines (though prizes and bonuses will only work for a while).[4] Similarly, dangerous work may require special perks and hazard pay, or people may simply refuse to work. However, tedious and dangerous work environments don't follow the Theory Y rule of providing healthy and respectful working environments, so this critique may support McGregor's theories rather than disprove them. Sadly, even though we know better, Theory X workplaces with their carrot-and-stick rewards, punishments, and performance reviews exist everywhere today, even in businesses that falsely believe themselves to be flat, democratic, and empathic. Theory X still wields a lot of unhealthy power in the working world, whether the exterior prompts are negative and controlling, or whether they're positive and rewarding.

Newer theories of motivation build on McGregor and Maslow's work but highlight the crucial aspects of connection and belonging. In the 1970s and 1980s, psychology researchers Edward Deci and Richard Ryan focused on motivation (and the conditions that lead to demotivation and disengagement) and developed their acclaimed Self-Determination Theory, which focuses on motivation, human development, and psychological wellness.[5] Deci and Ryan found that the conditions that lead to healthy internal motivation are built on *competence* (the ability to interact skillfully and effectively in your environment), *autonomy* (the ability to choose, self-regulate, and make decisions about your own life), and *relatedness* (the presence of healthy connections and a sense of closeness, belonging, and often, love). If these three conditions of competence, autonomy, and relatedness are not present, then motivation will likely not be present either. Some people who arrive in the workplace with healthy internal motivation may maintain their inner drive even when these conditions aren't present, but in many unhealthy workplaces, these "passionate" workers are not usually treasured or protected — and may even be exploited for their passion.[6]

As we learned from the workplace mental health research I shared in the introduction, when the conditions that lead to feelings of competence, autonomy, and relatedness are not present, productivity suffers. But more importantly, human beings suffer and lose their motivation as their mental and emotional health drain away. In these unhealthy and demotivating workplaces, people must push themselves to work, or be coerced and manipulated into working. In unhealthy and emotionally unregulated workplaces, the carrots and sticks of Theory X are necessary, because nothing in the social structure supports healthy internal motivation. Deci and Ryan's theory helps us understand why: Coercive and controlling Theory X environments impede or erase competence, autonomy, and relatedness, while trust-based Theory Y environments support these aspects. In a Theory Y workplace, you don't need to manipulate or jolly or force people into working, because you're not interfering with their internal motivation. Theory Y environments support people's natural work ethic so that the carrot-and-stick approach is not required. But even if carrots or sticks were required, their effect would be only temporary.

There's an old saying: You can lead a horse to water, but you can't make her drink. Research into grades, awards, and competition in schools regularly show that they're counterproductive, and actually reduce internal motivation. Students become less able to work *unless* there's a reward offered.[7] Grades, performance appraisals (all forms, even the newest methods everyone is pushing), and merit pay have been shown to demotivate people, create unnecessary competition and conflict, and waste everyone's time.[8]

I had an email conversation about this with education reformer Alfie Kohn, whose groundbreaking work against competition, grading, gold stars, rewards, and punishments provides a road map toward truly respectful schools and workplaces (see his books in the recommended resources section).[9] He and I were discussing the nondemocratic, time-wasting, and motivation-killing effects of performance reviews and appraisals, and he wrote: "Peter Block [an organizational development consultant] once described such appraisals as 'the occasion at which you're reminded who owns you.'"

Kohn also noted that performance appraisals make people focus on the wrong things for the wrong reasons: "They encourage a 'please the boss' rather than 'improve the quality of work' mindset. They promote a misleading focus on the performance of solitary individuals, discouraging cooperation and overlooking the respects in which each person's performance actually reflects systemic factors. They undermine morale and intrinsic motivation. They cement into place a top-down control model and they create a temptation to set up pay-for-performance plans — i.e., extrinsic inducements, which, as you know, are not just ineffective but powerfully counterproductive."

Appraisals and rewards interfere with and destabilize people's *autonomy*, and competition attempts to make their *competence* into a public rather than private drive, which in turn interferes with their *relatedness* (colleagues become rivals and not peers). Competition, performance appraisals, awards, and hierarchies also tend to support narcissistic tendencies, or can even *create* them in otherwise healthy people who may have to sacrifice relatedness, turn their autonomy into isolation, and weaponize their competence in order to rise through the ranks (we'll explore the damage that hierarchies inflict on people on page 61).[10]

And as we've all seen, employee parties and retreats, gift baskets, group dinners, waffle makers in the break room, climbing walls, team-building exercises, free donuts, "fun" performance-based perks, employee of the month awards, the newest forms of performance reviews, and other attempts to make the workplace entertaining or competitive have no value whatsoever if management and owners don't know how to create a psychologically healthy and emotionally well-regulated structure for their workers.

Workers are not being fooled here. These carrot-and-stick approaches are no substitute for a healthy working environment, and their presence suggests that the environment wasn't healthy or workable in the first place.

There's another saying: People don't quit their jobs; they quit their managers. People only rarely leave jobs because the work is too difficult for them; instead, they leave because the social and emotional environment does not support competence, autonomy, or relatedness (or is just plain miserable). This saying, however, puts too much responsibility on managers. In many organizations, managers don't have the power to create an emotionally well-regulated workplace or even choose their own workflow or work groups. In fact, many well-meaning managers are actively stopped from creating healthy workplaces by their superiors, or by workers who refuse to trust them (because they've been manipulated, lied to, or abused before). Alongside this, there's a workplace-wide addiction to Theory X rewards, grades, contests, performance reviews, and punishments, which creates a demotivating environment, no matter how well-meaning individual managers may be. Many managers are held accountable for employee motivation and engagement, but they're provided only with tools that reduce both, which makes everyone's work difficult, frustrating, and unrewarding.

This workplace-wide failure to understand human motivation fascinates me, because we've already got a word in the English language that tells us exactly where motivation comes from: it's *emotion*. The Latin root for the word emotion is *emovere*: to move, excite, or motivate. Our emotions motivate us, move us, energize us (or slow us down, if necessary), and help us make sense of everything we experience. Rewards and punishments applied from the outside can affect us for a short while, but it is always our emotions that provide our main motivating force. Healthy and lasting motivation is internal and emotional, as is our work ethic and our ability to understand whether a workplace values us or is just trying to use and manipulate us.

If we know we're valued and respected, and if our competence, autonomy, and relatedness are supported, our emotions will let us know that we're in an emotionally well-regulated environment where we're respected — and therefore our motivation will be engaged.

But if we aren't respected or valued, our emotions won't be fooled by any kind of reward or punishment, and our motivation will plummet (as it should). Some workplaces try to pacify us with happy-peppy atmospheres or stirring vision statements focused on passion, but our emotions aren't fooled by any of this. We may complete our work, but our hearts won't be in it, and we may become one of those 7 out of 10 workers who are actively looking for better jobs while at work.

Motivation certainly comes from our emotions, but they do so much more than motivate us — they're a key part of our cognition and our ability to comprehend and navigate our world. Understanding how emotions work and how to work with them is crucial, not just in the workplace, but in every area of our lives.

Model 4: Discovering the Brilliance in Emotions

Imagine a place where you could find not just motivation, but honor, integrity, fairness, loyalty, good instincts, intuition, ingenuity, certainty, creativity, transformation, healing, delight, hope, and the ability to work skillfully on tasks and deadlines. All of these qualities and more live in your emotions.

Emotions are central to your basic awareness and cognition; they tell you how you're feeling and what's going on inside you and around you. Emotions provide you with the information and motivation you need in both your private life and your working life: They help you make sense of the world, and they help you think, decide, act, create, relate, dream, and heal. Each of your emotions is unique, and all of them contain specific forms of intelligence. Their presence in the workplace is required, and if we can all learn how to listen to and respect them, emotions can give us deep information about the actual conditions of our workplaces (no matter what our corporate mottos or vision statements claim). With the vital information our emotions bring to us, we can learn how to build functional and emotionally well-regulated workplaces that work for everyone.

In my work, I strive to make emotions as accessible as possible without oversimplifying them. I've found that organizing the emotions into four families helps people identify and work with them more easily. I'll introduce the emotions here in their four basic families and build on this information throughout the book. They are: the Anger Family, the Fear Family, the Sadness Family, and the Happiness Family. Each family of emotions contains a specific kind of intelligence that helps guide us so we can understand what's going on inside ourselves and in the world around us.

Emotions Are Vital Aspects of Your Social Intelligence

Before we learn about the four emotion families, I have an important note for you: Don't focus a lot of your attention on individuals in your past or current workplace. We've been taught, wrongly, to see emotions as belonging entirely to individuals. As such, many emotional management or mindfulness practices place the entire responsibility for emotions onto individuals, who are supposed to manage, suppress, or internally resolve their emotions in some way. The truth, however, is far more complex.

Emotions may belong to individuals in part, but because they're a key feature of our ability to understand and navigate the world, emotions also respond to our environment. Emotions tell us what's going on inside ourselves, certainly, but they also tell us what's happening around us. So, in regard to emotions in the workplace, if you see one worker displaying a lot of intense emotion (or repressing emotion), then yes, this may be something entirely restricted to that person (unless they're acting out emotions for others, which happens a lot in repressive workplaces — see the section on *Agitators* in chapter 3). But, if you see a trend in many workers' emotional responses and reactions, then there's definitely something going on in their social environment. We all respond emotionally to our social environment, which is why emotionally well-regulated social structures are so important for our emotional health and well-being.

Also, there's a huge ethical component to focusing on individual workers' emotional functioning, as DEI professional and workplace consultant Marion Langford pointed out in one of our Workers of the World meetings. Unless you're a licensed mental health professional and you have a worker's direct permission to delve into their personal life, you have no business interfering with their internal emotional functioning or assigning any psychological labels. None. Each worker's rights to privacy, dignity, and emotional autonomy must be respected, because as we saw earlier, the workplace environment itself is far more likely to be the cause of trouble than individuals are.

You may remember the percentages I shared in the introduction, where 63% to 85% of workers were found to be either depressed, trapped, or burnt-out. The workplace has a heartbreaking track record of emotional abuse — either intentionally, or through incompetence and a lack of emotionally well-regulated social structures. So, when people ask me to consult with individuals in their workplace who have (or are causing) emotional problems, I immediately look at the health of the workplace social structure. That's the first likely cause of any social or emotional difficulties.

And if the workplace structure is generally healthy, I then ask why and how this individual was allowed to fall so far out of balance before anyone spoke up? Why wasn't anything in place, and why was the workplace unable to respond effectively? If the person was struggling at home, was there any support for them, or were they expected to erase their difficulties and slap on a happy mask at work? What aspects of emotionally well-regulated social structures were missing, and why?

Workplaces are social groups, and in social groups, emotions do not just arise in individuals; they say something important about the group environment in nearly every instance. As you explore emotions in this new way, be aware of the powerful effects that the social environment has on people's emotions, behavior, motivation, and mental health.

Introducing the Four Emotion Families

An important key to learning how to work with emotions is to view them — all of them — as essential to your cognition and awareness. There are no negative emotions, and there are no positive emotions; as you'll see, every emotion has value, and every emotion can help you understand the true conditions in your life and your workplace.

The emotions see the truth and they tell the truth, and people with emotional awareness and emotional skills are more successful in relationships and jobs, because they can more easily see things as they are (people who repress or ignore emotions tend to miss important information). People with emotional awareness and emotional skills are also good at reading people and social situations, so they tend to be less susceptible to manipulation and control tactics — which is probably why people have tried (and failed) to remove emotions from the workplace for centuries. Thank goodness they've failed, because with the help of emotions (and our emotional skills), we can learn how to clearly identify the social and emotional problems that plague the workplace and address them so that the workplace can become a functional and livable environment.

The four emotion family tables that follow can help you understand what emotions do and which forms of intelligence they bring to you. With this information, you can learn how to work *with* emotions instead of working against them.

Emotions are key aspects of cognition and intelligence, and as such, I look at them very differently than you might be used to. I focus first on how and why they work, and then on which gifts, skills, and forms of intelligence they bring to us. As we explore the emotions, I won't tell you what to do to fix the emotions, because there's nothing to fix! Emotions contain intelligence, and you don't *fix* intelligence; you listen to it, pay attention to it, and use it to deepen your understanding of yourself and the world.

Because I see all emotions as aspects of intelligence — each with its own gifts, skills, and forms of genius — I developed a set of questions to help people engage directly with their emotions. Many of us have never learned to work *with* our emotions, especially powerful ones like anger, anxiety, depression, or joy. Most of us only know how to express our emotions outwardly without understanding exactly what we're doing (or what our emotions are trying to tell us). Or, we've learned to repress our emotions inwardly because we don't know what else to do with them. Sometimes emotions have been forbidden in our families, schools, workplaces, or cultures, but sometimes we simply have no idea what to do with our emotions, so we just repress them into oblivion. In both cases, whether we're expressing emotions without awareness or repressing them without skill, we're throwing our emotions away. And in so doing, we're losing access to astonishing forms of energy and genius that don't exist anywhere else.

The questions for each emotion below may seem simple, but they do something that expression and repression cannot: They lean into the genius of the emotions and engage with them empathically and respectfully. These questions help us work directly with the skills and awareness that each emotion brings to us.

I trust that once you understand emotions in this way, your own emotional intelligence will help you think more effectively about them. We'll look at specific approaches to address emotions throughout this book, but as we meet them here, we won't try to solve, suppress, change, or fix them, because emotions are not problems.

We've mostly been taught to see emotions as problems instead of learning how they truly work, but emotions aren't problems and emotions don't *cause* problems; they bring us the instincts, motivation, skills, and intelligence we need to *solve* problems. When we can work respectfully with the intelligence inside our emotions, we'll have direct access to the awareness and tools we need to improve our own lives, improve the social and emotional environments of our relationships and workplaces, and then change the world.

Emotions are *that* powerful.

Understanding the Anger Family —
Boundaries, Rules, and Behavioral Guidelines

The emotions in the **Anger Family** (anger, guilt/shame, apathy, and hatred) tell us what's important and when a boundary has been crossed or a rule has been broken. These emotions help us set behavioral guidelines for ourselves and others.

In the context of the workplace, these emotions help us create and nurture our basic sense of security, competence, autonomy, and relatedness.

When any of these Anger Family emotions are very active in the workplace, they can point to a breakdown in rules, social agreements, and basic respect from owners and managers, between departments, or between individuals.

The Anger Family helps us identify, create, and uphold the boundaries, rules, ethics, and morals that individuals, relationships, and social groups depend upon. Note that apathy, which is a synonym for demotivation and disengagement, arises when the boundary-setting emotion of anger and the motivating forces of competence and autonomy are not respected or welcome in the environment. Many workplaces try to jolly or punish their workers out of apathy, which shows a complete misunderstanding of the purpose of this emotion. When apathy is present, it's a sign that the social structure is unhealthy and demotivating; it doesn't mean that people need punishments or parties.

What people need is an emotionally well-regulated environment where their emotions are understood and respected. In an environment of care and respect, people will have the emotional awareness they need to question and work with their emotions, and they'll have the emotional skills and social support they need to address the problems or opportunities their emotions alert them to.

Emotion	Questions	Gifts and Skills
ANGER arises when people's self-image, behaviors, values, or interpersonal boundaries are challenged — or when they see them challenged in someone else.	*What do I value?* *What must be protected and restored?*	Honor, certainty, healthy self-esteem, proper boundaries, healthy detachment, and protection of ourselves and others.
APATHY is a protective mask for anger, and it arises in situations where people are not able or willing to work with their anger openly.	*What is being avoided?* *What must be made conscious?*	Detachment, boundary-setting, separation, taking a time-out, and protection of the self in an unhealthy or inappropriate environment.
GUILT AND SHAME arise to make sure that people don't hurt, embarrass, or dehumanize themselves or others.	*Who has been hurt?* *What must be made right?*	Integrity, self-respect, making amends, behavioral rules and guidelines, behavioral change, and work quality.

Emotion	Questions	Gifts and Skills
HATRED arises in the presence of things people cannot accept in themselves (and despise in others).	*What has fallen into my shadow?* *What must be reintegrated?*	Hatred can be an emergency signal in the workplace that, if handled skillfully, can lead to deep interpersonal awareness, sudden evolution, and the ability to address prejudice and bias openly.*

*HR and workplace safety note: If people are expressing hatred in the workplace and they have no emotional skills, they will likely devolve into abuse or bullying, both of which create an unacceptably hostile workplace environment. Abuse and bullying in the workplace are illegal and need to be addressed and resolved immediately. Emotional skills are always essential, but when powerful emotions like hatred arise, these skills are absolutely crucial. If people can't manage their emotions and they're hurting others at work, HR must step in.

Healthy communication processes (which we'll explore in chapter 5) make room for the vital emotions in the Anger Family to have a voice and contribute their intelligence to individual workers and the working community as a whole.

Understanding the Fear Family —
Instincts, Intuition, Orienting, and Action
The emotions in the **Fear Family** (fear, anxiety, confusion, jealousy, envy, and panic) contain intuition and instincts. These emotions help us orient to our surroundings, notice change, novelty, or hazards, and take effective action.

In the workplace, these emotions help people keep abreast of all of their tasks and tools and stay aware of any impediments or hazards that would impact their work and their working community. Jealousy and envy in particular keep an eye on fairness, equality, loyalty, and relatedness.

When any of these Fear Family emotions are very active in the workplace, they can point to serious issues such as a lack of appropriate safety regulations and practices, unregulated relationship conflict, widespread inequality, unfair or improperly managed workloads, and inadequate time management and/or workflow processes.

Emotion	Questions/Actions	Gifts and Skills
FEAR arises to help people focus on the present moment, access their instincts and intuition, and tune into changes in their immediate environment.	*What action should be taken?*	Intuition, instincts, focus, clarity, awareness, attentiveness, and readiness.
ANXIETY is focused on the future — it arises to help people look ahead and identify the tasks they need to complete and the deadlines they need to meet.	*What brought this feeling forward?* *What **truly** needs to get done?*	Foresight, focus, task-completion, procrastination alert, planning, organization, and awareness of future problems and needs.
CONFUSION is a protective mask for fear and anxiety, and it arises when people have too much to process all at once. Confusion can give people a much-needed time-out.	*What is my intention?* *What action should be taken?*	Soft awareness, spaciness, flexibility, taking a time-out, and protection against overload.

Emotion	Questions/Actions	Gifts and Skills
JEALOUSY arises when people's connection to love, loyalty, or security in their relationships is challenged.	*What has been betrayed?* *What must be healed and restored?*	Commitment, security, love, connection, belonging, loyalty, and the ability to create and maintain healthy relationships.
ENVY arises when people's connection to material security, resources, or recognition is challenged.	*What has been betrayed?* *What must be made right?*	Fairness, security, access to resources, proper recognition, self-preservation, and the promotion of equality and justice.
PANIC arises when people face threats to their survival. Panic gives them three life-saving choices: fight, flee, or freeze.	*Just listen to your body — don't think, just react.* *Your body is a survival expert, and it will keep you safe.*	Sudden energy, intense attention, the ability to protect the self and others, absolute stillness, and survival in the face of shock and danger.*

*HR and workplace safety note: Many of us try to talk people out of their feelings of panic and anxiety, but these emotions should not be ignored! If a worker is feeling panic about the workplace or its process, check to see if there are any hazards; there likely are. Many workplace disasters occur after workers' panicky concerns, fears, and anxieties are belittled or ignored.

The Fear Family keeps us and the people around us safe, it upholds equity and fairness, and it keeps an eye on our workloads. Note the connection between fear, anxiety, and the protective state of confusion. If workers are anxious a great deal of the time, or if they drop into confusion, it's likely that their workloads are not being metered out or managed appropriately, or that the number of tasks and the timing of deadlines are unrealistic. The presence of Fear Family emotions is an important warning about trouble in fundamental areas of work relationships, workflow, and workplace safety.

Sadly, the Fear Family emotions are often ignored or treated as signs of cowardice, and an overwhelming percentage of workers (85% in the study I shared on page 3) would not communicate their valid fears, anxieties, or panicky feelings upward, even when those emotions were pointing to serious or life-threatening situations. Creating workable communication processes in the workplace is vital, and making sure that the Fear Family emotions are welcomed and listened to can literally save lives.

**Understanding the Sadness Family —
Stopping, Letting Go, and Recovering**

The emotions in the **Sadness Family** (sadness, grief, depression, and the suicidal urge) help us release things that aren't working and mourn things that are gone so that we can relax, let go, and rejuvenate ourselves.

In the workplace, these emotions can help people make smooth transitions, deal with loss and change, and identify processes and ideas that can't work and need to be changed.

When Sadness Family emotions are very active in the workplace, they can point to badly handled transitions, unmourned losses, and serious functional issues that are not being taken seriously or dealt with effectively.

Emotion	Questions	Gifts and Skills
SADNESS arises to help people let go of things that aren't working. If they can let go, they'll be able to relax, recover, and revitalize themselves.	*What must be released?* *What must be rejuvenated?*	Relaxation, rejuvenation, the ability to identify waste, outdated ideas, and unworkable processes, and the ability to let go.
GRIEF arises when people have lost something — a person, an idea, a belief, a possession, or a situation — that has died or will never come back.	*What must be mourned?* *What must be released completely?*	Sorrow, the ability to identify and mourn losses, remembrance, acceptance of loss, deep release, and honoring of the lost idea, situation, person, or possession.
SITUATIONAL DEPRESSION arises when things are not working well, and people lose the energy to keep going in the ways they previously did. There's always an important reason for situational depression to arise.	*Where has my energy gone?* *Why was it sent away?*	Ingenious stagnation, stillness, awareness of dysfunction and difficulties, warning of future trouble, intelligent restriction of energy, and a reality check.

Emotion	Questions	Gifts and Skills
THE SUICIDAL URGE arises when something in people's lives needs to end — but it's not their actual, physical life! It's important to reach out for help and identify the situation or thing that needs to end so that people can get their lives back.	*What idea or behavior must end now?* *What can I no longer tolerate?*	The ability to identify abuse, futility, and completely unworkable situations; certainty, finality, freedom, transformation, and rebirth.*

*In my Dynamic Emotional Integration work, I help people understand that suicidal urges have a place in the emotional realm, but that physical death is not required. Instead, we focus the intense laser-focus of the suicidal urge on the person's painful or unlivable situation and bring the powerful genius of this emotion to bear; it arises when things are very bad indeed, but it does not require the physical death of the person!

HR and workplace safety note: If a worker expresses suicidal ideation, get help from an employee assistance counselor or your local crisis center or lifeline immediately. When the suicidal urge is present, emotional skills and social support can literally save people's lives.

The Sadness Family takes a regular inventory of what we have, what we need, what we've lost, and what we need to lose in order to function well.

This important family of emotions tends to be ignored in the workplace (and the world at large), because loss and change are either avoided, dreaded, or handled very clumsily. As a result, hiring, onboarding processes, training and retraining, conflict management, disciplinary actions, demotions, firing, and transitions of all kinds tend to be handled haphazardly in many workplaces. Some organizations have workable processes for some of these normal transitions, but very few workplaces have healthy or appropriate processes for all of them (we'll explore many ways to create healthy transitions in chapter 6). This leaves the Sadness Family with a lot of unpaid work to do to keep people functioning in the face of transitions and loss. It's not surprising that situational depression (disengagement is one sign) is so widespread in the workplace. This form of depression (which is different from conditions such as major, bipolar, or postpartum depression) arises in response to situations that are unworkable or are heading that way. Situational depression in the workplace is a warning sign of ongoing, unaddressed dysfunction that not only disturbs workers, but also may disrupt the future viability of the business.

Welcoming the Sadness Family into the workplace is key to creating a humane and functional environment where humans can do their best work and face their losses in a changing and uncertain world.

Understanding the Happiness Family —
Hope, Confidence, and Inspiration
The emotions in the **Happiness Family** (happiness, contentment, and joy) help us look around ourselves or toward the future with hope, satisfaction, and delight.

Sadly, many workplaces focus unhealthy amounts of attention on these emotions, which means that their presence is often engineered or manufactured (or faked). I call this a *toxic positivity bias* that can lead people and businesses to avoid problems and miss clear signs (from the other three emotion families) that their plans and ideas aren't grounded in reality.

TOXIC POSITIVITY BIAS

A dangerously mistaken belief that the allegedly positive emotions are the only emotions that should be felt or shared in the workplace. This bias causes extensive suffering as people suppress all forbidden emotions, lose their emotional awareness and skills, and become unable to address serious problems that *require* the gifts, skills, and genius in the forbidden emotions.

Left to their own devices, however, these emotions help people understand when the ideas, actions, and future of a business group are sound. However, when Happiness Family emotions are very active in a workplace, they can signal that the emotions in the other three families are being actively suppressed.

Emotion	Statements	Gifts and Skills
HAPPINESS arises to help people look around themselves and toward the future with hope and enjoyment.	*Thank you for this lively celebration!*	Amusement, hope, delight, playfulness, and belief in a bright future.
CONTENTMENT arises after people have accomplished something, and it helps them look at themselves with pride and satisfaction.	*Thank you for renewing my faith in myself!*	Satisfaction, self-esteem, confidence, healthy pride, and a healthy work ethic.
JOY arises to help people feel a blissful sense of open-hearted connection to others, to ideas, or to experiences.	*Thank you for this wonderful moment!*	Expansion, inspiration, brilliance, bliss, and a new vision for the future.

Most workplaces want to deal *only* with the Happiness Family. Many managers dream of happy, engaged, and motivated workers who are content with their jobs. But this small family of three emotions can't create or maintain a healthy workplace without the entire emotional realm helping them set boundaries, watch out for hazards, and identify loss, waste, injustice, and inequality. All emotions are necessary.

In a healthy and emotionally well-regulated social structure, all emotions will be free to move forward and step back in a natural rhythm in response to changing situations. Some days, everyone will be happy and laughing, and on other days emotions such as apathy, anger, anxiety, sadness, envy, or depression may show up to help people identify problems that need to be addressed. Every emotion has its necessary time and place.

When you understand emotions as crucial aspects of cognition and intelligence, you'll be able to listen to them and welcome the gifts and skills they contribute. You won't need to create a toxic positivity bias by over-emphasizing the Happiness Family; instead, you'll learn how to treat these emotions with respect and empathy and let them work in their own ways as valued members of a whole and intelligent emotional realm.

This emotional wholeness is important for each of us as individuals, because working well with all of our emotions supports our mental and emotional health. However, this full-bodied emotional capacity can also help us develop a skill that's at the forefront of the workplace and everywhere else right now: *empathy*. The quality of our empathy, it turns out, is completely dependent upon our ability to work skillfully with every emotion we have (and not just the Happiness Family).

Model 5: Knowing That Empathy Is First and Foremost an Emotional Skill

Empathy is a hot topic in the business world, and while it should be, many people don't understand empathy well enough yet to bring it into the workplace safely or successfully. Study after study finds that workers who show empathy are rated as more effective, more approachable, and more professional than their less-engaged colleagues. And empathic managers are consistently shown to develop better communication and stronger team cohesion, while empathic healthcare professionals have higher patient satisfaction scores. However, dangerous levels of empathic burnout are rampant in healthcare and many high-empathy-demand occupations.[11]

Many people think that empathy is just about being nice, listening, or being available to people; and that's part of it. But empathy between people is primarily based on our ability to respond to the emotions of others from an emotionally aware place in ourselves. Therefore, empathy might look like this: When you're overwhelmed and cranky about a stubborn customer, your emotionally aware coworkers may intentionally ignore you so that you can have some privacy and calm yourself down. That may not look like niceness, but it's a highly empathic response to your needs. Of course, at other times, these same coworkers may give you a chance to complain out loud and act like a jerk, which *also* may not look like niceness, but it's excellent empathy. Empathy is completely situation-dependent, and it rarely looks the same from situation to situation (you can't achieve true empathy through a script, though many people try to). Empathy is our full-bodied, honest, and emotive ability to truly relate to others; it's a key component of the relatedness that supports our healthy motivation.

Empathy is a trait and a skill, yet as we all know, it can sometimes be hard work. If our workplace is emotionally well regulated, then our empathic work will likely be appreciated and supported. However, if our workplace is not emotionally well regulated, serious problems can arise when we're required to be very empathic (or *empathetic*; both are correct, but *empathic* is gaining traction in the US while *empathetic* tends to be a British usage) but don't receive any support for our empathic work.

For instance, the healthcare profession demands constant (and often enforced and scripted) empathy from its workers, and is seeing high absenteeism, regular turnover, widespread depression, empathic burnout, and a hidden epidemic of suicides among doctors, nurses, and other medical professionals.[12] Empathy in the workplace is essential, but it's *work*, and it needs to be treated seriously and supported intentionally so that empathic burnout does not occur.

Workplace empathy requirements enforce *relatedness*, which, along with competence and autonomy, is one of the three important aspects of motivation. However, if this relatedness is required but not supported, it can and does interfere with workers' sense of *competence* as they begin to burn out and lose their ability to maintain their emotional engagement and empathy. Removing the aspect of choice from a worker's empathy and relatedness also interferes with their sense of *autonomy*. When seen in this light, it's easy to track (and predict) disengagement and empathic burnout in a high-empathy-demand workplace that's not emotionally well regulated.

In part 2 of this book, we'll explore many ways to identify workplace empathy demands and create the well-regulated structures empathy workers (and each of us) require. We'll also develop a clear understanding of empathy so that we'll know what we're asking for in high-empathy-demand work, and why.

In my research on empathy, I've found that most people don't understand the different aspects of empathy and are not usually aware of the crucial social and emotional skills at the heart of empathy. Accordingly, most workplaces (and most people) have a hard time identifying the exact empathic and emotional demands they and their colleagues face, or the ways that their workplace culture can protect workers from overwhelm and burnout (or impact their health unnecessarily).

In my 2013 book, *The Art of Empathy*, I developed a model of empathy to help people organize their thinking and approach empathy with skill and clarity. This is my definition:

EMPATHY

A social and emotional skill that helps you feel and understand the emotions, circumstances, intentions, thoughts, and needs of others, such that you can offer sensitive, perceptive, and appropriate communication and support.

Emotional awareness is the first requirement for empathy, and empathy develops very early — usually before the age of 2.[13] As we mature in our social and emotional skills, we become able to empathize with more awareness and precision, and by the time we enter the workplace, most of us have decades of empathic experience to fall back on. Empathy is second nature to most of us; it's unconscious, and because of this, we often aren't able to identify the steps we take to empathize or what aspects of empathy we're using (or overusing, most likely) at work. I developed a model of empathy to help you understand empathy more clearly so that you can employ it more intentionally (and more skillfully).

The Six Essential Aspects of Empathy

I developed my Six Essential Aspects of Empathy model to help make empathy easier to understand, utilize, and manage, especially for people who are experiencing empathic burnout or are heading there. I also built it to help people who struggle with not having *enough* empathic awareness. This six-aspect model can help people understand exactly where their empathy is overused or underdeveloped.

The first five of these six aspects come from research (though they aren't linked together in this way). I brought them together to help people understand the building blocks of empathy. The sixth aspect is a concept I added to help people envision empathy at a more complete level than the research currently makes room for. With the help of this model, people can develop their empathy at any stage of their lives (or balance their empathy if they're hyper-sensitive, hyper-empathic, or facing empathic burnout).

The Six Essential Aspects of Empathy are:

1. **Emotion Recognition (also known as Emotion Contagion):** Before empathy can take place, you need to sense that an emotion is occurring — or that an emotion or response is expected of you. Empathy relies upon your ability to detect, feel, and share emotions. Empathy is first and foremost an emotional skill that helps you know what's happening or what to expect.

2. **Empathic Accuracy:** This is your ability to accurately identify and understand context, emotions, and intentions in yourself and others so that you can choose appropriate responses and take suitable actions.

My Emotional Vocabulary List in the appendix can help you learn how to identify emotions with granularity and accuracy.

3. **Emotion Regulation:** In order to empathize effectively, you need to understand, regulate, and work well with your own emotions. When you can regulate your emotions, you'll tend to respond skillfully in the presence of your own and others' emotions (rather than being overtaken or knocked out of commission by them). Your ability to work with emotions is the key to healthy empathy, and an emotionally well-regulated social structure can support your emotion regulation skills beautifully. Conversely, a poorly regulated social structure will reliably lead to emotional overwhelm and empathic burnout.

4. **Perspective Taking:** This skill helps you imaginatively see situations through the eyes of others, and sense — from their perspective — what they might be feeling, wanting, or needing.

5. **Concern for Others:** This is your capacity for care and compassion, which helps you engage and empathize in ways that display your concern and humanity. In general, when people talk about empathy in the workplace, they are talking about Concern for Others, and possibly Perspective Taking. There tends to be very little awareness of (or support for) the vital first three aspects of empathy.

6. **Perceptive Engagement:** This is your ability to respond, act on, and communicate your empathy to others. This full expression of your empathy is dependent upon the first five aspects, which help you empathize or act wisely (if action is needed) in a way that works for others. Perceptive Engagement combines your capacity to sense and accurately identify the emotions of others, skillfully regulate your own emotions, take the perspective of others, focus on them with care and concern, and then engage empathically based upon your perceptions.

This model helps people understand empathy as a process and not a magical gift. I developed it to address the troubles people can have with empathy in both directions; some people struggle because they're hyper-empathic and experience *too much* Emotion Recognition, for example, while others struggle with hypo-empathy because they don't pick up *enough* emotions and signals from others. In *The Art of Empathy*, I help people learn to balance all six aspects so that they can empathize comfortably and skillfully, no matter where they start out on the empathic scale.

Many workplaces require empathy from their workers, but don't know enough about empathy to create the supportive environment their workers need. I notice that workplace empathy usually focuses on the final three aspects (Perspective Taking, Concern for Others, and Perceptive Engagement), but essentially ignores the foundational first three (Emotion Recognition, Empathic Accuracy, and Emotion Regulation), as if empathy arises out of thin air. Sometimes, workplaces offer training in reflective listening or Perspective Taking to increase customer-focused empathy, but because the workplace has such a troubled relationship with emotions, the social and emotional support high-empathy-demand workers require is often missing.

The unspoken message seems to be: We want your empathy, but leave your emotions at the door, and take care of yourself somehow, on your own time. Sadly, because workplace empathy *requires* emotions, emotional skills, and emotional support, pushing emotions out of the process leads reliably to workplace conflict, demotivation, depression, and burnout — *as it should*. Workers in high-empathy-demand professions require extensive support so they can manage their empathic workloads and protect their mental health. If they don't receive that support, their emotions will likely (and should) go on strike.

As we learn how emotions, motivation, and empathy function in ourselves and in the workplace, we'll rely on the five foundational models we covered in this chapter and apply them to real-world situations. As a reminder, they are:

1. Identifying Emotional Awareness and Emotional Skills
2. Developing Emotionally Well-Regulated Social Structures
3. Understanding Where Motivation Really Comes From
4. Discovering the Brilliance in Emotions
5. The Six Essential Aspects of Empathy

All five of these models directly impact our mental and emotional health, our capacity for engagement, and our ability to do our best work.

We've explored a lot of ideas and models so far, and in the next chapter, I'll share two case studies that bring all of these ideas together. I want us to step into the real world of work so that you can see how these ideas connect, and how they can help you build and maintain a naturally motivating, empathically healthy, and emotionally well-regulated working environment.

2

Five Models and Two Studies:
The Power of Emotions at Work

We've already explored five foundational models that can help us build and maintain emotionally well-regulated workplaces. Now, let's bring these models into the real world and observe them working (and failing) in two case studies.

In the first case, we meet Natalie, a high-end spa manager who asked for my help because her workers were in a mutiny. In the second case, we meet Mateo, who came to me after his staff accused him of not being empathic.

Natalie and Mateo are not actual individuals; these case studies are a combination of many stories. I'm sharing them here to help you see the five models in action, and also because you've probably already seen situations like these in your own working life. However, you may not have been able to identify all of the emotional and empathic undercurrents that were at play.

In these case studies, we'll identify the emotional, empathic, and motivational issues at play in Natalie's and Mateo's workplace difficulties. I also want you to see how simple it is to address seemingly insurmountable workplace problems when you know how to listen to and respect the genius inside the emotions; they're not the problem, they're *pointing to* the problem.

In this chapter, I'll also introduce you to some important concepts that we'll explore throughout the rest of this book: emotional labor, repair stations, the damaging nature of hierarchies, and the importance of large-group social skills.

Case Study: Are Natalie's Workers Spoiled Brats?

Natalie asked me for help because her staff was full of "spoiled brat children." Natalie managed a high-end spa at a luxury resort, and her staff of thirty men and women were the bodyworkers and aestheticians who served the resort's wealthy clientele. Natalie wanted me to train her staff and teach them emotional and empathic skills because many of them behaved thoughtlessly with her and with each other.

I was immediately concerned, and asked about their treatment of spa guests, but Natalie assured me that her staff treated clients with care and professionalism. Natalie's staff had emotional and empathic skills in the treatment rooms; the problems only occurred when clients weren't present (their "frontstage" behaviors were professional, but their backstage behaviors told a very different story). Scheduling had become a nightmare, staff members were squabbling and jockeying for power, Natalie felt isolated and disrespected, and morale and motivation were very low.

Natalie had fired the loudest, angriest, and most stubborn worker, but nothing improved (see the section on Agitators in chapter 3 to understand why). In fact, the problems got worse and the anger had now spread throughout the staff. This was not an emotionally well-regulated workplace; it was a miserable place for everyone (except the pampered spa guests, who didn't notice the troubles at all).

I had provided career development consulting to Natalie for many years, and I knew her to be an organizational genius who could identify logic-and-flow problems in any business and fix them as easily as you or I might tie our shoes. But I also knew that her people-management skills were not as good as her logistical skills; she had an intense work ethic and no patience for shenanigans. She and I often joked about people who came to work to live out their unhealed childhood traumas, earn money, and as an afterthought, do their jobs. Her staff seemed to be personifying this behavior, yet because they were treating the spa guests with care and empathy, I knew that something deeper was going on.

Service workers do a lot of *emotional labor*, where they display specific emotions and manage their own and their client's emotions as a part of doing their work (we'll explore this labor in chapter 3).[1] Personal service workers in occupations such as massage therapy, salon services, spa and resort reception, or hotel work are also given a great deal of responsibility for each client's experience of the environment — and of course, the more expensive the environment, the more extensive that responsibility is.

EMOTIONAL LABOR

Sociologist Arlie Hochschild's concept of the paid work you do to display or suppress specific emotions and emotional responses in the context of your job.

Personal service workers like Natalie's staff are supposed to soothe and cater to clients while physically and emotionally embodying the promises of the business. In a real way, they *are* the experience of the spa or the high-end environment, and their capacity for empathic relatedness is crucial. High-end personal service work requires a *ton* of emotional labor and empathy; it's heavy lifting and hard going in many cases. And sadly, this heavy lifting is usually not supported by managers or owners.

Natalie's staff were skilled at frontstage emotional labor and empathy. They displayed clear emotional and empathic skills with their clients, they handled needy and demanding clients gracefully, and the spa was doing well with lots of repeat business. But in the backstage, there was a great deal of anger being directed at Natalie, and there was a lot of infighting, envy, and jockeying for position among the staff. Scheduling had become a weekly nightmare where anger and envy were only increasing; it was rough. I know from my work that anger arises when people's boundaries and basic needs are being disrespected and that envy arises in response to inequality and injustice, so I wanted to know more about the working conditions at this spa. The anger and envy told me that there were issues of disrespect and unfairness in the spa, but I knew Natalie to be a fair and deeply respectful person — so why were these staff members attacking her (and each other)?

I focused on their workplace environment first and asked Natalie about her staff's schedule: how many breaks they had, what their service turnaround was (their time between clients), and where their breaks were taken. As I suspected, their turnarounds were short (10 minutes between clients) and there was no break room to speak of because most of the space in the spa had been dedicated to income-generating treatment rooms and guest-pampering waiting lounges. Natalie's thirty-person staff shared a small, drab, windowless locker room with a mini-fridge and a usually cluttered table with four chairs. Most of these bodyworkers avoided the break room and spent their required 15-minute breaks and lunch breaks walking around the crowded resort or sitting in a busy lounge area near the bar with their earbuds in. In these luxurious surroundings, these hardworking people had no place to rest or be alone; they had no *repair stations* at all.

REPAIR STATIONS

Sociologist Erving Goffman's concept of protected backstage areas where people can be real and honest about what they're facing, or where they can rest and get away from the frontstage demands of their lives or their jobs. Repair stations in the workplace can be physical spaces such as break rooms or smoking balconies, or they can be social spaces such as intentional communication practices or trusting relationships.

The Importance of Repair Stations

We all require rest, privacy, and what sociologist Erving Goffman called "repair stations," which are backstage spaces where we can let down our guard, speak the truth, and take a break from our frontstage or work-related behaviors and our emotional and empathic labor.[2] Even in our relaxed home lives, where we often have control over our time and our emotional labor, we need rest, privacy, and backstage repair stations (private bedrooms can be excellent repair stations, but so can loving relationships with friends and pets).

Every workplace needs repair stations (which don't have to be complex or expensive; see chapter 6), and when workers like Natalie's are expected to do extensive emotional labor and high-empathy-demand work as the public face of high-end service environments, they need very good repair stations indeed. Natalie's emotional laborers, however, had nothing; just a sad and shabby room in an otherwise well-furnished and opulent spa. This lack of care and respect reduced all aspects of these workers' motivation: competence, autonomy, *and* relatedness. That break room was not just gloomy and ugly — it reminded them every day of how powerless they were, and how unimportant their needs and their lives were to the resort owners. But they never saw the owners; they only saw Natalie, and unfortunately, she took the brunt of their hurt, pain, envy, and anger.

Emotional labor and high-empathy-demand work need to be managed expertly, because these forms of labor reliably lead to burnout in a poorly managed work environment. Sadly, Natalie was good at managing every other form of labor *except* emotional and empathic labor, and she expected her workers to behave well regardless of what their working conditions were. It's how she was raised, and it's a value she's carried throughout her life. In a way, her logical, business-like demeanor *was* her protective repair station; it helped her remain self-contained and separate from the emotional needs of others. Because of this, she was unaware of the stress that a lack of privacy and downtime were creating in her always-emotionally-available, yet emotionally disrespected and demotivated staff.

Natalie could intellectually understand the concepts of emotional labor and repair stations, but she wasn't able to perform skilled Perspective Taking with her frustrated staff (likely because they were making her life so difficult). She couldn't see things from their perspective, and she didn't realize that they were showing many signs of impending burnout. Natalie's Concern for Others also didn't kick in because her staff were acting out instead of communicating clearly. As such, she couldn't see the many valid reasons for their problems — she only saw brats.

In an emotionally well-regulated workplace, Natalie and her staff would have had many ways to speak about the stressors they were experiencing, but in this spa, they could only silence themselves, act out, jockey for power, attack, or be attacked.

The solution to Natalie's situation took some time. She did not have the temperament to supervise emotional laborers, the resort owners were too far removed to help, and Natalie, frankly, didn't have any interest in managing people when she had no true authority to make necessary changes. That was not where her genius lived. Her logistical skills were not being utilized well and she was expected to do heavy emotional labor that had no meaning for her. She was as burnt-out as her staff, when it came right down to it.

Because there were serious trust issues, I didn't work directly with Natalie's staff; they would not have been open to outside interference (and their emotions were providing all of the intelligence and energy they needed in any case). Instead of adding another person to this volatile mix, I worked in the background to help Natalie plan her exit strategy so that the spa would continue to flourish with a different (more people-focused) manager.

Over the following months, Natalie and I made small changes and watched how her staff responded; she took over one larger treatment space to create a real break room (the windowless room was redesigned to become an esthetician's station), and crucially, she asked the staff to design their own break room as a community. Because Natalie gave her people a sense of autonomy, competence, and choice, and a repair station of their own design, the attacks and infighting relieved to a great extent. They regained a sense of power and importance, and their shared task restored some of their caring relatedness with each other, which relieved a lot of their relationship strife and helped them retrieve their internal motivation. Natalie also made ingenious changes to the spa schedule so that everyone would have the option of 25-minute turnarounds if they needed them.

Notice that I didn't give Natalie's staff anger-management training or emotional intelligence training — I worked on the workplace structure, because their emotions were telling the absolute truth about their unworkable working environment. There was no need to train these emotionally skilled empathy professionals; they did high-end emotional labor and high-empathy-demand work every day. They didn't need to learn how to subdue their normal and necessary emotional responses to their miserable workplace — and they certainly didn't need to learn how to empathize; what they needed was a supportive and emotionally well-regulated social structure with functional repair stations and intelligent scheduling.

Their treatment of Natalie (and each other) was unskilled, and their responses were disruptive, but their emotions and reactions were correct. The situation was not workable, the social structure was dysfunctional and damaging to them, and their emotions were correct. Their protest was not a sign of emotional incompetence; it was a sign that their dignity, their autonomy, and their normal human emotions had no voice, no position, and no support in that workplace. So, we changed that, and *voilà*, the situation evened out and the intense emotions were no longer required on a daily basis. Their anger and envy didn't need to be on high alert because we listened and took appropriate and emotionally supportive actions to address the problems their emotions were so clearly pointing to.

Natalie left within a year (after she had trained a more people-focused manager), and she's now building her own sports apparel company. To generate income while her business is in its infancy, she's consulting with spas and resorts across the country. She flies in, finds the problems, suggests new processes and structures, and helps spas become better run and more profitable while protecting the time and privacy of their emotional laborers and empathy workers. Natalie works from her strengths now, and she's happy to be out of the people-managing business. Her empathic genius lives in the area of structure, finance, flow, and process improvement. People and their emotions just aren't that interesting to her, and that's perfectly fine. Empathy is not simply a person-to-person skill; empathy is our basic capacity to relate. Discovering where her empathy and interests flourished helped Natalie find work that suited her — and her emotions.

Case Study: Is Mateo Unempathic?

Mateo contacted me after his employees complained about his lack of empathy. That always perks up my ears, because a true lack of empathy is very rare. Empathy develops early, and empathy impairment can be a response to neglect or abuse at a specific stage of infancy, or it can be the result of a rare neurological condition.[3] But even among neglected, abused, and neurologically atypical children, empathy can and does develop; we are a highly social and empathically resilient species.

I asked Mateo for more information. He's a brilliant and well-traveled Spanish-American attorney who had started work at a large international aid organization when he was in his late thirties. This was a very late start for someone who wanted to work in the field, and even though he spoke five languages and had an elite education in international law, Mateo was at the end of a long line for promotions, behind people who had been at the organization since college and knew the lay of the land.

Though he had quit smoking a few years back, Mateo started up again so that he could join a group of workers who gathered on a balcony for regular smoking breaks.[4] In that fog of smoke, Mateo developed relationships and learned the social and emotional ins and outs of this complex multinational organization. He learned who had power (which is often not the person in charge). He learned about people coming and going, new positions being created, interpersonal connections and strife, and how the entire workplace functioned socially and logistically. Mateo's natural social skills and his capacity for relatedness helped him develop competence in this new social world. Within a year, he had been promoted three times, and was soon a director in charge of his own department of all-female managers, two of whom were his smoking buddies.

Mateo's social success suggested to me that his empathy and relationship skills were highly functional — and in talking to him, I noted that he read my emotional cues accurately, tracked with me, responded appropriately, laughed with me, and displayed concern and frustration about the situation. He also tried to employ Perspective Taking with the people who had called him unempathic so that he could see what they saw, but he was still confused (so was I). Mateo had well-developed emotional awareness, emotional skills, and empathy; he wasn't unavailable, socially uncomfortable, unaware, self-absorbed, manipulative, or lacking in empathic skills, so I focused my attention on the social situation rather than on his empathy levels. I especially focused on the hierarchical structure of his workplace, because hierarchies create social and emotional trouble all by themselves.

How Hierarchies Can Reduce Empathy — and Encourage Narcissism

Mateo's organization was a complex, formal hierarchy where people worked in an unequal pyramid structure: interns, aid workers, and administrative staff at the bottom, managers above them, directors above them, section chiefs above them, and international governments above the whole organization. This organization's pay grades, responsibilities, and access to information were laid out in a rigid and highly segregated (Theory X) way — in stark contrast to the democratic, friendly, and informal (Theory Y) world of the smoking balcony.

But the existence of the smoking balcony wasn't a coincidence. When hierarchies enforce layers and separations and control people's access to power and influence, significant social imbalances are created — and these imbalances affect people's emotions and motivation negatively. Hierarchies enforce artificial and formalized relationships that reduce competence, autonomy, and relatedness — and in response, informal relationships and groups like the smoking balcony will need to arise so that people can restore these vital qualities and retrieve their internal motivation once again.

Social systems are not as controllable as we like to believe they are; instead, they're living, evolving entities that continually equalize themselves and develop their own internal rules, even (and especially if) we try to enforce rules or control from the top down or from the outside in. Backstage repair stations like the smoking balcony are necessary in all social structures (Natalie's spa workers were destabilized because they had no repair stations), but in rigid and hierarchical bureaucracies, informal repair stations are essential for the health and well-being of all.

Hierarchies are by their very nature unbalanced, unequal, and often dehumanizing, and people inside them must work to balance themselves and equalize their relationships. Individuals and groups require warm and supportive relationships, equal access to information, and equality in general.

This equality and balance support competence, autonomy, and relatedness, but if equality and balance don't exist in the formal social structure, they will arise in informal repair stations such as the smoking balcony, lunchtime groups, texting chains, carpools, or in fabled water cooler conversations. Mateo knew this instinctively; it's why he went out on that balcony in the first place, and it was an ingenious move. He introduced himself to a true center of information and access in that artificially segregated and rigidly controlled hierarchy, and he entered into what I call the *gossip network*, which is a crucial part of any social structure.

GOSSIP NETWORKS

In contrast to formal information networks that exist to support the formal power structure, these are essential informal networks that contain extensive social, emotional, and empathic information about the complex inner workings of a workplace or a group. We work to make these vital networks ethical, supportive, and empathic.

Gossip has a terrible reputation because many people use it as a form of social violence, but that's not gossip's fault! At its heart, gossip is simply (and powerfully) an informal communication process that exists in all relationships, all genders, all ages, and all social structures (we'll explore the surprising and essential genius of gossip in chapter 5). The informal communication practice of gossip is a type of repair station that's present in every human relationship and every group, and it becomes essential in formalized, segregated, and unequal structures like Mateo's aid organization.

In that balcony gossip network, Mateo had accessed the vital, living heart of his organization, and he gained crucial social and emotional knowledge that helped him succeed. But when he became a director, he no longer had free time or the need to be out on that balcony. He also stopped smoking when he took over his department and shifted his friendships to professional relationships. This sudden shift was the reason his managers were complaining about his empathy; his smoking buddies were destabilized by losing their informal relationships with him.

I asked, and yes, the complaints originated with the two women who had been his smoking buddies, and they had gathered allies among the other managers in his department. Their fear, anger, and jealousy arose (rightfully so) in response to this sudden loss of closeness, but there was no way for them to speak about what they truly felt in this depersonalizing bureaucracy; instead, they had to create a new repair station, which was an unhealthy gossip network focused on Mateo's alleged lack of empathy.

The alarm that Mateo's managers felt, and their accusation that he was unempathic weren't completely off base — they weren't true *yet*, but their accusation might have become true over time because unhealthy hierarchies can negatively affect the empathy and humanity of the people inside them.

There's a troubling dynamic that occurs in power-based hierarchies of any kind, and Mateo fell into it when he began to distance himself from his managers. The general rule of thumb in hierarchies is that we must study and understand the needs of the people above us; we must know and work with the people at our level; but we may not need to pay deep attention to the people below us at all. Our access to power in a hierarchy may depend upon our ability to create transactional, upward-focused relationships rather than empathic ones, and we may lose our awareness of and empathy for the people below us (and eventually, for everyone else).

Mateo was inadvertently heading in this troubling direction, because in unhealthy hierarchies, most people need to focus their empathy and their intelligence laterally and upward to survive. In Mateo's organization, this meant that he needed to focus on other directors, section chiefs, and government bureaucrats; those were the "important" people in his working life now. The demands of the hierarchy and his absence from the smoking balcony threatened to reduce his empathic capacity, and though his staff's concerns were correct, they weren't able to clearly identify what they were seeing. They were right to be alarmed, however, because the unequal social positioning in a hierarchy can create unempathic and narcissistic behavior in otherwise emotionally healthy people, and it can create a perfect environment for people with narcissistic personality disorder (NPD) to flourish.

Hierarchies and inequality create transactional, rewards-based, power-grabbing social environments that will naturally bring forth powerful emotional responses against injustice (such as anger, envy, jealousy, depression, anxiety, and other necessary emotions). But in emotionally unregulated hierarchies, these correct and necessary emotional responses will be suppressed and shunned. Emotionally healthy people will usually lose their motivation or leave, and the only people who'll remain are those who flourish in the presence of inequality, transactional and unempathic relationships, emotional suppression, and competition.

We love to think of ourselves as rugged individuals who aren't fazed by the external world, but this isn't how human nature works; we're all deeply affected by our relationships and social structures, as the research on workplace mental health clearly shows. Without supportive social structures, we tend to suffer or even lose our emotional and empathic abilities (which might have happened to Mateo if he had continued in his distanced hierarchical role). And it's important to note that NPD, which is a condition of reduced empathy, impaired shame, heightened competitiveness, and an inflated sense of self-worth, is very rare — it's found in less than 1% of the population. But in emotionally unregulated and competitive hierarchies such as the military, medical schools, police departments, and the corporate world, you may find large groupings of people with narcissistic behavior or actual NPD.

For instance, studies have found that 20% of military personnel and 17% of first-year medical students display signs of NPD, while some studies have suggested that 50% of CEOs have narcissistic tendencies or full-fledged NPD.[5] Rigid hierarchies and competition attract, reward, and preferentially select for manipulative, competitive, unempathic, and narcissistic behavior and NPD. Superiority *requires* inferiors and a lack of healthy relatedness, and it creates a perfect (yet empathically devastating) environment for people who don't actually know how to function in healthy, empathic, or equality-based relationships.

It's sort of sweet, in a strange way, that we've built structures where emotionally unaware and empathically delayed people can flourish and make a living. But if we didn't *mean* to create a breeding ground for narcissism and empathy deficits, then we've got some serious reorganization to do! If you find that you've inadvertently created an organization with wide disparities in salary and power, segregated departments, top-down management, a carrot-and-stick reward system, and a rigid hierarchy (or any one of these things), you'll very likely be surrounded by conflict, injustice, inequality, bullying, demotivation, and misery. If you'd like to address this situation, the principles in this book can help you and your colleagues develop new skills and awareness, an emotionally well-regulated social structure, and a flexible and livable environment that treats everyone with respect and empathy. Segregated and competitive hierarchies can't do any of these things well, if at all.

It was once thought that hierarchical workplaces had some sort of value, even though they're based on Theory X (workers must be graded, rewarded, punished, and controlled or they won't work) and are deeply demotivating structures. However, many organizational behavior professionals, such as Edgar Schein and Lindred Greer, no longer believe that hierarchical structures are appropriate for 21st century workers.[6] This is especially important to understand in light of the fact that people no longer work for the same company all their lives, or even for more than 4 years (on average in the US).[7] Rigid, hierarchical, Theory X organizations cannot retain a stable workforce, because good people can and certainly will leave. The new understanding is that workplaces must become more democratic and develop flexible networks built on equality-based, Theory Y adult relationships.

During this pandemic, we're seeing newly home-based workers relishing their freedom, and we're seeing some hierarchical businesses learning how to function democratically because they cannot exert power over workers in the old ways. Some organizations are playing the old, tired game and installing keystroke trackers and timers on people's home-based computers, but many are learning how to treat their workers with empathy and dignity. I hope this humanizing trend continues.

The old structures — the rigid hierarchies that separated people unnaturally and treated workers like schoolchildren — are showing their age and crumbling. Healthier and more democratic organizations are slowly taking their place, and they tend to be flat rather than hierarchical and treat adults as adults. In humane and democratic workplaces, there are generally no managers of people's behavior (and there are no performance appraisals either). Instead, the work speaks for itself and people are held accountable in more natural and respectful ways; workers are trusted and surrounded with support rather than managed. (Some famous examples of flat, democratic, and manager-free workplaces are Semco Partners in Brazil and GORE-TEX in the US. GORE-TEX founder W. L. "Bill" Gore called the flexible networks at his company *lattices*.[8])

In Mateo's organization, the smoking balcony acted as a flat, democratic, Theory Y space where workers could be together as equals and friends. This balcony repair station protected workers from the emotionally unregulated, motivation-damaging, and empathy-reducing influence of their rigid hierarchy.

Mateo's move away from the informality of the balcony and into a more rigid form of professionalism wasn't unempathic, it was just the way things were done in that impersonal and unequal social structure. However, it had the effect of suddenly removing relatedness and belonging that were already well developed; it was a shock. While his mistake was understandable, it was a doozy. Mateo's smoking buddies didn't just lose their relatedness to him, but they also lost the sense of autonomy and social competence that they had all created together on that balcony. Their jealousy, fear, and anger were alerting them to the loss, certainly, but also to the dangers of losing Mateo's friendship. Because this formal, bureaucratic aid organization wasn't an emotionally well-regulated social structure (at all), Mateo's managers had no way to talk about what had happened to them, except to attack Mateo's character and his empathic abilities. It was painful for him, but he understood that his organization gave them no other language and no other social or emotional tools to address this wrong.

Restoring Empathy in Simple Ways (Once You Understand How Empathy Works)

My consultation with Mateo was a quick fix, because he had not been in his position of power long enough to truly lose his empathy. Hierarchical social structures tend to seek out, create, and reward unempathic and even narcissistic behaviors in the people who rise to the top, but Mateo hadn't been damaged in that way yet. Thank goodness.

There was nothing we could do about the built-in inequalities or the inflexible, dehumanizing structure of the organization, but we could rehumanize Mateo's relationships. He and I focused on the specific aspect of empathy that the women were complaining about (it was Concern for Others — they felt that he no longer cared for or about them). We also explored his sudden shift away from the balcony, and the leadership behaviors that were required in the formal hierarchy that were being misinterpreted as a lack of empathy.

We developed ways for Mateo to spend more friendly, informal break times with his managers without sacrificing the efficiency and professionalism that he expected from them or from himself. Problem solved; empathy reengaged. Actually, the empathy had never been disengaged — we simply restored some of the vital informality that the hierarchy and Mateo's new position had erased. Now, Mateo's working group had access to their own friendly repair station and informal gossip network that included Mateo instead of further isolating him (and thankfully, Mateo didn't need to start smoking again to build it).

We'll explore many ways to create healthy repair stations in part 2 so that you and your colleagues can build emotionally well-regulated social structures. We'll also focus on what I call *large-group social skills*, which many of us haven't been able to develop because we've only worked in emotionally unregulated workplaces.

LARGE-GROUP SOCIAL SKILLS

Our ability to understand, navigate, relate, and work successfully within large and interconnected groups such as extended families, schools, committees, workplaces, and organizations.

Large-Group Social Skills Are Uncommon

Many people assume that social and emotional skills are acquired in childhood, and that adults develop workplace-focused social skills as a continuation of that childhood process. However, those assumptions are often wrong. Unless you grew up in a large family that owned a business where you worked for many years in many different positions, it's unlikely that you developed the multilayered social and emotional skills you need to work with (or manage) large groups of adults. And even if you did grow up in a family business, your family may not have learned or taught you these skills either.

Instead, most of us learn our large-group social skills at school. Sadly, those skills don't translate reliably to the working world, because schools are made for children. Schools are artificially segregated by age (and sometimes by sex) and teachers usually have power over (not with) the students, who often create alliances to protect themselves from the effects of this top-down form of social control. Schools also tend to be demotivating due to their use of grades and rewards that interfere with autonomy and competence (and relatedness).[9] It's hard to develop healthy social skills or a self-determined work ethic in the unequal and demotivating Theory X environment of most schools.

Many of us come to the workplace directly from school where, for the most part, we were not involved in the decisions that affected our lives. As students, we usually had little to no say about our schedules, the curriculum, our teachers, or the setup of our classrooms. We didn't control the duration of our work, our relaxation, our exercise, or our private time. We may not have had any repair stations or even a basic right to privacy or autonomy. We were also not the equals of our teachers, the principal, the school board, or our parents and guardians at home. For 12 years or more, we learned how to obey and make our way in a large-group environment that was deeply unequal, and where our true needs could only exist in relationship to whatever authority figures wanted. Many people think that this unequal and choiceless approach is a necessary way to train and educate children in large groups, and sadly, in our crowded, underfunded, and test-focused educational environment, they may be correct. However, this training, which interferes with all three aspects of motivation (competence, autonomy, and relatedness), and is rarely offered in an emotionally well-regulated environment, creates many problems as people mature and enter the workforce.

Because there's no clear transition out of the powerlessness of being a student (even graduate education involves relative voicelessness and choicelessness) — and no training on how to create and nurture complex adult relationships in large groups — many of us bring our student behaviors to the workplace.[10] We sit in our chairs or cubicles, do our assignments because someone in power told us to, and we get our grades, which in the workplace translates into access, attention from higher ups, money, or promotions. But we don't tend to behave as equals, and many of us bring a child's view of group behavior into our working lives. It's all we know.

When inequality, conflict, pain, and trouble occur at work, many of us tend to do what we did as powerless and voiceless schoolchildren. We act out with the information our emotions give us, but we often don't know why. We may silence ourselves with apathy or depression, we may create unhealthy alliances among our peers with poorly managed jealousy and envy, or we may act out in anger, anxiety, or even panic (and so forth) — but we don't often make clear-eyed decisions about our situation. In school, we could almost never make mature or entirely autonomous decisions, so it's not surprising that we struggle as adults to navigate the workplace successfully or address our troubles directly. We can see this in Mateo's and Natalie's situations: Mateo's staff communicated their necessary jealousy laterally within their gossip network and then called him unempathic, which was an attack on his character rather than a mature form of communication. Mateo needed help to decipher what was going on because this wasn't direct or effective communication (it was also incorrect). Natalie's staff, on the other hand, communicated their necessary anger and envy only through their troubling behaviors; no one even bothered to speak up or explain the problems in a way that Natalie could understand. None of these otherwise skilled and intelligent professionals knew how to speak directly to Mateo or Natalie about problems that affected them, their workplace, and their lives.

But Mateo and Natalie had unintentionally contributed to these problems. When people become managers and bosses, they may unconsciously behave like distant, teacher-like or principal-like authority figures, as Mateo did when he shifted away from casual friendliness, or as Natalie did when she described her staff as bratty children. These detached and controlling roles didn't suit Mateo or Natalie, and they didn't support their workers at all, yet both of these highly intelligent people adopted unworkable roles without realizing it. Their workers viewed both Mateo and Natalie as having power over them (not with them); therefore, no one attempted to communicate appropriately about the troubles. No one even had the language to do so. In fact, while everyone was unconsciously trapped in their school-based social roles, only their emotions knew what was happening in those artificial, disempowering, demotivating, and emotionally unregulated environments.

Many managers work to avoid top-down, controlling behaviors, and that's a great start. But most management training programs don't teach about emotions, empathy, motivation, or large-group behaviors — and they also bring school-based ideas of authority and obedience into the workplace by giving managers more power and authority than they would (or should) have in equality-based adult relationships. Bosses and owners struggle, too, because they're not taught about emotions, empathy, or large-group behaviors either. And they're often sold the old, tired story about needing to assert authoritarian, hierarchical, Theory X control over their worker-children.

Even HR professionals have little to no training in emotions, empathy, how groups operate, or how individuals find or create their places in those groups. HR professionals are also required to monitor, grade, and even punish workers as if they are inferiors or children, and not fellow adults. This can mean that HR departments, which should be places for workers to find support, are often viewed with suspicion or even hostility. No wonder we all struggle, and no wonder there have been thousands of workplace books and millions of workplace consultants who try to fix what's wrong. If any of those approaches worked, surely they would have worked by now. The reason they haven't worked is that the way we think about work is deeply confused (or even ignorant) when it comes to emotions, empathy, and motivation, and it's (mostly) unconsciously working from a failed child-versus-authority-figure model that causes misery for everyone.

As it stands now, the modern workplace as an entity is set up to fail because it doesn't understand or provide for adult human needs and realities. Luckily, we can change that, and it's really not so difficult once we understand emotions, empathy, motivation, and how to create emotionally well-regulated adult social structures. The work Mateo and Natalie did to address the troubles in their workplaces wasn't rocket science; they simply had to consider the human needs and emotional realities of their colleagues and use their power and empathy in service to their fellow workers. And it was the emotions in both cases that told them exactly where the problems were. The solutions they came up with were empathic and kind, but they were also good business. Mateo's troubled work relationships would eventually affect everyone's productivity and mental health, while Natalie's staff were essentially in a mutiny that was tearing the spa apart. There is no value to letting people suffer, and there is no profit in remaining ignorant about emotions, empathy, motivation, and human needs.

The modern workplace has stolen a great deal from all of us. It has eaten up our time; it has thrown us into relationships and groups without giving us the support or information we need to thrive; it has treated us as if we are untrustworthy children; it has expected us to manage people as if they are beneath us; it has diminished our emotional, empathic, and communication skills; and it has caused entirely unecessary suffering (and even death). People like Mateo, or Natalie's staff, are expected to be empathic, but very few workplaces know what empathy is, how it works, or even that it *is* work. Therefore, emotional laborers and high-empathy-demand workers tend to do their important work without any support or recognition. The workplace as a socio-emotional model has failed us, yet we humans created it, and we can recreate it so that it will finally be a worthwhile place to spend our time and our energy.

Laying the Foundation for Your Unique Healthy Workplace

I have called the modern workplace an *unintentional community*, because in most cases, people are thrown into groups without clear models for adult working relationships or effective emotional skills, empathic skills, or communication processes. As a result, workplace cultures tend to arise in the shadows, where indirect communication, hidden repair stations, troubling gossip networks, workplace bullying, and rebellions can take hold. This is not the fault of individuals; the social and emotional troubles we see in the workplace are predictable when we understand emotions, empathy, motivation, and social groups. Thankfully, these troubles can be addressed, and healthy changes can occur; we just need to creatively re-envision and alter our workplace social structures so that people and their emotions can have freedom of expression in a healthy and emotionally well-regulated environment.

UNINTENTIONAL COMMUNITY

A group of people who are thrown together haphazardly without dependable communication processes, emotional skills, empathy skills, or clear models for relationships or conflict. Sadly, most workplaces are unintentional communities.

There's a model I use in teaching that will be very helpful as we think about changing our workplace behaviors and our approach to emotions. It's the consciousness and competence model that helps us observe how people learn and develop new skills.[11] This well-known model explores the flow and dance between consciousness and unconsciousness, and between competence and incompetence.

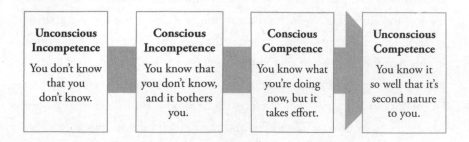

Unconscious Incompetence
You don't know that you don't know.

Conscious Incompetence
You know that you don't know, and it bothers you.

Conscious Competence
You know what you're doing now, but it takes effort.

Unconscious Competence
You know it so well that it's second nature to you.

Most of us have been taught to avoid anything that makes us look or feel incompetent, but as the left side of this model shows, incompetence is an important part of any learning process.

We like to think of ourselves as conscious and competent at everything (at all times), but that's not how learning or mastery work. Unconsciousness *and* incompetence are equally vital to the process of learning and growing.

For most of us, information about emotions, empathy, and social groups lives on the incompetent left side of this model. We may not realize that we don't know what we're doing — or we may know something is wrong but have no idea what to do about it. Because we unconsciously bring our school-based behaviors into the workplace, and because the workplace is unconscious about emotions, many of us function socially in Unconscious Incompetence — we don't see or understand our behavior; it's just how things *are*, and we don't question it. If we're uncomfortable or miserable at work — angry, depressed, envious, anxious, and so forth — we may move into *Conscious* Incompetence, where we know something is wrong, but we can't figure out what to do (and it bothers us). The emotions bring us into consciousness, which is a vital aspect of every learning process, and if we know how to access their genius, we can move toward social and emotional competence.

As we step into the competent right side of this model, we'll develop Conscious Competence in regard to emotions, empathy, motivation, and the creation of emotionally well-regulated social structures built for self-motivated adults. It will be work, and we'll struggle and likely step back into Conscious *Incompetence*, but the important thing is that we won't ever fall all the way back to the beginning again; we won't become unconscious. We're conscious of the problems now and we understand something about our areas of incompetence. We're on the learning journey and our incompetence is absolutely necessary — otherwise, we'd never grow or evolve. But notice in this pathway that when something (such as a practice, skill, or behavior) becomes second nature, unconsciousness will arise again, and you'll be in Unconscious *Competence*. For instance, think of how incompetent people are when they learn how to ride a bike, and how much intense conscious effort they need just to remain upright. But when they have enough experience, bike-riding becomes second nature to them, and they don't have to think about it at all; they become Unconsciously Competent. Unconsciousness is as important to true learning as incompetence is. It's a lovely model.

And luckily, it's not hard to become conscious about how emotions, empathy, communication, and social groups work, because we've all been in groups and relationships all of our lives. We have competence there, even if it's unconscious or hidden almost entirely in our emotional responses. We all have social skills, emotional skills, and empathic skills that we use every day, even if our social structures are very badly managed, and even if we have no words for what we're doing. We've all found ways to identify healthy authority figures and groups, and how to survive terrible ones. We've all found ways to create repair stations or enter gossip networks to share our emotional information. We may not know exactly what we're doing — we may be unconscious — but we're doing it.

When Mateo's staff complained about his empathy, they were using a current buzzword to talk about the sudden and jarring inequality in their relationships with him; their emotions helped them become *conscious* of the problem, but they misattributed it to empathy because they had no other language. When Natalie called her struggling staff "spoiled brat children," she was witnessing their schoolyard behaviors correctly, even if she had little conscious awareness about why they were gathering together, or how she and the resort owners had unconsciously created an inhumane workplace where her staff had no direct way to communicate about the lack of respect and support they were enduring. Their emotions told them the truth, but because the spa was an emotionally unregulated environment, they had no way to work with this excellent emotional information consciously or respectfully.

Our emotions and empathy are always working to motivate us, to help us become conscious and competent, to help us develop our relationships, and to help us navigate through the workplace social world and get our best work done. These emotional processes are already occurring, often beneath our conscious awareness, so the next step in the learning process is to develop our conscious awareness of these processes so that we can build a healthy, empathically sound, and emotionally well-regulated workplace for everyone. As we learn new ways to work with emotions, empathy, and motivation in adult working groups, remember this dance between consciousness and unconsciousness, and between competence and incompetence. All four are necessary for healthy learning, change, and growth.

This model will also help us as we learn to perform what's called *empathic design*. When I first heard that term a few years ago, I was so excited to know what it meant. Someone told me that it's a design process where you:

1. Confer with the people who will use whatever you design.
2. Design the thing and present it to the people.
3. Make changes if the thing doesn't work for the people.

I laughed and asked, "Wait, isn't that just *good* design?" Empathy is a buzzword these days, and people love to slap the word onto just about everything, so let's just go with it. As we gather the tools we need to empathically design our workplace social structures, let's remember that the process of good, empathic design involves watching how the structure works, getting feedback from people and their emotions, and being willing to change and update the structure to better serve everyone's needs. Empathic design is a continual process of moving back and forth between competence and incompetence, and between consciousness and unconsciousness — as every meaningful learning process does. Here's to the empathic adventure of learning how to design our own healthy and emotionally well-regulated workplaces.

EMPATHIC DESIGN

A design process that focuses on the end users' needs and emotions, and employs multiple tryouts and redesigns until the end product meets those needs.

In the next chapter, we'll explore the emotional labor and empathic work that make our workplaces function but are often performed unconsciously and without support. We'll learn how to identify this work so that we can consciously build emotional and empathic support into our workplace social systems.

3

Identifying Emotional Labor
and Empathic Workloads

I
n all social structures, people learn how to care for each other — so it's
natural for workplace colleagues to pick up the slack when someone is
sick, overwhelmed, or overworked. This is a sign of a healthy community, as long as picking up the slack is voluntary, consciously done, and of
short duration.

But there's a different kind of slack work that occurs in emotionally
unregulated workplaces, where individuals need to perform unpaid and
unsupported emotional labor or empathic heavy lifting to stabilize their
workplace community. This labor can understandably lead to fatigue and
conflict, but because this labor isn't written into anyone's job description,
workers may not understand what's happening to them. Emotions such as
anger, jealousy, envy, anxiety, or depression may arise to address the problems,
but if people don't have emotional skills, they may shut down their emotions
with unhealthy repression or act them out with unhealthy expression.

People rarely act out emotionally without reason; I see these unacknowledged emotional laborers as providing emotional balance in
a larger structure that *requires* whatever behaviors they're displaying.
These people may not be entirely conscious about what they're doing
(they and their emotions may be drawn into these behaviors unconsciously), but their emotions are usually telling the truth about what's
occurring. We saw this with Natalie's difficult, struggling spa workers
(whose emotions were signaling the absolute truth about inequality and

their impending burnout), and we saw it with Mateo's managers (whose emotions had correctly identified an endangering loss of relatedness with him). People respond emotionally to what's going on in their social groups; their emotions tell them what's happening and how they feel about it. How they respond and react to their emotions depends a great deal on their individual emotional skills — but it also depends on whether they're in an emotionally well-regulated social structure or not.

In an emotionally *unregulated* structure, nearly all emotional and social responses will be unconscious and unskilled — people will likely step back into their school-based or childhood behaviors in response to the problems they experience.

Most of us like to think of ourselves as unique individuals who are in control of our own behaviors, and there is some truth to that. But our social environment — our relationships, the rules at play, and the social structure — is a powerful determining factor in how we'll be able to respond in any given situation. If we and the people around us have emotional skills, communication skills, healthy relationships, respect, and support, then we'll have options when our emotions tell us that something's wrong. We'll be able to grow beyond childhood and beyond school to learn new ways to be competent in our adult relationships. But if we're in an emotionally unregulated and demotivating environment, then we won't have healthy options for emotional expression and we'll fall back (often unconsciously) to what we learned elsewhere. Or, we'll fall into unpaid emotional labor that may work for a while, but usually isn't noticed or supported and may lead to burnout. In these unhealthy social environments, we'll often experience discomfort, misunderstandings, and misery — not because *we* are broken, but because the social system cannot or will not support us properly.

And sadly, when we see misery in the workplace, we often add to the existing social and emotional problems by mistakenly focusing our attention on individuals, as I mentioned earlier. People waste so much time focusing on the problems of individuals in the workplace (or in any unhealthy relationship or group) when it's usually the social system that's at fault. It's very difficult for an individual to maintain healthy social and emotional skills in an environment that does not support those skills. In fact, in emotionally unregulated workplaces, it's very common for talented, mature, and socially aware people to leave after they become depressed, angry, apathetic, and demotivated. They understand enough about their emotions to know that the workplace itself is the cause of their misery, and they'll search for someplace better. The people who are left behind tend not to be as aware; they may be unconscious about their own emotional reactions, and though they may realize that their workplace is unhealthy, they may only be able to act out their school- and childhood-based behaviors, which means that the workplace will become even more emotionally unregulated and troubled (if these school-based behaviors include bullying, see the Workplace Bullying Resources on page 253).[1]

Unconsciously Incompetent managers and business leaders will often see this trouble but completely misunderstand and misattribute it to individuals and their work ethic. They may bring in consultants and coaches, they may force new workplace processes or behaviors onto their workers, they may implement rewards and punishments, they may enforce team-building exercises or retreats, or they may enforce artificial happiness with dance parties, corporate mindfulness trainings, snack wagons, ping-pong tables, or by assigning "Funbassadors" (I kid you not). In essence, they will treat their workers as if they are misbehaving children who need to be trained, shaped, punished, or jollied with treats and bribes.

But the social structure will remain unchanged and emotionally unregulated, and now there will be new problems that no one can address because new processes were enforced from the top down (or because happiness is the only emotion that's allowed). In response, motivation will plummet (as it should), communication will go underground into secret repair stations and gossip networks, and misery will be baked into the entire system. It's a workplace-wide catastrophe.

As I pointed out earlier, emotions don't just belong to individuals; they're a crucial part of our social intelligence, and they carry vital information about what's going on in our social world. Workplace emotional difficulties are sometimes isolated to one person, but more often than not, they're pinpoint-accurate responses to destabilized or dysfunctional social systems. If we make the mistake of focusing on individuals, or if we treat their normal emotional responses as problems or character flaws, we'll misread the situation entirely and fix the wrong things for the wrong reasons while the real problems only intensify. And remember the ethical component here: All workers have rights to emotional privacy, dignity, and autonomy. A worker's internal emotional functioning belongs to them and is not usually the issue; the emotional atmosphere in the workplace social structure nearly always is.

But if we cannot see the structure because we're still viewing the world through a powerless child's eyes, or because we've mistakenly taken on a distant or unapproachable position of authority, then all we can do is focus unprofitably and incorrectly on individuals. And even in situations of workplace bullying, where individuals *are* creating problems, the workplace social structure must be held accountable. Why is the workplace so emotionally unregulated and unsafe? Why is bullying tolerated? Why aren't victims able to report abuse and be supported? Why are there no effective mechanisms of emotional regulation and care?

As we learn how to identify the emotional and empathic demands in our workplaces, we'll be able to see how a poorly managed environment will create reliable problems for groups and individuals. Emotionally unregulated social systems will interfere with relationships, lead to self-silencing or exaggerated emotional responses, and reduce the motivating factors of competence, autonomy, and relatedness. As a result, consistent patterns of demotivation and workplace misery will follow.

However, you'll also see people (or entire departments) performing unpaid and unrecognized emotional and empathic labor because there are glaring unmet needs in the social structure. People will naturally react to unequal and unjust social systems, and some will step forward to carry the weight for others. However, this unsupported emotional labor and empathic work can be draining, so it's important to become aware of it. It's normal for people to pick up the slack for each other, but doing so should be a conscious choice; no one should be forced to do unpaid emotional and empathic labor just because their workplace is emotionally unregulated.

Understanding Emotional Labor, Emotion Work, and Empathy Work

We'll look at specific kinds of emotional laborers and empathic workers in this chapter, but first, let's define these types of work so that we can become conscious about them. It's important to know what these often-hidden forms of emotional and empathic labor involve so that we can begin to envision new and functional ways for this labor to become conscious, well regulated, and sustainable in our workplaces and in our lives.

Emotional labor is a marvelous concept that we touched on lightly in chapter 2. It was developed by sociologist Arlie Hochschild and explored in her famous 1983 book, *The Managed Heart*. Emotional labor is the paid work we do to manage or generate our emotions, such as the required happiness and friendliness that flight attendants are expected to display no matter how they're treated or how they feel. Or the required anger and unfriendliness that bill collectors are expected to display, no matter how they were raised to treat people or how they feel about people who are struggling financially. Emotional labor is an often unacknowledged yet crucial aspect of many (but not all) occupations.

EMOTIONAL LABOR

Sociologist Arlie Hochschild's concept of the paid work you do to display or suppress specific emotions and emotional responses in the context of your job.

For instance, Natalie's spa staff did heavy emotional labor to create the public face of a calming and nurturing environment for their upscale clients, but Mateo's managers worked mostly within their own departments and weren't expected to suppress or display specific emotions in order to get their jobs done. Mateo's staff had to behave themselves and treat each other humanely, but their pay wasn't based on their ability to perform the emotional labor of suppressing or overemphasizing specific emotions (as Natalie's staff had to do).

Emotional labor is usually (but not always) required in public-facing jobs where people have to cater to the needs of customers (or get customers to do something such as buy a car or pay a bill). Workers who do a lot of emotional labor require a lot of emotional support, but sadly, very few high-emotional-labor workplaces provide this support. As a result, burnout is common for emotional laborers. This burnout is completely unnecessary, but because emotions and emotional labor are not usually recognized or understood, many high-emotional-labor workplaces see high absenteeism, conflict, apathy, depression, burnout, and continual staff turnover.

Jobs that aren't public facing, such as research and development, office work, shipping, or manufacturing tend not to require a great deal of emotional labor. These low-emotional-labor jobs still require emotionally well-regulated social structures, but their workers don't usually need the advanced support that heavy-lifting emotional laborers do.

Emotion work is another concept developed by Arlie Hochschild. Emotion work is a more encompassing term that includes the work we do (paid or unpaid) to manage our emotions or the emotions of others in order to keep our relationships and our social world running smoothly.[2] For instance, you do emotion work when you choose not to snap at someone you love when they're being annoying. You also do emotion work when you're in a deep and empathic relationship so that you can maintain your connection and let your partner know how important they are to you. Some of your emotion work will be draining, but a lot of it is nourishing, and the key is to make sure that there's an even balance between draining and nourishment in your emotion work (see page 117 to measure this balance in your own emotion work).

EMOTION WORK

Sociologist Arlie Hochschild's concept of the work you do outside of your paid position to manage your own emotions or the emotions of others to sustain your relationships and the smooth flow of everyday life.

For instance, if you do a great deal of draining emotion work at home with struggling children or ill parents, it's important to have an equal or greater amount of nourishing emotion work in your life, which you'll receive from loving and funny friends, mates, siblings, coworkers, and/or therapeutic relationships. Emotionally well-regulated relationships and social structures are necessary for everyone, but they're crucial for people who perform a lot of emotional labor or a lot of draining emotion work.

Empathy work is a concept that I've developed. It encompasses both paid emotional labor and unpaid emotion work, and also includes a specialized awareness of multiple emotions, empathy, and large-group social skills. For instance, healthcare and counseling professionals in high-empathy-demand positions are empathy workers *and* emotional laborers, because they not only need to display or suppress specific emotions, but they also need to understand a great deal about the emotions and needs of others through the empathic skills of Emotion Recognition, Empathic Accuracy, and Perspective Taking (see page 48 for a reminder of the six aspects of empathy). Empathy workers also need to have extensive Emotion Regulation skills, a natural store of Concern for Others, and be able to perform skilled Perceptive Engagement within large groups.

EMPATHY WORK

My conceptualization of an extensive and multilayered form of emotion work that involves an understanding of emotions, empathy, relationships, social structures, and large-group social skills.

What Mateo did out on that smoking balcony was empathy work, because it required much more than one-on-one emotion work; he needed to understand complex social relationships and social structures and take many different perspectives so that he could navigate skillfully in the deeply segregated hierarchy of his international aid organization. Natalie, on the other hand, did not have strong skills in empathy work; while she could do one-on-one emotion work with individuals, the more complex and intertwined behaviors of her spa staff were mostly invisible to her. Unlike Mateo, Natalie did not have the wide-ranging Empathic Accuracy and Perspective Taking skills she needed to empathize skillfully with large groups of people or see things from their perspective; her empathic abilities were focused on systems and processes rather than on people.*

*HR and hiring note: It's crucial for hiring managers to seek out empathy workers like Mateo for people-management positions, and not to force workers like Natalie (whose genius and empathy are focused on systems) to manage people. So much workplace misery occurs because we don't yet understand emotional labor, emotion work, or empathy work. We don't yet understand the differences between them, and we don't yet know how to build emotionally well-regulated workplaces that bring this unpaid work into conscious awareness. We also don't understand how to identify and hire people into roles that support their natural skills. Empathy work is a unique form of work, and not everyone can do it; that's okay. What's not okay is when people like Natalie are expected to be empathy workers when it's not their area of expertise.

Observing These Three Forms of Work

We don't all have jobs where emotional labor (such as displaying continuous friendliness or continuous anger) is required; however, we all do emotion work in our close relationships and we all do some form of empathy work in group relationships or in complex, high-empathy-demand jobs like counseling or healthcare.

The distinctions between these forms of work are important to understand, not just in hiring, but in everyday situations. We need to know what kinds of work we're expected to do and what kinds of support we can depend on (or create, if we're in positions of influence). We also need to know what kinds of emotional and empathic work our colleagues are doing so that we'll know how to support them, and how much we can ask of them at any given time.

Here's an example: If you know that your coworker deals with rude and insensitive customers, and that he's required to do heavy emotional labor to maintain a façade of friendliness and professionalism, you would know not to load him up with your own emotional needs or stories about your own troubles. You would treat his work as *real* work, and you would provide support, give him a break, or simply make eye contact and roll your eyes to let him know that you see what's going on. You might even provide a repair station for him by welcoming his need to down-regulate and chat or gossip between customer contacts. Of course, you would need to monitor your own emotional health and well-being before you offered your ear and your time — you don't want both of you to burn out — but you would have a clear understanding of what he was doing, what you were doing, and why.

In most workplaces, this kind of understanding doesn't exist, and people perform unregulated and unsupported emotional labor, emotion work, and empathy work every day. Most workplaces are emotionally unregulated, and therefore, no one is responsible for or aware of what's going on (except our emotions, of course). Therefore, workers are left to their own devices to find private spaces to rest, regulate their emotions, develop supportive relationships, or create repair stations. We know that most workers aren't provided with the support they need for their emotional and empathic work; however, some workers (in retail, service work, healthcare, and gig work, among others) aren't even allowed to *create* that support for themselves. As a result, all aspects of workplace morale and motivation will break down — as they should.

If my concept of emotional OSHA was more widespread, we'd have standards in place for the care and protection of emotional laborers, emotion workers, and empathy workers. Sadly, we don't; not yet. But we do have this book, and we have each other. So, as you look at your own emotional and empathic work and at the work of your colleagues, it's important to treat what you're all doing as *work* — and often, as draining or even dangerous work. We haven't been trained to notice or identify this work, so we'll be in Conscious Incompetence about it at first, but we can learn how to identify the different emotional and empathic responsibilities that people take upon themselves to bring balance to an unbalanced and emotionally unregulated workplace.

Empathy work, for instance, is a vital survival strategy in large social structures that are unjust and unequal. Empathy work is also a requirement for people from non-dominant groups and people who have been marginalized. For instance, I came into the workplace in the 1980s and 1990s, when women had to work harder and be more skilled than men if they wanted to be seen as equals (sadly, that's still true). I arrived in the workplace with Mateo-like skills in empathy work, and because of that I was generally able to rise through the ranks fairly quickly. However, I never achieved parity with the men at work (many of whom were not as educated or as hardworking as I was). Creating my own business was the only way I could achieve what I needed to achieve; sadly, the only way that I could work in a just and emotionally well-regulated workplace was to create it for myself.[3]

As you know, gender is not the only area of inequality that impedes and injures workers. Workers who are members of any non-dominant racial, religious, or ethnic group here in the US (and elsewhere) are also tasked with a great deal of unpaid and unacknowledged empathy work and emotion work as they navigate through unequal workplace cultures that do not consider their needs. And sadly, even if these workers are geniuses at empathy work, many do not achieve parity with workers from the dominant group (who are usually, but not always, White, able-bodied, Christian, heterosexual males who support the concept of binary gender).

A similar requirement for heavy and unequal empathy work exists for disabled workers, LGBTQIA+ workers, older workers, and also for any worker who is a minority in a particular workplace. For instance, my husband, Tino, went back to school in his fifties to fulfill his dream of becoming a nurse, but his presence as an older male in nursing school was both unnaturally privileged and constantly questioned. He was not completely part of the inner circle of female nurses, and he had to navigate his relationships skillfully to be seen as a part of the team (patients regularly misidentified Tino as a doctor, which was frustrating and painful for him). He stepped away from the idea of bedside nursing due to the many ways he was unable to navigate the gender chasm (many female patients don't want male nurses, and many female nurses aren't welcoming toward male colleagues). He's currently in a management position where he's separated by hierarchy from the bedside nurses, and while we're glad he has a steady job, it's sad that his dream of being a nurse had to be amended and reduced because he's not the correct age or gender.

As you explore the world of emotion work and empathy work, take a close look at people who are members of non-dominant or marginalized groups. They'll usually be doing a great deal of skilled yet unpaid emotion work and empathy work in order to navigate through a social world that was not created with them in mind. We'll revisit this important and unequal work in the section on diversity, equity, and inclusion on page 108.

In the following sections, I'll describe four different types of emotion workers and empathy workers that I call *Keystones*, but I don't mean for these to be rigid categories. I don't want you to search for these people at your workplace as if these roles are set in stone. You may not have anyone performing these specific roles; the roles people take in your workplace may be entirely different, and you should create your own titles for the roles you see.

KEYSTONES

Workers who perform (usually unpaid) emotion work or empathy work to fill in the social and emotional gaps in an emotionally unregulated workplace.

People may also take on multiple roles or switch roles depending on the situation. I'm presenting these concepts to help you take more of an eagle-eyed view of your workplace so that you can develop stronger large-group social skills and an awareness of the different types of emotion work and empathy work you and your colleagues may be doing. Feel free to add as many new categories and roles as you like.

If you find anyone in your workplace taking on these Keystone roles, don't blame them; thank them and get them support. And don't try to fix them; they're not broken! People who take on a great deal of emotional or empathic responsibility in the workplace are responding to trouble that's already there. Your Keystone workers are not the problem and they're not *causing* the problem; they're *responding* to the problem.

Identifying Your Keystones: Ambassadors and Connectors

Keystones, in my terminology, are people who pick up the social and emotional slack in troubled and emotionally unregulated social structures. Keystones perform unpaid emotion work and empathy work, and they provide extensive support in unsupportive workplaces.

In architecture, a keystone is a crucial stone or brick that's placed at the top of an arch, and even though it's placed last, it's the stone that helps the entire structure bear weight. Keystones in the workplace are like real keystones; they tend to arise when the social and emotional structure is incomplete or unbalanced. They may be the people everyone goes to with their troubles and concerns (regardless of their job title) — and you'll often find Keystones in small departments that function well even if the larger organization is dysfunctional. These are people who create an enclosed environment of emotional regulation, care, concern, empathy, and justice, even in unhealthy workplaces.

In our Workers of the World meetings, no one could recall an entirely healthy or emotionally well-regulated workplace, but many of us remembered small healthy departments that were run by empathic Keystone managers. We also recalled special, welcoming Keystone workers that I call *Ambassadors*.

AMBASSADORS

Workers who take on the (usually unpaid) task of welcoming and training new people in a workplace where there are no effective onboarding processes.

Many workplaces have onboarding processes that train new workers in the nuts and bolts of their jobs, but don't teach them how to fit into the workplace culture. This is a glaring deficiency that usually calls for Ambassadors, who introduce new workers to the ins and outs of the workplace social world. Ambassadors will befriend new workers, tell them about informal rules, let them know who's kind, who's a bit difficult, who's having trouble with whom, and what's the best day to submit requests for supplies. They may also tell new workers about the actual power structure, which is almost never the power structure on the hierarchy charts; they'll know which assistants actually run things and which supervisors have been promoted above their level of competence. Ambassadors are usually keyed into workplace gossip networks, and they provide a welcoming social and emotional repair station for new people.

Ambassadors often build a supportive social structure around themselves, but they're rarely the people in power. As we learned in the section on hierarchies in chapter 2, people in positions of power are often separated from the everyday life of the business; they know their own jobs and what the people at their level and above them need (and they may have a long-range view of the organization's future), but they may not have the time or the empathic capacity to focus on the everyday needs of the people below them.

Ambassadors are invaluable to new hires and the entire organization; they help the workplace function. But they're often unrecognized, or they may get saddled with unpaid onboarding work because they're so good at it. Ambassadors often struggle because they do a tremendous amount of high-level empathy work, usually without support or recognition. They may become depressed (this can help them protect their energy), they may become envious (in response to the inequality and injustice they witness), and they may become angry (as a result of being disrespected or seeing their colleagues treated poorly). In some cases, Ambassadors may share these emotions in the complex social networks they've created, and they may start a rebellion in the workplace. It's unfortunate, but I don't blame them. Ambassadors are amazingly valuable empathy workers, but most workplaces don't even notice them; they just take advantage of their skills.

It's necessary to identify and develop culturally intelligent Ambassadors and provide extensive support for them, but most workplaces don't identify their Ambassadors and don't have any training or support systems in place for them. In emotionally unregulated and socially troubled workplaces, Ambassadors are necessary, and often, so are the Keystone workers I call *Connectors*.

CONNECTORS

Workers who develop and maintain relationships throughout the entire workplace structure. Connectors are especially valuable in large bureaucracies, workplaces that have expanded quickly, or workplaces that are fragmented by artificial or hierarchical divisions between people.

Mateo functioned as a Connector, or a skilled empathy worker who understands the entire social structure and can work deftly with many different people throughout the organization. You'll find many Connectors in rigid hierarchies like Mateo's international aid organization; they're important everywhere, but in rigid and segregated social structures, Connectors can make the difference between a livable working environment and a demotivating, mechanistic, or dehumanizing one.

Though Mateo's staff didn't have the terminology to identify him as a Connector, their alarm at losing closeness with him was correct; his extensive understanding of the organization protected everyone in his sphere, and they needed to maintain their close personal contact with his Connector abilities, empathic skills, and large-group social awareness. When he unconsciously took on a distant, school-principal-type role, he destabilized the sense of belonging and relatedness in his entire department.

Hierarchical social structures (especially if they're based on Theory X control methods) can destabilize relationships, reduce empathy, and create an emotionally miserable environment of injustice, inequality, and demotivation. In response, many Keystones will have to arise in order to keep these rigid, unempathic, and emotionally unregulated social structures functioning. If you're struggling under the weight of a damaging hierarchical system, the principles in this book can help you and your colleagues develop new skills and awareness, an emotionally well-regulated social structure, and a flexible, democratic, and livable environment that treats adults with respect and empathy. Theory X hierarchies can't do any of these things well, if at all.

Ambassadors and Connectors are rarely at the top of hierarchies because they're usually highly empathic people who don't value competition. Ambassadors tend to work somewhere in the middle of hierarchies, and they usually have the empathic capacity to pay attention to everyone in the structure, even if no one else has the time or energy to do so. Connectors often rise higher than Ambassadors in hierarchical structures, but the higher they rise, the less likely they are to maintain their Connector status. When Mateo became a director and began to separate himself from his people, he was mistakenly stepping away from his valuable Connector role of understanding and engaging with everyone, regardless of where they were in the hierarchy. His team members were correct to react and challenge him; Mateo had not lost his empathy, but he was in danger of doing so. Thank goodness his people listened to their emotions and spoke up.

In our Workers of the World meetings, we discovered that healthy work groups were usually created by individual Connector managers who built an atmosphere of equality, justice, and emotional regulation in their area of influence. As I mentioned earlier, none of us could recall an entire workplace that implemented and maintained a healthy social environment; only individual Connector managers were able to do that in their small areas of influence, often without drawing too much attention to themselves. Usually, these small healthy islands in otherwise emotionally unregulated workplaces would be left alone because they were productive and didn't cause any problems. These Connector managers didn't receive much recognition or support from their larger organizations, but at least they and their colleagues were allowed to work undisturbed.

It's important to identify your own unpaid Ambassadors and Connectors, because their presence speaks to trouble in the areas of onboarding, training, emotions, relationships, hierarchy, or support (or all six) that are not being addressed by anyone except these often-unrecognized people. Your Ambassadors and Connectors are vital empathy workers, and they need to have a voice and multifaceted support. If you don't have any authority to make changes in your organization, you can at least support your Keystone people (or yourself if you are one), speak to them openly about the importance of what they do (and thank them), and perhaps share this book with them.

If you *do* have the authority to make changes, and you want to identify the different kinds of Keystones in your own business, you may need an outsider to help you. Keystones are valuable empathy workers who tend to rise up in response to unmet needs, unseen problems, unacknowledged (or built-in) inequalities, and unspoken injustices that — because emotions have been pushed out of the workplace — no one has been able to address openly or effectively. A person from the outside (such as an organizational development consultant or an employee assistance professional), who hasn't been socialized or silenced by the specific problems in your organization, would have more freedom to see what everyone else has been trained to ignore. Of course, this outsider should work as a respectful peer, and not come barging in to enforce new processes or top-down rules; this situation requires a skilled empathy worker who knows how to listen, how to observe, and how to trust and rely upon your workers' native social and emotional intelligence.

Supporting an Ambassador or Connector will usually require a period of careful listening, a willingness to make changes, and the ability to be in Conscious Incompetence as you learn about what you didn't know. With your newly conscious awareness, you can begin to build an emotionally well-regulated social structure and restore everyone's competence, autonomy, and relatedness (and give your Keystone workers a break). Ambassadors and Connectors can continue doing their important work, but this work can now be identified, respected, requested, supported, and paid for. Thankfully, in an emotionally well-regulated social structure, Ambassadors and Connectors will no longer be the only people performing these duties; the work of building and maintaining an emotionally healthy and empathically aware organization will now be distributed more equally across the entire group (as it always should have been).

Beyond Ambassadors and Connectors, there are other kinds of emotional and empathic roles that I see in emotionally unregulated organizations. In these roles, people may take on specific communication duties or act out specific emotions when there's conflict (that no one will speak of openly) or when there's emotional suppression at play.

Identifying Two More Keystones: Peacemakers and Agitators

A Peacemaker is a kind of Connector who may do their work in a small department, or between a small number of people who need to work together even though there's no formal way for them to do so. You'll often see Peacemakers cross departmental lines and act as translators between, for instance, the needs of the art department and the needs of the shipping department. Often, these two departments will develop their own internal language, their own processes, and their own sense of reality and time that doesn't mesh well with other departments at all. Shipping may need something tomorrow to meet a sudden demand in orders, while the art department is accustomed to having four weeks to think about a new product or process before they even put pen to paper. You'll see this same kind of miscommunication and conflict between accounting and research and design departments, between customer service and manufacturing, between process improvement departments and line workers, and so on. Peacemakers are empathy workers who bring social and emotional awareness to neglected, disconnected, or conflict-generating areas of their organizations.

PEACEMAKERS

Workers who do emotion work and empathy work to smooth out troubled relationships between disconnected or conflicting departments and/or individuals.

In an emotionally unregulated workplace where divisions between departments are too rigid, Peacemakers will arise because they have to arise. Their empathy work is necessary if anyone wants to get their work done, and they tend to become skilled at understanding everyone's needs within the context of their departments; they understand individual needs in terms of who can get the job done and when, and they understand customer needs in terms of getting the product or the process out on time. Peacemakers are empathy-work geniuses who often do a tremendous amount of emotion work *and* emotional labor to manage their emotions in the face of inefficiency, turf-protecting behaviors, inequality, and multiple breakdowns in organizational design and communication. It's a lot to expect anyone to do, and burnout is common among Peacemakers.

If you've got a worker who can get a department to hurry up, who can translate between two departments or people, or who can understand the flows and different social structures of multiple areas of your business, you've got a Peacemaker. You'll also find Peacemakers as assistants and go-betweens for individuals who are brilliant workers, but have few social skills, or for individuals who have power and don't pay attention to the rules that everyone else must follow. Peacemakers help processes and relationships work more smoothly. And, like Ambassadors and Connectors, Peacemakers may do their jobs so well that no one in the organization has to face the consequences of baked-in problems, injustice, inequality, or a long-standing lack of interdepartmental communication. The presence of a Peacemaker means that things may have been sideways and dysfunctional in your organization for a while, and that your people, departments, and processes need to be reintegrated. Peacemakers tend to arise in the presence of structural fragmentation that leads to a loss of healthy relationships, workable communication, and smooth workflows.

Agitators, on the other hand, tend to arise in situations of emotional repression and unworkable communication in a rigid or hierarchical environment. In Natalie's spa, where the well-being of the massage therapists and aestheticians was not even on the map (and the owners were invisible), a single Agitator arose and took all of the heat as the other workers repressed their anger and envy and presented a face of calm and healing to their spa guests. This Agitator became an emotional surrogate for her colleagues, and she essentially acted out their anger and envy for them. Natalie did what she could to work with this person, but because this Agitator's emotions seemed out of proportion, Natalie made the mistake of isolating and then firing her. Peace and stability did not follow.

AGITATORS

Workers who act out unwelcome emotions in an emotionally repressive or empathically unskilled workplace community.

Without their Agitator to speak for them, the rest of the staff were destabilized and disrupted, and they could no longer keep their emotions at a simmer. The problems that required an Agitator were still there, and sadly, getting rid of the Agitator only made things worse.

While it's true that some workers are cranky, stubborn, or troubled, the overwhelmingly unhealthy and often-abusive conditions in the modern workplace are far more likely to be at fault than individuals are. Sadly, individuals are almost always identified, blamed, counseled, coached, punished, demoted, or put on notice while the larger social and emotional atmosphere of the workplace is left completely untouched (except through lip service to organizational values and the vision statement, or some such nonsense). The social repercussions of individual blaming can be extremely toxic: angry people are silenced or fired, depressed people are pacified or ignored, and envious or anxious people are shamed (and so forth). In response, most people learn to silence their emotions and just get through each day because everyone sees that honest emotions are not only unwelcome in the workplace, but they're also punishable offenses.

Though having an Agitator in your workplace can be disruptive (to say the least), there's a blessing that needs to be given to a person who will continue to feel and express difficult or forbidden emotions in a repressive environment. Agitating is a kind of emotional swashbuckling, but it's exhausting, and Agitators need support.

If I had been called in before Natalie fired her Agitator, I might have gone to the resort in person to work directly with her, because she held a wealth of information about what was truly happening in that opulent, unjust, and artificially calm spa environment. But because she had been banished and the pressure regulation she provided was gone, I suspected that anyone associated with Natalie or the resort's owners would be unwelcome. I had to work in the background because this important Keystone (*of course* Agitators are Keystones!) had been removed, and the social system was too destabilized to receive any new person, process, or information. We got it turned around, but I have to tell you that when Natalie told me she had fired her Agitator, I inwardly swore up a blue streak! Agitators are priceless Keystones — not *in spite of* the difficult information they bring to the surface, but *because* of it. Tragically, because we don't understand emotions and have been deluded into believing that they don't belong in the workplace, we ignore, suppress, try to fix, or fire priceless Agitators every day.

And let me say this again: Yes, some workers bring their pre-existing emotional difficulties into the workplace, and they may disturb or destabilize others due to internal struggles that they aren't able to address yet. They may not be community Agitators in the way that I have described here; they may just be agitating. (If they're bullying and abusing people, then of course it's time to involve HR or ask your local labor board to step in; see the Workplace Bullying Resources on page 253).

In an emotionally well-regulated workplace, however, individual emotional struggles are not insurmountable problems, because the workplace atmosphere itself won't make things worse. There will be many ways for people to talk about their emotions without being blamed or shunned, because emotions will be seen as information and not as character flaws. However, in an emotionally *unregulated* workplace, people's internal emotional struggles may intensify because now they're in an unhealthy social environment that intentionally suppresses emotional awareness, and they're surrounded by people who are struggling (as they are) just to get through each day. Blaming workers for their emotional struggles without turning a critical eye toward the social structure of their workplace is a recipe for misery and failure. We won't be doing that.

Remember that people *live* at work. Many of us spend more time at work than we spend with our families or our mates, yet most of our attention is focused on the relationships in our private lives. We do a lot of emotion work at home, we read self-help books, see therapists, or go on vacations and retreats to support these relationships, even though they're not the relationships that take up most of our time and energy.

Our work relationships and work environments are crucial to our health and well-being, and we have a right to develop healthy workplace relationships that increase our sense of belonging, relatedness, and love. We have a right to live and work in welcoming and emotionally well-regulated workplaces, yet we aren't usually able to influence them in any real way. Not openly, anyway. Problems in our workplace are usually signaled by the presence of Keystones, but if people don't know how to identify Keystones or decipher what their presence says about the social and emotional conditions in the workplace, the problems will just intensify. That needs to change; we need to realize that the presence of any sort of Keystone is a sign of unbalanced or broken workplace relationships, processes, emotion regulation, or the social structure as a whole.

The presence of anyone who is doing extensive, unpaid emotion work or empathy work within your organization is a sign of trouble in your workplace. This trouble could stem from inequality, communication breakdown, emotional suppression, departmental fragmentation, improper onboarding, poor training, lack of support, uncareful management, hierarchical injustice, unhealthy competition, or a lack of organizational awareness from the top down. Keystones arise because they have to arise, not because certain workers are nice, responsible, empathic, or emotionally expressive. We may feel proud of our unpaid Ambassadors and Connectors, or of our Peacemakers, but they're signs of trouble in our workplace in the exact same way that an Agitator is a sign of trouble. These Keystones arise because the structure is failing and needs to be reinforced (or reformed).

Using the Genius in Emotions to Support Your Keystones

I'm bringing back the emotion charts from chapter 1 so that you can identify the information each emotion is bringing forward. As you think about your Keystones, take a look at which emotions they're working with and why. If your Peacemakers, Ambassadors, or Connectors are managing emotions or helping others to repress emotions, look at the gifts and skills in those emotions to reveal the underlying emotional rules in your organization (these may surprise you). If you have an Agitator who's expressing the emotions everyone else has suppressed, look at the gifts and skills those emotions contain. What are those emotions signaling about your social structure, and how can the gifts, skills, and genius in these emotions help you build a healthier social structure that's emotionally well regulated?

As you read through these charts, remember that the four types of Keystones I listed are not the only ones. You may see entirely different types of Keystones in your workplace because we're all unique and each workplace is its own world. Whatever Keystone behaviors you see, follow the emotions; they carry the genius you need to solve the problems that your Keystone workers are responding to.

Understanding the Anger Family —
Boundaries, Rules, and Behaviors

The emotions in the **Anger Family** (anger, guilt/shame, apathy, and hatred) tell us what's important and when a boundary has been crossed or a rule has been broken. These emotions help us set behavioral guidelines for ourselves and others. Generally (because the Anger Family is so unwelcome), Agitators (or authoritarian managers and bosses) will be the only people who can openly express these emotions.

If you have an Agitator who has taken over the work of these Anger Family emotions, there has likely been a serious or long-standing breach of rules, social agreements, and a lack of basic respect from owners and managers, between departments, or between individuals. Thank your Agitator, take their complaints seriously, and recruit their (paid) help as you get to work on the problems your Agitator has been pointing out (see the many communication practices in chapter 5 for support). No one should ever have to carry or express emotions for an entire community; your Agitator deserves thanks, a break, and lots of support.

Emotion	Questions	Gifts and Skills
ANGER arises when people's self-image, behaviors, values, or interpersonal boundaries are challenged — or when they see them challenged in someone else.	*What do I value?* *What must be protected and restored?*	Honor, certainty, healthy self-esteem, proper boundaries, healthy detachment, and protection of ourselves and others.

Emotion	Questions	Gifts and Skills
APATHY is a protective mask for anger, and it arises in situations where people are not able or willing to work with their anger openly.	*What is being avoided?* *What must be made conscious?*	Detachment, boundary-setting, separation, taking a time-out, and protection of the self in an unhealthy or inappropriate environment.
GUILT AND SHAME arise to make sure that people don't hurt, embarrass, or dehumanize themselves or others.	*Who has been hurt?* *What must be made right?*	Integrity, self-respect, making amends, behavioral rules and guidelines, behavioral change, and work quality.
HATRED arises in the presence of things people cannot accept in themselves (and despise in others).	*What has fallen into my shadow?* *What must be reintegrated?*	Hatred can be an emergency signal in the workplace that, if handled skillfully, can lead to deep interpersonal awareness, sudden evolution, and the ability to address prejudice and bias openly.*

*HR and workplace safety note: If people are expressing hatred in the workplace and they have no emotional skills, they will likely devolve into abuse or bullying, both of which create an unacceptably hostile workplace environment. Abuse and bullying in the workplace are illegal and need to be addressed and resolved immediately. Emotional skills are always essential, but when powerful emotions like hatred arise, these skills are absolutely crucial. If people can't manage their emotions and they're hurting others at work, HR must step in.

Understanding the Fear Family —
Instincts, Intuition, Orienting, and Action

The emotions in the **Fear Family** (fear, anxiety, confusion, jealousy, envy, and panic) contain intuition and instincts. These emotions help us orient to our surroundings, notice change, novelty, or hazards, and take effective actions. Jealousy and envy in particular keep an eye on fairness, equality, loyalty, and relatedness.

Most (or all) of your Keystones will need to step forward if the Fear Family emotions are being ignored. Peacemakers and Connectors may step forward when fairness, equality, communication, and relatedness are threatened (and the workplace is emotionally unregulated), while Ambassadors may become impromptu workplace safety captains. Agitators may be the only people who can point out serious issues — such as a lack of appropriate safety regulations, unregulated relationship conflict, widespread inequality, unfair or improperly managed workloads, and/or inadequate time management and workflow processes. These Fear Family emotions carry crucial information, so if you find your Keystone workers focusing on them, please treat this as a serious warning.

Thank the Keystones who have taken on this necessary work, give them a (paid) voice in the remediation of these serious problems, and study the information in part 2 of this book. There's a lot of work to do, but the emotions and your now-recognized Keystone workers can (and will) help you.

Emotion	Questions/Actions	Gifts and Skills
FEAR arises to help people focus on the present moment, access their instincts and intuition, and tune into changes in their immediate environment.	*What action should be taken?*	Intuition, instincts, focus, clarity, awareness, attentiveness, and readiness.

Emotion	Questions/Actions	Gifts and Skills
ANXIETY is focused on the future — it arises to help people look ahead and identify the tasks they need to complete and the deadlines they need to meet.	*What brought this feeling forward?* *What **truly** needs to get done?*	Foresight, focus, task-completion, procrastination alert, planning, organization, and awareness of future problems and needs.
CONFUSION is a protective mask for fear and anxiety, and it arises when people have too much to process all at once. Confusion can give people a much-needed time-out.	*What is my intention?* *What action should be taken?*	Soft awareness, spaciness, flexibility, taking a time-out, and protection against overload.
JEALOUSY arises when people's connection to love, loyalty, or security in their relationships is challenged.	*What has been betrayed?* *What must be healed and restored?*	Commitment, security, love, connection, belonging, loyalty, and the ability to create and maintain healthy relationships.

Emotion	Questions/Actions	Gifts and Skills
ENVY arises when people's connection to material security, resources, or recognition is challenged.	*What has been betrayed?* *What must be made right?*	Fairness, security, access to resources, proper recognition, self-preservation, and the promotion of equality and justice.
PANIC arises when people face threats to their survival. Panic gives them three life-saving choices: fight, flee, or freeze.	*Just listen to your body — don't think, just react. Your body is a survival expert, and it will keep you safe.*	Sudden energy, intense attention, the ability to protect the self and others, absolute stillness, and survival in the face of shock and danger.*

*HR and workplace safety note: Many of us try to talk people out of their feelings of panic and anxiety, but these emotions should not be ignored! If a worker is feeling panic about the workplace or its process, check to see if there are any hazards; there likely are. Many workplace disasters occur after workers' panicky concerns, fears, and anxieties are belittled or ignored.

Understanding the Sadness Family — Stopping, Letting Go, and Recovering

The emotions in the **Sadness Family** (sadness, grief, depression, and the suicidal urge) help us release things that aren't working and mourn things that are gone so that we can relax, let go, and rejuvenate ourselves. When these emotions are welcome in a social structure, they can help people make smooth transitions, deal with loss and change, and identify processes and ideas that can't work or need to be changed significantly (or deleted completely).

When the Sadness Family emotions are not welcome, Ambassadors and Peacemakers will need to step forward to manage and smooth over badly handled transitions, unmourned losses, and functional issues that are not being taken seriously (or dealt with effectively). In an unrealistically positive workplace culture, Agitators may also step forward to feel and express the Sadness Family emotions that others aren't allowed to feel. Thank these Keystone workers, welcome their (paid) input on the problems they've been managing, and focus your attention on the communication workflows in chapter 5 and the section on Emotionally Agile Transitions in chapter 6.

Emotion	Questions	Gifts and Skills
SADNESS arises to help people let go of things that aren't working. If they can let go, they'll be able to relax, recover, and revitalize themselves.	*What must be released?* *What must be rejuvenated?*	Relaxation, rejuvenation, the ability to identify waste, outdated ideas, and unworkable processes, and the ability to let go.
GRIEF arises when people have lost something — a person, an idea, a belief, a possession, or a situation — that has died or will never come back.	*What must be mourned?* *What must be released completely?*	Sorrow, the ability to identify and mourn losses, remembrance, acceptance of loss, deep release, and honoring of the lost idea, situation, person, or possession.

Emotion	Questions	Gifts and Skills
SITUATIONAL DEPRESSION arises when things are not working well and people lose the energy to keep going in the ways they previously did. There's always an important reason for situational depression to arise.	*Where has my energy gone?* *Why was it sent away?*	Ingenious stagnation, stillness, awareness of dysfunction and difficulties, warning of future trouble, intelligent restriction of energy, and a reality check.
THE SUICIDAL URGE arises when something in people's lives needs to end — but it's not their actual, physical life! It's important to reach out for help and identify the situation or thing that needs to end so that people can get their lives back.	*What idea or behavior must end now?* *What can I no longer tolerate?*	The ability to identify abuse, futility, and completely unworkable situations; certainty, finality, freedom, transformation, and rebirth.*

*In my Dynamic Emotional Integration work, I help people understand that suicidal urges have a place in the emotional realm, but that physical death is not required. Instead, we focus the intense laser-focus of the suicidal urge on the person's painful or unlivable situation and bring the powerful genius of this emotion to bear; it arises when things are very bad indeed, but it does not require the physical death of the person!

HR and workplace safety note: If a worker expresses suicidal ideation, get help from an employee assistance counselor or your local crisis center or lifeline immediately. When the suicidal urge is present, emotional skills and social support can literally save people's lives.

Understanding the Happiness Family —
Hope, Confidence, and Inspiration

The emotions in the **Happiness Family** (happiness, contentment, and joy) help us look around ourselves or toward the future with hope, satisfaction, and delight. Sadly, many workplaces focus unhealthy amounts of attention on these emotions, which means that their presence is often engineered or manufactured (or faked).

In an emotionally unregulated workplace with a toxic positivity bias, Connectors, Peacemakers, and Ambassadors will do a lot of unpaid work to keep everybody happy and to actively squelch the other emotions; it's *exhausting*. In response to this emotional suppression and imbalance, one or more Agitators may step forward to express all of the emotions that are forbidden, which is *also* exhausting. Thank all of these Keystones, give them some (paid) time off, and invite their (paid) input as you get to work on all of the practices and processes in this book. A good place to start is the section on A Different Kind of Complaints Department on page 152.

Emotion	Statements	Gifts and Skills
HAPPINESS arises to help people look around themselves and toward the future with hope and enjoyment.	*Thank you for this lively celebration!*	Amusement, hope, delight, playfulness, and belief in a bright future.

Emotion	Statements	Gifts and Skills
CONTENTMENT arises after people have accomplished something, and it helps them look at themselves with pride and satisfaction.	*Thank you for renewing my faith in myself!*	Satisfaction, self-esteem, confidence, healthy pride, and a healthy work ethic.
JOY arises to help people feel a blissful sense of open-hearted connection to others, to ideas, or to experiences.	*Thank you for this wonderful moment!*	Expansion, inspiration, brilliance, bliss, and a new vision for the future.

In a healthy and emotionally well-regulated social structure, all of the emotions in all of these families will be welcome, and no one person will have to express them for others, suppress them, become an unpaid Keystone, or act as a translator or go-between because the social structure is dysfunctional. The emotions and their gifts will be treated as powerful personal and communal tools, not just for the work that needs to be done, but also for the health and well-being of everyone in the workplace. Unsupported emotional labor and emotion work, unacknowledged empathic work, unaddressed emotional or empathic inequalities, and any unresolved or unspoken conflict — all of these can be identified and addressed when people have free and open access to the gifts, skills, and genius that live inside all of their emotions.

As the emotions are welcomed back into the workplace (even though they never left) and people have permission to speak openly about the situations their emotions have identified, the unique emotional and empathic demands of your workplace will become clearer. This awareness is important for everyone, but it can be particularly supportive for anyone who's a member of a non-dominant or marginalized group, because their empathy work usually transcends these Keystone categories.

The Emotion Work and Empathy Work of Diversity, Equity, and Inclusion

Here in the US, the reality of systemic racism, sexism, homophobia, transphobia, ableism (discrimination against the disabled), ageism, classism, and religious intolerance (along with many other systemic prejudices) has become painfully obvious. In response, people everywhere — especially in the workplace — have been rushing to become educated about these glaring systemic inequalities. My Dynamic Emotional Integration colleague Amanda Ball and I have been studying antibias, antiracist, and diversity materials for many years, and we've been grateful for them. However, we've found that many (most?) don't work well with emotions. They don't clearly identify the disproportionate amount of emotion work and empathy work that people from non-dominant groups must do to make it through each day.[4] And most don't fully appreciate the new and unaccustomed emotion work and empathy work that people from dominant groups are having to learn from scratch now that systemic prejudice and discrimination are being tackled in organizations, schools, and the media.

If you're a member of a marginalized or non-dominant group in an emotionally unregulated workplace, you're likely doing emotion work and empathy work most of the time. For instance, a lone Deaf woman in a workplace full of hearing people will not only have to do her own work, but she may have to act as a kind of Ambassador to her deafness so that hearing people will feel comfortable. Yet even so, hearing people may still call to her across a room or speak when they're walking away from her so she can't make out what they're saying. She'll perform extensive emotion work, yet even if she's a genius at it, it won't make much of a difference, or not for long, anyway.

Jim Sinclair, a nonbinary Autistic activist, describes the extensive empathy work Autistic people have to perform in non-autistic spaces, where they must become what they call "a self-narrating zoo exhibit" for neurologically typical people who are fascinated (or offended) by their differences.[5] Men in heavily female-centric workplaces, or nonbinary people in heavily gender-binary workplaces may have to perform continual empathy work to deal with expectations that come from gender prejudice — *especially* if those expectations are unspoken. And non-White workers in White-centric workplaces may have to become racial Ambassadors, Connectors, and Peacemakers, and also do emotional heavy lifting in order to suppress their natural emotional responses to everyday bias and prejudice (because their honest responses might endanger their position as "safe" or acceptable members of their groups).

Being a member of a non-dominant or marginalized group in an emotionally unregulated social structure can require endless amounts of unsupported emotion work and empathy work; it can be *exhausting*. In unequal and unaware environments, casual, everyday ignorance can be a constant underlying influence — almost like the hum of a machine that the dominant people can't hear (because they live inside the machine). Culturally insensitive acts such as focusing on Christmas but completely ignoring Ramadan, Lunar New Year, Hanukkah, Yom Kippur, Kwanzaa, or Diwali (and many other celebrations) tells people that they and their cultures are not valued, even though no one in the machine may have intended to offend or exclude them. People from dominant groups may not mean to injure people, yet their very dominance (and the ignorance that's built into systems of dominance) does that all by itself.

As our awareness of systemic inequality and injustice increases, we're seeing many dominant-class people struggling mightily with the shameful implications of their dominance, and with the (mostly) unintentional damage they're doing to so many marginalized and vulnerable people. This new awareness is requiring a lot of new and unaccustomed emotion work for dominant people in the areas of shame, grief, panic, and rage, and it's also requiring extensive learning and retraining.

Someone online joked that when White people hear about systemic racism, they join a book club. That's funny and true, but the learning that's occurring in these book clubs is not a joke. Systemic bias, racism, and prejudice don't live in individuals; they're a part of the cultural machine. Until we engage in intentional learning, we White people may have no idea of the damage that our (often) unknowing support of systemic racism, oppression, and exclusion are doing every single day. (Who would think that Christmas parties would be a problem?) Dominant-group people who want to challenge systems of dominance must read, study, feel all of their emotions, ask questions, and learn how to listen to people who have been damaged by their dominance. It's crucial work, but it's difficult, clumsy, emotionally intense, and painful. And in the context of the workplace, this work absolutely cannot be done in a couple of antibias trainings or with a new corporate vision statement. This work requires systemic awareness and accountability from the dominant people themselves, yet the cultural machine works continually and powerfully to keep dominant people unaware and unaccountable.

For instance, as a White heterosexual woman, I've learned with shock, shame, horror, and rage that I've been thoroughly socialized to see my skin color, my hair texture, my heterosexuality, my binary representation of gender, my culture, my media figures and literature, and my rituals as normal, and to see everyone else as unusual, "ethnic," exotic, or even abnormal. But I never would have said any of that openly. Not only because it's unempathic, but because I didn't know that I had accepted any of these ideas; not consciously anyway.

I wasn't taught explicit White supremacy or heteronormativity, but I *was* socialized into the machine. For instance, my K–12 education, especially in US history, taught me almost nothing real about slavery, our decimation of Indigenous peoples, our incarceration of Japanese Americans in World War II, our antisemitic unwillingness to accept refugees fleeing from Nazi Germany, the horrors of Jim Crow laws, and our medical establishment's grotesque history of experimenting on non-White people and people with physical and mental disabilities. I had no idea about the decades-long and entirely legal effort to deny African American, Hispanic/Latinx, Indigenous, Asian, and Jewish people the right to rent or buy homes freely.[6] I didn't know about real life; I lived in a protected bubble of hierarchical dominance, and I was trained to be ignorant about reality — not by evil individuals, but by a fully operational cultural machine of racism, inequality, and injustice.

I was educated and socialized to be Unconsciously Competent at everyday White supremacy, heteronormativity, ageism, ableism, and so many other forms of prejudice. Of course, I knew about racism, inequality, prejudice, and exclusion, but my schooling and most of my cultural references whitewashed most of it or assured me that these bad things were all in the past. I was raised in a fully White-supremacist, unequal, and unjust culture, yet I had no true awareness of that. Realizing this fact was horrifying, and of course I played the "I'm not racist or prejudiced" game for a while. However, I kept listening to the genius in my shame, grief, panic, horror, and rage — and read a mountain of books — and eventually became able to identify my position at the near-top of the US dominance hierarchy.[7]

And by going through that deeply emotive process, I saw the emotional and empathic problem that hinders the work of antiracism, social justice, and freedom for all. Dominance of any kind — gender, race, ability, religion, culture, and so on — is a hierarchy, and as we explored in chapter 2, hierarchies can decrease empathy and increase narcissism in people at the top. I was trained in every possible way — even in my Northern California liberal hippie-ish upbringing — to support an unequal, unjust, unempathic, and narcissistic system of oppression without even knowing I was doing it.

People at the top of systemic dominance hierarchies are socialized from birth to see themselves as superior, and they learn, as all people trapped in hierarchies must, to focus their empathic attention laterally and upward. Many dominant people actually lose their ability to empathize with the people below them; they become Unconsciously Competent in the ways of dominance, and Unconsciously *Incompetent* at seeing, understanding, or addressing the pain of non-dominant people and groups. They don't even know what they don't know.

I told you all that to tell you this: Systems of dominance, exclusion, and injustice train dominant people to be unempathic and unaware puppets in the system, such that dominant people (and their emotions) may have *no idea* about the extent of the damage they perpetrate every day. They may have to be *told*, for instance, that expecting Black workers to wear their hair straight is a racist act. Or that expecting disabled workers to make everyone else feel comfortable is exclusionary and ableist. Or that building a workplace where only men can achieve positions of power (surprise!) is sexist, and so forth. They and their emotions have to be *made* aware of things that everyone below them can see clearly.

Yet even if they become consciously aware of these acts of racism, prejudice, and exclusion, they will slip back regularly if they don't have the reliable, everyday social and emotional support they need to consciously re-engage their empathy and heal from decades of enforced ignorance and cultural narcissism. This is a deeply emotive process, and people may seesaw back and forth between Conscious Incompetence and Conscious Competence for years. If people cannot work with their emotions, they cannot truly enter this work.

If your workplace is looking into antibias or diversity and inclusion trainings where dominant-class people are forbidden to feel or express their natural emotional reactions to prejudice, injustice, or bias, *run*. These trainings will not and cannot work, and in fact, many of them will create a backlash, or give people a false sense of having done something about systemic injustice. That's nonsense. If people's emotions are not welcome in this deeply emotive process — and remember that emotions are the foundation of everything you think and all of your behaviors (including prejudice and empathy) — then the process will certainly fail.

And that's a crying shame, because the work of dismantling systems of dominance and hierarchy must be done by and with people from the dominant class; this work can't be pushed entirely onto the people who have been dominated. People in non-dominant positions carry vital and irreplaceable information about systems of oppression, and that information must be heard, treasured, and acted upon. But the deeply emotive and empathic work of dismantling systems of dominance and oppression must also be done by dominant people because they wield a great deal of power and influence (just by living in their own skin or having grown up in their own neighborhood), whether they intended to have this power or not. And if dominant people are going to be able to do this work, they must have access to all of their emotions and the full-bodied empathic badassery that those emotions help them develop.

The emotional suppression and ignorance baked into most antibias and diversity trainings is not unusual — we've all been taught to distrust or even hate emotions, and the workplace is an emotion-bashing disaster area. Thankfully, there are some people who are working to bring the emotions into this work and to help dominant people learn how to empathize fully. Resmaa Menakem's somatic work is brilliant. Tiffany Jana's work on erasing systems of bias in workplaces is marvelous. Ibram X. Kendi's work on antiracism and the history of racism in the US is stunning in its scope (you can find all of these people in the Recommended Resources section). So, the work is being done, but it's not fully available yet. The anti-emotion bias is still too strong.

This is clearly a deep subject that deserves its own book, but here in this book, it's essential to understand the place of emotions in workplace diversity, equity, and inclusion efforts. Empathy is first and foremost an emotional skill, and if emotions are forbidden in these efforts, then the powerful empathy that's required to help dominant people awaken and heal cannot and will not arise. Emotions are vital and they must be included in all inclusion work.

I'm writing about my antiracism and antibias work as a White woman because in 2016 (and again in 2020) White women like me voted for and supported a president and a party that based their power on openly racist, sexist, ableist, anti-immigrant, Islamophobic, antisemitic, homophobic, and transphobic words and actions. I know some of these women, and they see themselves as caring and empathic people. And they *are* — but only laterally and upwardly. They didn't have the time, support, or emotional knowledge they needed to read a mountain of books or dive into the intense emotions that arose during Barack Obama's presidency, and so they retreated to the safe, familiar, and unempathic cultural narcissism of their dominance.

Our work toward antiracism, antibias, diversity, equity, and inclusion is deeply emotional and powerfully empathic. We need to welcome the emotions into this process — likely by working with affinity groups first, and then by bringing people together (once they have emotional and empathic skills) to tear down the systems of dominance that have injured every single one of us.

Humans built these systems of dominance, and humans must dismantle them. But we can only do that if we have full access to the power in our emotions, which will give us full access to the deep and wide-ranging empathy we need to do this vital and world-changing work.

Emotional and Empathic Awareness Supports Everyone

When people have access to their emotions and they can identify their emotional labor, emotion work, empathy work, or Keystone status, they'll certainly become more aware and awake about what's happening in their relationships and their social structures. But if everyone in the workplace has equal and shared access to this information, the entire community can awaken, come alive, and become more inclusive, equality-focused, just, and emotionally well regulated.

Now that we have a sense for the different kinds of emotional and empathic work people do in the workplace, let's look at the quantity and quality of that work. The simple inventories in the next chapter can help you identify how much of this work you're doing and whether it nourishes and feeds you, or drains and exhausts you.

4

Is Your Emotion Work
Nourishing or Draining?

t's important to bring conscious awareness to the types and amount of emotional and empathic work you do, but gaining this awareness can be difficult when so many of the rules and expectations for this work are unspoken or hidden. I developed some quick inventories to help bring all of this work into the light of day.

In this chapter, I'm going to simplify things and combine emotional labor, emotion work, and empathy work together under the broad category of *emotion work*. When I work in organizations, I use this one simple category to help people learn about the overall emotional and empathic condition of their lives, their work, and their workplace community.

I usually introduce these inventories as a communal activity (I post large inventories on the wall or whiteboard and have everyone score themselves communally) so that workers can understand more about each other and the work they share. However, taking these inventories individually can give you good information about your current situation. When you become conscious of the quantity and quality of emotional and empathic work you do, you can begin to approach it strategically.

These inventories are meant to give you a simple overview of the emotion work you're doing, but of course you can be more explicit if you want to focus on the specifics of your work. You can fill out each inventory three times: once for your paid emotional labor, once for your unpaid emotion work, and once for your paid or unpaid empathy work; it's up to you. You can also fill out an inventory for the extra work you do as a marginalized person in your workplace or your personal life.

However, the most important thing to focus on in these inventories is not so much the *type* of emotional or empathic work you do, but *where* you do this work, *how much* you do, and whether it's nourishing or draining for you.

Nourishing emotion work occurs when people listen to you, respect you, empathize with you, and welcome your emotional and empathic intelligence. Some examples are: very close friends who engage with you as deeply and empathically as you engage with them; coworkers who notice, respect, support, and return your emotional and empathic work; and a love partner who is loyal, engaged, available, and emotionally open with you. In an emotionally well-regulated relationship or environment (at home or at work), people will be much more likely to nourish each other; the relationship or the environment won't drain them.

Draining emotion work, on the other hand, occurs when people ignore you, disrespect you, burden you, or ignore your emotional and empathic work and intelligence. Some examples are: family members who expect a lot but rarely give back; coworkers who load you up with emotional or empathic work but ignore your needs and don't support you; or a love partner who doesn't listen, doesn't respect you, or isn't available. These draining relationships are in and of themselves emotionally unregulated social structures, but they usually take their cues from larger unhealthy structures: the family of origin in the case of intimate relationships, the workplace as a whole in the case of work relationships, and the region or country in the case of racism, prejudice, inequality, and mistreatment. These draining relationships and systems need to be addressed, and you'll need support to endure them (and to become free of them). Remember that no aspect of Maslow's pyramid can work properly without the crucial foundation of closeness, belonging, and love. Emotionally draining relationships and environments deprive us of the reciprocal and caring relationships we need to thrive.

Taking an Inventory of Your Emotion Work

I've divided the following inventories into separate environments so that you can observe the emotion work differences between the private and public areas of your home life and work life. As you think about the four environments below, consider whether the emotional and empathic work you do in them is mostly nourishing or mostly draining. At home, you'll look at your most intimate relationships and your more casual friendships. In the workplace, you'll look at the backstage work you do with your colleagues as well as the frontstage work you do with the public or other departments.

You may even want to add another row if you've got multiple internal workplace environments, such as your own work group, a management group, a marketing group, a process improvement group, and so forth.

This first inventory can help you start to explore the emotional and empathic effects that different relationships and environments have on you. In this first inventory, please place an X in the box that describes the quality of your work.

Emotion Work Environment	Nourishing?	Draining?
At home with the people closest to you		
Outside your home with friends and family		
At work with your colleagues and support people		
At work with your clients or the public		

Note that a single environment can be both nourishing *and* draining. For instance, you may have a very loving home where your emotional needs are met beautifully, yet a child, parent, or roommate in your home may be ill or struggling. In this instance, you might place an X in both the Nourishing *and* Draining categories.

As you identify the *quality* of the emotional and empathic work you do, you can also identify the *quantity* of the work you do with a simple 0–2 scale:

0:   Little to no emotion work required (for instance, if you live or work alone, and you aren't taking care of others).

1:   A reliable or manageable amount of emotion work required.

2:   A great deal of emotion work required (for instance, caring for an ill family member, Peacemaking between fighting coworkers, or tending to a deeply intimate and involved relationship).

Of course, your emotional workload changes regularly, but in this second inventory below, please focus on the relative *amount* of emotion work you currently do in these environments. Instead of a simple X, please place the number 0, 1, or 2 in the Nourishing and Draining columns, and then total both columns.

Emotion Work Environment	Nourishing?	Draining?
At home with the people closest to you		
Outside your home with friends and family		
At work with your colleagues and support people		

Emotion Work Environment	Nourishing?	Draining?
At work with your clients or the public		
Totals:		

In this inventory, too, a single situation can be both Nourishing *and* Draining. For instance, in a very healthy and emotionally well-regulated workplace, you and your colleagues could be dealing with a workplace crisis, a financial downturn, or the sudden loss of a colleague. In this instance, you might place a 2 in both the Nourishing *and* Draining categories; things are very difficult at work, but you have the relatedness, connection, and support you need to function well in the face of these difficulties.

If you find high draining numbers in one environment or in your entire inventory, you should have high nourishing numbers as well. If you don't have balance in (and support for) your emotion work, you may struggle. You may feel depressed (because your situation is not workable), you may feel angry (because your and others' values and boundaries are not being respected), you may feel envious or jealous (about people who are treated better or who are allowed to drain others without repercussions), you may feel anxious (because you have too much to do and not enough resources to keep yourself going), and so forth. Your emotions will naturally respond to draining inequalities, injustices, and a lack of support in your relationships and social environments, and in your emotional and empathic workloads.

If you're a member of a non-dominant or marginalized group, you may find that your totals are high in the draining column and low in the nourishing column. For that, I am deeply sorry, and I hope that you have loving relationships at home and many repair stations at work to help you navigate in an unequal and unempathic environment. It is my hope that the tools and concepts in this book will help you protect yourself and find the peace, nourishment, and safety you deserve.

Something else to look out for is a specialized form of empathy work that's *built* to be draining. I call it *non-reciprocal empathy work*, and it's very common in the medical and mental health professions. Doctors, nurses, therapists, and social workers are expected to be completely focused on their patients and clients, and to meet every need they can identify. But the patients and clients usually are not allowed to respond in kind. The extensive empathy work in healthcare is set up specifically so that patients and clients cannot build an equal or reciprocal human relationship with their healthcare providers. Therapy and social work have rigid rules that forbid outside contact with clients, and there is no reciprocity we can offer to our doctors or nurses, except showing up on time and following their orders and advice. This creates a highly unequal and draining situation that neither the mental health profession nor the healthcare profession has addressed appropriately (because emotions are unwelcome and empathy is treated as a one-way tool), and the consequences are grim.

The rates of addiction, divorce, stress-related disease, major depression, anxiety disorders, and even suicides are much higher among these professionals than they are in the general population — and these statistics are hidden from view, which is another sign of the lack of care and reciprocity these professionals labor under.[1] Most healthcare professionals are taught to hide their difficulties and despair, and to treat their normal emotional reactions to unsupported and non-reciprocal emotional and empathic work as personal character flaws. It's a tragic and literally life-endangering situation.

Addressing the dangers that the healthcare field has created through enforcing non-reciprocal empathy work is beyond the scope of this book, but I brought it up so that you can begin to think about the reciprocity of any work that you do. If you're a Keystone, is anyone supporting your vital empathy work? If you're doing heavy emotional labor on the phones at work, are there any repair stations (page 56), gossip networks (page 62), or mental health breaks available to you? If you're a non-dominant or marginalized person at work, is there anything in place to support you? If you're doing a lot of emotion work at home, is anyone available to give you a break? Where is the necessary reciprocity and nourishment?

Because you see, emotional labor is *labor*. Emotion work is *work*. Empathy work is *work*. They are not soft skills or free gifts that spring forth from the endless fountain of your private emotional life. This is work that's required in every relationship and every workplace, and reciprocity is necessary, or people will become drained, enraged, depressed, ill, despairing, or all five at once. Your important emotional and empathic work needs to be recognized, respected, and supported.

Is anyone recognizing your work? Is there any type of emotional OSHA in your home or your workplace? Is anyone (besides you) watching out for your well-being? And is this emotional and empathic work suitable for you?

For instance, Natalie was placed in a heavy-empathy-work position at the spa that didn't suit her at all. It wasn't where her interests were, and it wasn't where her empathy was focused. If anyone had understood the empathy-work requirements of that position, Natalie would have had the knowledge she needed to avoid the draining spa job and choose another occupation where her particular empathic genius would be welcomed and valued.

As you think about your balance of nourishing and draining emotion work, note whether there's reciprocity and whether your social environments are emotionally well regulated. These reflection questions may help:

- In which environment(s) do you experience the most nourishing emotion work?
- In which environment(s) do you experience the most draining emotion work?
- What are some differences between these nourishing and draining environments?

These simple inventories and questions about your social structures can help you develop a greater empathic capacity for the empathic aspects of Emotion Recognition, Empathic Accuracy, and Perspective Taking. You can also use these inventories to understand more about the emotional and empathic workloads of the people in your life.

Identifying the Emotion Work of Your Colleagues

If you think back to the Keystones I described in the previous chapter (Ambassadors, Connectors, Peacemakers, and Agitators), see if you can place one or more of them in the second inventory on page 118. How much nourishing and draining work do they do? What are their total scores? Do they have the support they need, or are they struggling because no one is respecting their vital work?

And as you look back at the emotion tables on pages 36–44, think about which emotions these various Keystone workers might be feeling in their emotionally unregulated social structures. Which emotions would step forward to help them identify problems, and which gifts and skills do those emotions contain? And ask yourself: "Have I been in any social environments where these necessary emotions were noticed, respected, or supported?"

Now, do the same for one or two of your real colleagues. How much nourishing and draining work do you think they're doing, and what are their total scores? Which emotions would you expect them to be feeling, and are those emotions welcomed or supported in your workplace? These simple exercises in empathic Perspective Taking can help you learn how to imaginatively put yourself in the place of another, which increases your empathy and your emotional awareness. These exercises can also help you develop an eye for the emotional currents that flow through large-group social structures.

In emotionally unregulated social structures, we're usually working so hard to get through the day that we don't take the time to look around ourselves and observe the bigger picture. My suspicion is that in many workplaces, that's the point; the people in power don't want workers to have the time or energy to develop large-group social skills and critical awareness of emotions, empathy, reciprocity, and justice in the workplace social structure. Well too bad for the people in power! These skills are necessary, and we all have the right and the responsibility to develop them.

These very simple emotion work inventories can help you identify the quality and quantity of your own and your colleagues' work — and in so doing, you'll increase your large-group social skills, your emotional awareness, and your empathic capacity.

You can even use these inventories to observe the emotion work in entire departments. For instance, what's the difference between the emotion work of the customer service department in contrast to the custodial staff, the manufacturing department, or the management team? Which department does the most draining work (and are they being supported), and which does the most nourishing work (and why)? Is any department doing entirely non-reciprocal empathy work? Why? And can anything be done to help the people in that department avoid burnout? Understanding the emotional and empathic work that's being done throughout your workplace can increase your large-group social awareness and widen your Concern for Others and your capacity for Perceptive Engagement.

It's also important to understand how your colleagues show up to start their workdays. Do you know anything about their home environments or the balance of nourishing and draining work they do there? Are they arriving at work with a surplus of emotional energy and empathic skills, or are they dragging themselves in and slapping a smile over their drained faces, focusing on their tasks, and perhaps trying not to think too much about their difficulties at home?

When you start your workday or begin a meeting, are people invited to share how they're feeling? Even one sentence from each person can help the group take the emotional temperature of their community. This awareness can support people's large-group social skills, certainly, but it can also help them become more effective as team members. If people know that their colleagues are tired or suffering, or energized and looking for new projects, they'll be able to plan their workflows accordingly. And if people have some idea about the amount of emotion work they and their colleagues are doing at home *and* at work, they can develop clearer Perspective Taking abilities and Concern for Others. Though most of us live at work, we also have lives outside of work, and our whole lives affect our ability to show up and get our work done.

This whole-life focus is important, and it's why I like to post these inventories up on the wall with entire workplace groups, so that everyone can see what kinds of emotion work their colleagues do, and whether they're being drained or nourished in each area of their lives. If there are imbalances, everyone can see them, and the existing emotional intelligence that's already in the group can be put to work.

Each working community's emotional and empathic requirements are different, and each group's solutions are unique, but if everyone can see the emotional situation clearly, then everyone can address it intelligently — as a community. As a workplace consultant, I can then act as a guide and supporter instead of an outside "expert" who enforces solutions from the outside in or the top down.

If people are given the tools they need to understand emotions, emotional labor, and empathy work, their large-group social skills will expand and mature. When everyone has the tools and knowledge they need to identify their own and their community's issues, then everyone can get to work on them. In following their own emotional intelligence and doing their own work, workers will maintain and strengthen their relationships and sense of belonging, identify and improve their repair stations and gossip networks (see chapters 6 and 7), recognize and learn to support their Keystones, and maintain their competence, autonomy, and relatedness. Though many changes (and lots of Conscious Incompetence) may be required, this respectful and worker-empowering approach ensures that these changes won't reduce motivation or destabilize workers' lives, as so many change processes that are enforced from the outside or imposed from above reliably do.

We've all been in organizations that implemented the newest tools and processes, and after a period of interest, we watched as those newfangled ideas fell away. Soon enough, another process would come along, and that one would stick for a few months. Then, yet another process would get forced into the system, because the first two didn't "take." Well, of course they didn't take, and of course the third one will fail in a few months too. These enforced, alien, exterior processes don't respect the pre-existing (though usually suppressed) emotional intelligence, empathy, competence, autonomy, and relatedness that the working community has already developed. If workplace tools and processes don't respect those things (and most don't), they will fail.

Change that's emotionally intelligent, empathically sound, and naturally motivating must come from within the community itself, and workers must be treated with respect, empathy, and dignity. Workplace communities may need support and ideas, but only the people in those communities (and their emotions) can reliably identify their own issues, agree upon their own social processes and structures, and maintain those processes and structures over time. Anything else, no matter how popular it is, will reliably fail, or will require so much training, retraining, attention, and maintenance that it will actually get in the way of productivity.

The only empathically sound way to create and maintain an emotionally well-regulated social structure is to trust the emotional intelligence of the people who already live and work within it. The genius is in the people already; it's in their emotions and their responses to the workplace as it is. It's in the repair stations they've created and the Keystones who are holding things together. It's in their emotional labor, emotion work, and empathy work and the ways they've all learned to manage this work. The gifts, skills, and answers are already there, and when workplace communities have access to their own emotional genius, they can move out of Unconscious Incompetence together, and head toward the kind of democratic, inclusive, naturally motivating, and supportive working environments they (and we) have always deserved.

Building an Emotionally Well-Regulated Social Structure, Together

We've explored many topics so far, and I want to acknowledge that we've been on a journey through a troubled social environment that may feel utterly broken. I won't argue with you; it is broken. The troubles of the workplace can be overwhelming to think about and feel into, especially since most of us have traumatic memories about rotten workplaces we survived or are surviving now. It can feel unmanageable, which is why so many people avoid thinking too much about the emotions. It's also why so many workplaces enforce emotionally unwise fixes (one after the other) from the outside, or just give up because the problems feel too big.

I focus on the emotions in my work because they hold the answers to all of these problems, and they always have. As I wrote in the introduction, our work in this book doesn't involve heavy emotional lifting; it involves seeing what has been hidden and acknowledging what has been silenced. It involves moving from Unconscious Incompetence in regard to emotions in the workplace, and entering into *Conscious* Incompetence, which is the first important step in learning anything new. It's an uncomfortable step, yes, but discomfort has a purpose in all learning and all growth; we have to become conscious of our difficulties or we won't know what we're doing because we won't know what the problems are or where our incompetence lives.

We're in that place now; we're conscious of the problems, and we're learning a group of concepts that will help us address the problems in new ways. Right now, we're Consciously Incompetent, which is the perfect place to be. We might feel anger, shame, sadness, anxiety, or other emotions (skip back to the emotion tables on pages 36–44 to identify the gifts and skills within these emotions), but we now know that these emotions are necessary — they're bringing us valuable forms of intelligence. We might be clumsy and sort of clueless about which emotions we feel, but we're learning how to feel them and how to identify the skills and intelligence they bring us.

Learning to feel your emotions with clarity is not as difficult as you might think. Vocabulary is the magic key, and when you can increase your emotional vocabulary, you can increase your ability to tune into yourself and others. I've included my Emotional Vocabulary List in the appendix to help you identify what you're feeling at many different levels of activation, which will help you develop the first three aspects of empathy: Emotion Recognition, Empathic Accuracy, and Emotion Regulation.

This vocabulary list can also support you as you learn to identify the emotions your loved ones and colleagues may be feeling (of course, you would *ask* about your impressions and not *tell* people how they're feeling in order to respect their privacy, emotional autonomy, and dignity). Learning how to identify the emotions of others while trusting their own emotional awareness can help you develop more precise empathy, better Perspective Taking, and a stronger Concern for Others, which will mean that your empathy (and your empathy work) will result in clearer Perceptive Engagement.

As it is with learning any new skill, developing your emotional vocabulary will take practice; all of these skills and concepts will take practice. As we work through the rest of this book, we'll head into *Conscious* Competence together. It will take work to apply these new skills and concepts, but this work will lead us someplace new and worthwhile because we've taken the time to become conscious of the problems we face.

As we move forward from here, I want to return to the model of the emotionally well-regulated social structure we looked at in chapter 1. When you filled out your inventories a few pages back, you may have identified nourishing and well-regulated relationships or social structures in your own life, and that's wonderful. But if you're dealing with mostly draining, unequal, unregulated, or unsupportive relationships and social structures, it can help to take a closer look at the nine aspects that make up a well-regulated structure so that you'll know where the problems are and where changes need to be made.

Under each of the nine aspects below, I've included information on the three aspects that support motivation so that you can see how these structures support your competence, autonomy, and relatedness. I've also included the seventeen emotions (see the charts on pages 36–44) so that you can see how well-regulated structures support your emotional awareness and skills. Finally, I've included the Six Essential Aspects of Empathy (see page 48) so that you can observe how each aspect of an emotionally well-regulated social structure can support you and your community. As you'll see, each of these nine aspects engage most of the aspects of motivation, all of your emotions, and all of your essential aspects of empathy, but I want you to see them laid out clearly.

All nine aspects of emotionally well-regulated social structures are vital to the health and well-being of individual workers and their workplace communities:

1. **Emotions are spoken of openly, and people have workable emotional vocabularies.**
     » **Motivating factors engaged:** All three
     » **Emotional gifts and skills supported:** All seventeen
     » **Aspects of empathy supported:** All six

The emotion tables (see pages 36–44) can help you and the people around you begin to learn about the gifts and skills each emotion brings to you. These tables can also help you understand why emotions arise. When you can see emotions as necessary, purposeful, and valuable, you'll be much more willing to speak about them openly and listen when other people speak about them. My Emotional Vocabulary List in the appendix will help greatly, because a precise emotional vocabulary can help you learn to identify and regulate your emotions more skillfully. Vocabulary is essential for understanding.

2. **Mistakes and conflicts are addressed without avoidance, hostility, or blaming.**
    » **Motivating factors engaged:** All three
    » **Emotional gifts and skills supported:** All seventeen
    » **Aspects of empathy supported:** All six

So much suffering and waste are generated when people's mistakes and conflicts are handled badly. Even one badly handled mistake or conflict can cast a pall over a relationship or an entire workplace for months or even years. In chapter 5, we'll explore simple communication processes that can help people treat mistakes and conflicts as important information and opportunities for awareness (instead of character flaws or signs of failure).

3. **You can be honest about mistakes and conflicts without being blamed or shunned.**
    » **Motivating factors engaged:** All three
    » **Emotional gifts and skills supported:** All seventeen
    » **Aspects of empathy supported:** All six

When you and your colleagues are able to speak openly about emotions and you have ways to communicate about mistakes and conflicts, no one will be made into a scapegoat or pushed out of the community when inevitable problems occur. In an emotionally well-regulated social structure, troubles are accepted as a regular part of real life, conflicts are dealt with appropriately, and all emotions are welcomed, not just the happy-peppy ones.

4. **Your emotions and sensitivities are noticed and respected.**
   » **Motivating factors engaged:** Competence and relatedness
   » **Emotional gifts and skills supported:** All seventeen
   » **Aspects of empathy supported:** All six

This fourth aspect builds on the first three; when you share an emotional vocabulary and can communicate clearly about emotions, mistakes, conflicts, successes, and real life in a safe and welcoming environment, you and everyone around you will be treated with care and respect.

5. **You notice and respect the emotions and sensitivities of others.**
   » **Motivating factors engaged:** Competence and relatedness
   » **Emotional gifts and skills supported:** All seventeen
   » **Aspects of empathy supported:** All six

In emotionally unhealthy environments, many people don't have the time or energy to care deeply about others; they're merely surviving. In an emotionally well-regulated environment, on the other hand, people can breathe, emotionally speaking. They have the energy, focus, vocabulary, and ability to utilize their empathy in healthy ways, instead of becoming unpaid or unacknowledged Keystones. When you and your emotions are welcomed and you have reliable ways to communicate about mistakes, conflicts, sensitives, and real life, you'll have the skills and nourishment you need to notice and respect others and treat them with care and respect.

6. **Your emotional awareness and skills are openly requested and respected.**
   » **Motivating factors engaged:** All three
   » **Emotional gifts and skills supported:** All seventeen
   » **Aspects of empathy supported:** All six

In emotionally well-regulated social structures there won't be glaring holes in the system that need to be filled unconsciously. If you tend to perform Keystone behaviors, you and others will be able to identify and fix the problems in the structure instead of loading you down with endless, unpaid empathy work. If you lean toward Ambassador duties at work, there will be a way to explore and implement better onboarding processes. If you find yourself Peacemaking, there will be ways to identify unhealthy segregation between people or departments, and so forth. You won't be isolated or unrecognized, and your emotional skills and empathic abilities will be seen as valuable talents (and not as exploitable tendencies).

7. **You openly request and respect the emotional awareness and skills of others.**
   » **Motivating factors engaged:** All three
   » **Emotional gifts and skills supported:** All seventeen
   » **Aspects of empathy supported:** All six

In an emotionally well-regulated environment, you'll be aware of the emotional labor, emotion work, and empathy work that everyone is doing, and you'll respect people's time and need for support. You'll also have the language you need to speak about this work openly. Your ability to recognize and speak about previously hidden emotion work and empathy work is a huge gift, and it will increase your emotional skills and your empathic capacities.

8. You and others feel safe enough and supported enough to speak the truth even if it might destabilize relationships or processes.

    » **Motivating factors engaged:** All three
    » **Emotional gifts and skills supported:** All seventeen
    » **Aspects of empathy supported:** All six

Workers of the World member and workplace consultant Sheila Diggs suggested this aspect, because she's seen that all work groups need to be able to speak the truth without fear of being shamed or retaliated against. When you and your colleagues have emotional skills and communication processes to rely on, and you're nourished by your social structure, you can weather conflicts and difficulties without fearing the loss of your place, your relationships, or your job. In the introduction, I shared research that found that 85% of workers refused to speak openly about trouble at work, even if that trouble was serious; emotionally unregulated workplace environments silenced these workers completely. This is a complete shame, and it speaks directly to the problems caused by kicking emotions out of the workplace. Emotions are crucial to everything we think, believe, and do, and if emotions are silenced, we cannot function. Our relationships cannot function, and our workplaces cannot function. When we can't access our emotions and we can't openly address conflicts, mistakes, or problems, we become trapped. In emotionally well-regulated social structures, on the other hand, people have the courage, sense of belonging, and support they need to speak the truth even when the truth is painful or destabilizing.

9. The social structure welcomes you, nourishes you, and revitalizes you.

    » **Motivating factors engaged:** All three
    » **Emotional gifts and skills supported:** All seventeen
    » **Aspects of empathy supported:** All six

In a healthy and emotionally well-regulated social structure, you'll be respected, supported, and cared for. Even if your emotional labor with customers is draining, even if your empathy work at work or at home is difficult, and even if your job itself is empathically strenuous, your emotionally well-regulated social structure can support you, nourish you, and provide you with healthy community in good times, in bad times, and in all the times in between.

Building a welcoming, democratic, inclusive, and emotionally well-regulated social structure requires a shift in focus (toward the emotions instead of away from them) and time spent in Conscious Incompetence. But at its heart, none of this work is difficult. It simply requires listening to emotions and respecting them. It requires being aware of emotional and empathic work *as work*, and addressing both if they're unpaid, unrecognized, draining, and/or non-reciprocal. It requires supporting people's competence, autonomy, and relatedness, and it requires treating people with empathy, respect, and kindness. That's not hard! The workplace as an entity has made it hard by ignorantly exiling emotions, but the emotions never left; they're an intrinsic part of every thought we have, every action we take, every idea we think up, every dream we envision, and every behavior we perform. The emotions never left, and this is not difficult work; it's deeply human work, and we're all fully able to do it.

However, this work does require that you give yourself permission to make mistakes, notice them, and fix them — all of which you can do in an emotionally well-regulated social structure. You don't have to be perfect; you just have to be real and honest — and your emotions will certainly help you do that. Listen to them.

If you and your colleagues make any changes that bring forward emotional concerns or suppress any emotions, you can stop and regroup. If you make any changes that disengage competence, autonomy, or relatedness, you can stop and regroup. If you make any changes that overburden or shut down any aspects of empathy, you can stop and regroup. If you make any changes that create the need for unpaid or unsupported Ambassadors, Connectors, Peacemakers, or Agitators (or whatever Keystone types you've identified in your organization), you can stop and regroup.

You can always step back, listen to the genius in the emotions that come forward, and reorganize your approach. This is the process of truly empathic design: You and your community think up some clever new thing, try it to see if it works, and fix it if it doesn't. And if you get lost, you can rely upon the consciousness and competence model to find yourself again. You can always shift back into Conscious Incompetence if you went too fast, or too far, or in the wrong direction. The emotions will tell you clearly when you move in the wrong direction with the wrong intentions, bless them. Listen to their wisdom and trust them. They know what they're doing, and they always have.

PART 2

Building Your Unique Healthy Workplace

5

Creating Communication Workflows
for Everyday Emotional Issues

have yet to find a workplace — in more than 40 years of searching — where there are defined and accessible processes to help workers deal with everyday social difficulties. I'm not talking about big problems such as workplace injuries, workplace bullying, or sexual harassment — there are formal HR processes for those situations, plus labor laws, labor commissions, and each country's version of OSHA. What I'm talking about are very simple communication difficulties that may occur several times each day.

I always ask, "Do your workers have a process for requesting attention from a busy person or asking someone to take over a task for them?" And I am met with blank stares. "What about asking a sensitive question without offending someone? Asking for help? Admitting that they made a mistake?" More blank stares. Crickets even.

When workers aren't provided with reliable ways to communicate about everyday interpersonal situations, they must cobble together methods from their private lives, from their schoolyard training, from previous jobs, or from thin air. This is an absurd waste of everyone's time, and it impedes workplace efficiency and emotional regulation from the word go. When workers don't even know how to ask each other questions or communicate their concerns, they'll trip over each other and create mini conflicts throughout each day — usually without meaning to. They'll also have to ramp up their unpaid empathy work and become Peacemakers just to navigate through unspoken issues, unmet needs, mistaken assumptions, and difficult relationships — and they won't be able to speak openly about any of it. Belonging and relatedness will suffer, multiple repair stations and gossip networks will have to arise just to keep everything (sort of) functional, and the workplace will be uncomfortable, inefficient, and wildly more likely to create the conditions that lead to employee silence about serious workplace problems.

When people don't have the tools they need to deal with simple, everyday communication issues, they won't develop a sense of interpersonal competence, and they'll often be too preoccupied or drained to deal with larger issues. Poor or nonexistent communication processes leave people unsupported and create unnecessary conflict throughout the workplace. This is an unsafe situation for everyone, but luckily, the solution is simple: Help workers develop effective skills for everyday difficulties, and they'll have the energy, support, competence, sense of belonging, and skills they need to communicate effectively when critical problems occur. We'll explore those skills in this chapter.

Another requirement in any communal environment is that people need to have access to privacy, relatedness, and comfort — physically as well as emotionally. These spaces help us rest and regulate ourselves so that we can work more effectively, but sadly, this is yet another place where the workplace fails us and creates unnecessary and unprofitable conflict and discomfort.

Healthy and emotionally well-regulated organizations should provide dedicated, welcoming, and communally agreed upon break areas; ways to find quiet and privacy; methods to share crucial emotional and empathic information; and clear processes to help people make healthy transitions into, within, or out of the organization. In our Workers of the World meetings, no one could recall a single working environment that had all or even some of these features. As we saw in the introduction, the workplace has largely failed to create a healthy or emotionally well-regulated environment, but luckily, we and our emotions can do that. And workplace communities can do that by developing many ways to listen to the emotions and respond to the information they provide.

As I mentioned at the beginning of this book, my on-site workplace consulting processes are unusual because I don't separate workers from management, executives, or owners. I remove the silos and work with everyone in the workplace at the same time (Including part-time workers and custodial staff). Everyone receives the same information so that the entire community can share a common language, clear understanding of the unique (and shared) stressors they and their colleagues face, and a communally developed set of social, emotional, and communication skills to help their workplace social structure become functional, supportive, and nourishing for everyone. Even in hierarchical and segregated social structures, working communities can develop healthy communication skills, relationship skills, gossip networks, and self-care skills — individually and as a group.

None of the processes I'll suggest in this chapter or the next are difficult, and most don't cost anything (except the time to develop them); in fact, they're just common sense when you look at them through the lens of an emotionally well-regulated social structure. But, as we know, the workplace isn't emotionally well regulated, so most of these simple approaches will seem unusual, and may require you to shift into Conscious Incompetence as you learn to identify, create, and implement these processes. Let's start with the simplest foundation first.

Do You Have a Communication Workflow For . . . ?

Most workplaces have written and agreed-upon processes for workflows, but these processes overlook everyday social difficulties and expect people to figure them out on their own. I've written many employee manuals with step-by-step instructions for every task and workplace process, but none of them included information on how to deal with simple everyday communication problems such as asking a busy person for attention. In the workplace as an entity, there's a deeply rooted ignorance about the ways that our social lives, our workplace relationships, and our emotional responses affect every aspect of our workflow. This following list of questions highlights social and emotional workflows that regularly fail because people don't have processes or even language for them.

Of course, each workplace has its own unique questions and situations, but this list can help you begin to identify where communication in your own workplace reliably breaks down.

Does your entire workplace community have a known, shared, and reliable communication workflow for:

- Requesting attention from a busy person?
- Asking for help?
- Asking a sensitive question without offending people?
- Asking someone to do a job or a task for you?
- Admitting that you made a mistake?
- Letting someone else know that they made a mistake?
- Knowing whether an email, a face-to-face conversation, or a meeting is appropriate?
- Knowing whether a text or a phone call is appropriate?
- Communicating about problems?
- Communicating problems upward without danger?
- Dealing with conflict and challenges?

Most workplaces don't have clear-cut or reliable processes for any of these everyday situations, which means that each worker will need to learn them on their own (with any luck). This learning, however, will often occur nonverbally, through sighs, eye rolls, dirty looks, shaming, blaming, or shunning that established workers use to teach newcomers these unwritten and unspoken social rules — as if these new people *should have known*! When social processes are unspoken, unregulated, and taught only in unconscious ways, the social environment will be unstable and emotionally draining. The HR department may need to get involved (if they can), but you'll also see Ambassadors and Peacemakers leap into the fray because a crucial onboarding process (teaching and maintaining the social and emotional rules in the workplace) lives in a completely unconscious area of people's awareness. Informal repair stations and gossip networks will also arise because people need to figure out the lay of the land somehow.

Peacemakers may have a big job on their hands, because there's no way to tell when the next unregulated conflict over emails, interruptions, refilling the copy machine, or someone's *tone* is going to make things boil over. Anger may arise to help people set boundaries; envy and jealousy may arise because inequality, disloyalty, and unfairness will go unacknowledged; anxiety may arise because no one knows what the rules are or when the next mini conflict will disrupt everyone; depression and apathy may arise to help people create some sense of separation from the trouble; and panic may arise because people may dread the loss of their place in the social structure, their jobs, or their livelihoods. It's a draining, emotionally unregulated mess. It's no way to run a business and it's no way to live.

But luckily, it's a simple mess to clean up. Starting with my list of questions, your workplace community can identify everyday processes that reliably fall apart because there are no agreed-upon procedures for them. For instance, one workplace sales team I worked with found that every question on my workflow list was left out of their workplace procedures and onboarding processes; however, there were also daily conflicts about how people loaded the dishwasher in the staff kitchen, who should replace the heavy bottle in the water dispenser, and whose responsibility it was to replenish the printer trays with the correct size and color of copy paper.

These may seem like silly, tiny problems, but this was a very busy sales team that was being drained and pulled away from their work by communication breakdowns over simple, everyday tasks. These people weren't lazy or ignorant; they were hard working professionals, but their workplace didn't provide them with the social and emotional skills or support they needed — and the tension and conflict were pretty intense once we got to talking about these three problems. Before we explore their issue, let me share the guidelines I set for these meetings because it's important not to let them turn into pointless brawls.

Guidelines for Communication Workflow Meetings

Unspoken problems in an emotionally unregulated social structure can surface a lot of conflict, and that conflict needs to be approached in a way that doesn't cause more conflict! These guidelines can help people explore these problems and listen to the gifts and skills that their emotions are trying to contribute:

- I've created a free Communication Workflow Packet that includes instructions for running these meetings, the workflow list, and printable emotion tables and Emotional Vocabulary Lists for you and your team. This packet is available at karlamclaren.com/the -power-of-emotions-at-work.
- Everyone in the workplace needs to be involved; let them know what you're working on and call a community-wide meeting to identify communication breakdowns and build reliable new communication workflows.
- Plan for a 1- to 2-hour meeting, and let people know that you'll continue the discussion in another meeting (or meetings) because you won't get to everything in the first one.
- One week before the meeting: Give people the workflow list from my packet and have them add any other communication processes that regularly break down in your organization.
- One day before the meeting: Gather and organize these responses and send them out to everyone.
- On the day of the meeting: Print out the emotion tables and Emotional Vocabulary List (from my packet) for every participant.
- Tape large pieces of paper on the wall or use a flip chart or whiteboard so that someone can write down the concerns and wisdom that the community shares.
- Choose a trusted person from the middle or lower areas of the hierarchy to be the scribe. In an emotionally unregulated workplace, there will be (valid) distrust of managers and executives, and workers may silence themselves if their superiors have control of the magic markers.
- As you go through each broken communication process, ask people to call out the emotions they feel in response to it (from their Emotional Vocabulary List) and write them down on the paper or whiteboard for everyone to see.
- Focus the emotions on the broken *processes*, and not on each other. Yes, some people's behaviors will be more noticeable in

communication breakdowns, but no one can be on their best behavior when there are no rules, no reliable processes, and no support.

- Look at the gifts and skills of the emotions the group has listed, and note *why* the emotions are present; which forms of intelligence are being called to the scene?

- Create a new process with everyone's input and continue to pay attention to the emotions that arise.

- Once the communication process feels right, post it where everyone has access to it.

- Know that you may need to revisit these processes if they don't work as you thought they would. Realizing that something doesn't work is not a failure; it's a crucial part of the empathic design process and of the consciousness and competence model of learning (see page 73 for a reminder).

Now that we have these guidelines in place, let's walk through the problems this sales team had (I was their scribe).

Case Study: How Dishwasher Hassles Brought a Workplace Community Together

When the sales team gathered (along with people from other departments) and we addressed these three problems — the dishwasher, the water cooler, and the copy machine — people called out a lot of words in the anger area (frustrated, peeved, annoyed, irritated, offended, etc.). We looked at the emotions list and saw that this anger was a valid response because their boundaries and values (about cleanliness, respect, and accountability) were being disturbed all day, every day. Anger was required.

But as we started to think up fixes for these problems, people called out words like discouraged, disconnected, exhausted, and drained — which refer to depression, apathy, and resignation. I wondered why, but I listened. There was an overall fatigue and a sense that no fix would stick; every suggestion was slapped down because people were sure that it would all fall apart again. This was important information that most teams would be jollied or pushed into ignoring, but that would be a mistake. These emotions were telling us something important. Situational depression (which is different from deeper forms such as major depression, postpartum depression, or bipolar depression) reduces people's energy when things are unworkable somehow; it impedes people's ability to go forward with the wrong intentions for the wrong reasons at the wrong time. And apathy is a mask for anger that arises when people are in situations where their needs are unimportant or they can't speak openly for some reason. These people and their emotions were telling me clearly that forward movement and clear communication were unworkable at this point in the process. Therefore, we didn't go forward.

As we talked more about these mini conflict areas, it became clear that each of them was related to a lack of time — time to load or unload the dishwasher in a specific way, time to change the water bottle, time to load the printer, or time to identify who *should* do these things — everyone was equally swamped and pressed for time. More vocabulary words relating to anger, sadness, depression, and even hatred went onto the list along with many words relating to fatigue (exhausted, burnt-out, etc.). There was a lot going on here.

In this workplace, these seemingly minor conflicts brought forth some powerful shared emotions. Because we listened to these emotions with respect, everyone was able to see that their entire busy community needed basic physical support; they didn't need a colorful dishwasher schedule with childish stickers on it and they didn't need a water bottle captain — they were exhausted and they needed someone to care for them.

As it is in many workplaces (and homes and schools, etc.), the pace of modern life brings forth many important emotional responses that tell us how we feel about what's going on. But when everyone is overscheduled and overworked, this awareness tends to move into Unconscious Incompetence. We forget that being too busy and not having enough rest or support is unworkable because we're surrounded by it; it's in the water we drink and the air we breathe, and we lose our ability to identify it clearly. But our emotions remain conscious of it, and sometimes, *only* our emotions can tell us what's really going on.

In listening to their depression and fatigue, we all realized that the sales team needed to be supported rather than trained on proper copy paper etiquette or something ridiculous like that. They all *knew* how to refill the copy machine and load the dishwasher, but they didn't have time. That was the issue that was bringing their depression and apathy forward every time we tried to think up a solution. When we understood that, we were able to focus ourselves in a different direction: Did the team need to hire someone to help with their workload? We talked about that for a few minutes, but there wasn't enough space in the office or in the budget for a new salesperson, and they didn't think they had enough extra work to expand.

The custodial supervisor then suggested something, and the entire room relaxed (remember that I ask everyone to be a part of these meetings). He asked if there was enough money in the budget to hire him or one of his nighttime crew to come in for a few daytime hours, three days per week, to clean, organize, restock, and look after the physical condition of the office so that everyone could focus on their work. The effect on the group was immediate and soothing; they became quiet, but relaxed. They began to smile, and some people's eyes began to tear up — yes! Sadness had arrived to help people let go of the unworkable situation. They called out words like calm, relieved, hopeful, grateful, amused, and grounded. Hope and happiness were telling us that this idea looked good and felt appropriate.

Notice that we didn't highlight the emotions in the Happiness Family (happiness, contentment, and joy) or try to force them into the process. We didn't try to jolly people out of their discomfort or make everyone happy; that would have inserted a toxic positivity bias and would likely have silenced everyone. No, we listened to the honest emotions that came forward until it was natural and valid for the emotions in the Happiness Family to appear — which they did when the custodial supervisor listened closely and then suggested an excellent solution.

To their credit, the sales team members were concerned about the custodian's well-being; they wanted to make sure that he had enough sleep, that they were paying him enough, and that he knew where everything was (he did). When he was settled into his new routine, the workplace smoothed out; now, no one went thirsty because they couldn't lift the water bottle and no one had to fume or interrupt their day because the printer was out of legal-sized paper. Even better, the custodian, instead of being invisible, became a valued member of the daytime team. He shared their new communication processes and could address areas of need that he saw arising in the community. And it was all because everyone came together to focus serious attention on their emotional responses to seemingly unimportant workday processes — no matter how small.

Creating these new processes must be a community effort because there's rich and hidden intelligence in the community and in each person's emotions; if you don't include everyone, you won't be able to see the whole picture. And I will warn you now that there will be arguments; *of course*, there will be arguments when people are allowed to bring unconscious, poorly managed, and conflict-generating processes into the light of day. These arguments are important, because they'll help people daylight all of the issues that have been squashed and suppressed — and that's what you want to see. You want to understand the issues and the problems, because if you don't get a complete picture of what's going on, you won't be able to create any worthwhile solutions. However, you don't want these arguments to decay into attacks or pointless bickering.

By asking people to call out emotion words about the *process*, and by writing them on the wall charts, you can keep these arguments focused on the group and its natural responses to unclear and unsupported communication processes, rather than turning this into a gripe session about individuals. Issues between individuals need to be dealt with privately, either through HR (if they have the time and the skill) or a mediator, and *never* in group meetings. Calling out individuals is unkind and unwise; it damages competence, autonomy, and relatedness, and it can stifle and silence everyone in the workplace. These workflow process meetings need to be places where the emotions can come out and contribute their genius to the broken communication that everyone has been struggling with. No individual should be put on the hot seat; that's unempathic.

The wisdom of the emotions is always valuable, but it's priceless in situations where problems and conflicts have been swept under the rug. You'll need to make time to listen to the emotions, because they're often the only things that can tell you what's actually going on. These meetings may be lengthy at first, yet I've discovered that once people know how this process works, the meetings get shorter and shorter while life in the organization gets easier and easier. At first, because no focused time had ever been spent on these issues, and because people weren't able to speak about them openly, there's a lot to go over. But once people move through Conscious Incompetence and into Conscious *Competence*, the process evens out and the community learns how to regulate and care for each other. People also develop stronger emotional vocabularies and emotional awareness, which helps in every area of their social and emotional lives.

I'll walk you through a few more examples so you can see the unique workflows other teams created with the help of their emotions.

In the next example, I was working with a high-performing engineering firm that had just transitioned into what I call the Devil's Floorplan: an unwalled, boundaryless, open-plan office environment with long flat desks (we'll explore the disruptive emotional and empathic effects of this devilish floorplan on page 175). If I had known about the open-plan office, I probably wouldn't have agreed to work with them, because it's just a disastrous thing to do to people, but there I was.[1]

Case Study: Creating a Workflow for Disappointment

At an afternoon meeting devoted to working through my list (plus specific issues the group had identified), this high-intensity working group of fifteen engineers developed their own process flow for requesting attention from a busy person. This team had previously been able to wall themselves off from one another, and because of that, they hadn't had to develop many skills for interrupting busy people — and they were all *very* busy people. Now that they had no walls, no peace or quiet, and no privacy, their busyness had become an area of growing conflict. The central emotion words this team called out were related to anger and anxiety, but they also called out words related to jealousy and envy because some people (managers) could interrupt busy people with no repercussions while others felt that they couldn't interrupt anyone, ever. This hierarchical difference became clear to everyone, and to their credit, the managers apologized for the unfair distribution of interrupting power.

This is the process these professionals agreed on after about 15 minutes of conversation and argument. Of course, another group at a different workplace would have developed a different flow, but this is what worked for these people. I was their scribe, and I wrote their suggestions on a large sheet of paper on the wall so that everyone could see them:

- Get yourself focused; but be loose in your expectations.
- Be willing to accept no for an answer.
- Organize yourself before you make your request:
  » By the importance of the request;
  » By the time you will need;
  » And by urgency (communicate a specific time and day).
- A suggested format: "Do you have [X] minutes to talk to me about [subject] on [day and time]?"
- Remember that interruptions decrease focus, concentration, and efficiency — and that people will need time to get fully back into their workflow again.
- Therefore, should you make this request by email or by text? (For some team members, a text meant *more urgent* or *pay attention immediately*.)

Notice that this process flow warns people to be prepared for disappointment. It almost says, "Bring your sadness and get ready to let go of your needs; your request may be turned down." Also notice the highly structured flow of this process; these were engineers, so the structure is to be expected, but the regimentation of this process also speaks to the lack of structure in their physical workspace. This process flow feels unwelcoming to me, but an open-plan office environment often forces people to become highly regimented (or overly loose) in their workplace relationships. The Devil's Floorplan creates a lot of unnecessary noise, interruptions, and trouble, and this process helped the team function better.

Case Study: Addressing a Toxic Positivity Bias

At another organization, a marketing group needed to create a process for communicating problems upward without danger. This wasn't an abusive environment, but the management team had developed a *toxic positivity bias* that had a deeply silencing effect because no one wanted to be seen as "negative." Most of the emotions were unwelcome, and only the Happiness Family emotions were allowed. As you might expect, this unbalanced approach to emotions created a great deal of unpaid emotion work because people had to suppress most of their emotions. It also created a ton of unpaid empathy work as people struggled to say everything perfectly when they had to report a "negative" situation to management. Most people didn't report; they just glued on their happy masks and took care of problems silently or hoped that the problems would disappear somehow.

TOXIC POSITIVITY BIAS

A dangerously mistaken belief that the allegedly positive emotions are the only emotions that should be felt or shared in the workplace. This bias causes extensive suffering as people suppress all forbidden emotions, lose their emotional awareness and skills, and become unable to address serious problems that *require* the gifts, skills, and genius in the forbidden emotions.

As we explored new ways to talk about problems in our group meeting, people were obviously silencing themselves, so I brought up an actual problem from the outside (a supplier was very late on delivering important parts for a project), called out the emotions that arose in response to it, and walked everyone through the process of reporting it. Once people saw that they could call out words relating to "negative" emotions without danger, they were able to loosen up and focus on the problem (instead of wasting their energy trying to repress their emotions). This is the workflow process the team came up with:

- We need to set aside "problem times" in our weekly meetings where the entire focus is to look for problems.
- Everyone needs to be in the room together, and everyone gets an equal voice.
- We need to ask ourselves: What's keeping us up at night? What's bothering us? What's wrong?
- We'll write the problems on the whiteboard so that everyone can see them and add to them, if needed.
- We won't try to fix the problems right away unless they *are* fixable right away.
- We'll prioritize the problems together and carry unfixed problems over to the next meeting.
- Everyone can suggest solutions, as long as they're real solutions, and not just ways to avoid the problems.

Having permission to speak about problems brought forth a lot of authentic (instead of forced) hope, happiness, and laughter in this group, even though they were entering unknown territory. Writing their problems on the whiteboard and carrying them over to the next week was a huge step for this "sweep it under the happy rug" group, because problems had been treated as personal emotional failings rather than normal everyday business situations. They expressed fear and uncertainty about leaving problems visible on the whiteboard, but these were normal and necessary feelings because these workers were breaking old rules. They also expressed some shame and guilt; they were very conscious of their communal incompetence in regard to talking about problems. They needed each other's help and support as they learned new ways to communicate. We all do.

There's a wonderful international group called The Failure Institute (thefailureinstitute.com) that offers regular F*ckup Nights around the world for people to come and share their mistakes, failures, and blunders, and it's a wonderfully freeing idea.[2] I'd love to see F*ckup Nights and days instituted everywhere — in families, in schools, in workplaces, throughout the media and in politics. Can you imagine how much unnecessary suffering we could relieve if everyone knew that conflicts, mistakes, and failures were normal and expected — and a vital part of learning? Remember that incompetence is a central part of all real learning processes, and so is unconsciousness. We need to stumble, be clueless, and fail regularly, or we won't ever learn anything new.

When this marketing team welcomed everyone into these special "problem times" in their meetings, they were ensuring that no one would be alone in noticing or speaking about problems. These meetings and the simple workflow this group created reduced the amount of unpaid emotional labor and empathy work everyone had been doing, and people became increasingly able to speak the truth about problems and even f*ckups. These new problem-focused meetings became repair stations that increased everyone's sense of competence, relatedness, and trust in one another.

·◆◆◆·

As you can see from these three case studies, each team's workflows are unique; their issues are specific to them, and their solutions are tailored to fit their needs. What all of these workflow meetings share, however, is a trust in the intelligence of the emotions and a willingness to listen to them as conflicts are surfaced and new processes are developed. What I love about this workflow process is that it respects the native intelligence of each individual and each group. My job as a consultant is not to tell people how to do things, it's to remind them of the knowledge and resources that already exist inside them, in their emotions, and in their community.

Welcoming the emotions back into the workplace — or into any human relationship — can uncover powerful sources of ingenuity, empathy, and emotional genius. Emotions rock!

A Different Kind of Complaints Department

Not knowing how to talk about problems, conflicts, and mistakes creates a lot of unnecessary emotional upheaval in the organizations I've worked in and observed; there just aren't clear processes for these normal everyday situations.

In our Workers of the World (WoW) meetings, only two people recalled workplaces that had something in place to address the normal presence of conflicts in everyday situations. When WoW member Marion Langford was a manager, she told every new hire that they were expected to make five mistakes each year, and one supervisor that WoW member Bobbi McIntyre worked for told all new hires that they had six weeks to be knuckleheads. Both of these things were said in jest, and as a way to make room for normal human mistakes, but note that these excellent suggestions had limits after an initial period of freedom, even though the limits were set humorously. In most workplaces, these limits aren't a joke; there's an idea that we can set a time limit on mistakes, or that after a specific date, people will somehow develop large-group social skills and communication skills — and not make mistakes. Sadly, this is not true; people need regular support and reliable communication workflows, especially in the face of mistakes, conflicts, and problems.

We all need to have freely available "problem times" and F*ckup Days in our meetings and working lives because problems, conflicts, and mistakes are normal, no matter how long people have been in a workplace. We all need to have places where we can talk about mistakes and problems, conflicts and misunderstandings, things that frustrate and disturb us, and work situations that are not functioning. We need a place to complain!

I included the case of the marketing team who were damaged by a toxic positivity bias because this bias is *everywhere* in the workplace. This bias is not only toxic to individual emotional functioning, but it can silence necessary conversations about workplace troubles and even dangerous safety violations.[3] A positivity bias also interferes with *all nine* aspects of emotionally well-regulated social structures, as you can see on the next page:

1. Emotions are spoken of openly, and people have workable emotional vocabularies.
2. Mistakes and conflicts are addressed without avoidance, hostility, or blaming.
3. You can be honest about mistakes and difficult issues without being blamed or shunned.
4. Your emotions and sensitivities are noticed and respected.
5. You notice and respect the emotions and sensitivities of others.
6. Your emotional awareness and skills are openly requested and respected.
7. You openly request and respect the emotional awareness and skills of others.
8. You and others feel safe enough and supported enough to speak the truth even if it might destabilize relationships or processes.
9. The social structure welcomes you, nourishes you, and revitalizes you.

People *must* be allowed to feel their full range of emotions, and they *must* be allowed to speak up and complain about the hassles, troubles, problems, and hazards that they and their emotions identify. If people are not allowed to speak openly, all aspects of motivation (competence, auton omy, and relatedness) will plummet, and emotional and social turmoil will follow. People must be allowed to feel, to speak, to point out troubles and hazards, and to complain consciously, with the full support of their emotional awareness and skills, their empathy, and their ethics.

I teach three communication practices that can help with real learning and real life at work — especially when complaints, mistakes, or blunders arise. One is private, and you can use it whenever and wherever you need to, and two are shared practices that you can use with your colleagues (and with your friends and family). These three practices (beginning on the next page) are repair stations and mental health breaks that can help you:

- Identify your emotions and understand why they're present.
- Understand the difficulties and hazards you're facing.

- Clarify your responses to these difficulties.
- Clear the air.

All three practices give you regular access to "problem times" and F*ckup Days. As I mentioned, the first practice is an individual practice and the second two are partner practices. The two partner practices may not be welcome in your workplace, especially if it's an emotionally unregulated social structure or if it's struggling under a toxic positivity bias. But this first, individual practice is yours to use wherever and whenever you need it. I've found over the decades that this practice can keep me stable and healthy even (or especially) when I'm in rotten environments. It's called *Conscious Complaining*.[4]

Conscious Complaining for Yourself

Complaining is not usually allowed, but it's necessary because life isn't a bowl of cherries; trouble is everywhere. Our emotions will respond and react naturally to trouble, especially at work or in places where equality and justice are not available. We'll naturally feel anger, envy, depression, jealousy, fear, anxiety, and every other necessary emotion. But if we aren't allowed to speak about or share any of our real responses, we may suffer — not just from the rotten situation, but because our voices are suppressed and our emotional awareness is unwelcome.

I created this Conscious Complaining practice after reading a wonderful book called *Wishcraft: How to Get What You Really Want* by Barbara Sher. She teaches people to listen to their wishes and dreams, and to follow them into careers that suit them. But unlike many follow-your-dreams books, Sher's isn't full of unicorns and toxic positivity. She understands that following your dreams can be grueling and rough, and she created something called "Hard Times" to help people express their struggles. Sher, like many researchers after her, discovered that complaining (consciously and intentionally) doesn't bring people down; it lifts them up and restores their humor and hope, because they're keying into the power of their honest emotions and becoming clear about the difficulties they're facing. After a good complaining session, people can shake off, refocus themselves on the problems and possible solutions, and get back to the work at hand.

I named this practice *Conscious* Complaining to remind myself that I was bringing consciousness to my struggles, and also to detoxify the necessary act of complaining (which most people are taught to avoid at all costs). Workplaces aren't the only emotionally unregulated social structures that have a toxic positivity bias; very few people learn how to address problems, conflicts, or troubles at home or at school, and very few of us were taught to welcome all emotions as valuable aspects of our intelligence and awareness. Because of this, many of us are separated from the intelligence in our emotions. This practice reconnects us.

Conscious Complaining helps you speak the truth and connect to your honest emotional responses, no matter where you are, and no matter how poorly emotions are treated by the people around you. This practice can restore your emotional autonomy and competence even in the midst of emotional repression and emotional ignorance, and it's free, portable, and available to you whenever you need it.

How to Perform Conscious Complaining

Find a private, solitary place where you can really whine and gripe (or cry) about the frustration, hopelessness, and absurdity of your situation. This private place can be a physical space, or it can be something you create with a paper and pen if you can't find anywhere to speak aloud. Start your complaining with some sort of phrase, like "I'm complaining now!" If you're inside, you can complain to the walls or furniture, to a mirror, or to whatever feels right. If you're outside, you can complain to plants and trees, animals, nature, the sky, the ground, or your god. If you're complaining in writing, you can draw or just scribble if you can't find the words. You can also use the Emotional Vocabulary List in the appendix to find precise words for the specific intensity levels of the emotions you feel.

Complain out loud or continue writing for as long as you like (you'll be surprised at how quickly you'll feel done), then thank whatever you've been complaining to, and end your Conscious Complaining session by shaking off, putting your paper and pen aside, and doing something you really like to do.

Conscious Complaining gives a voice to your emotions, which restores your flow, your energy, and your hope. When you have full permission to complain in this intentional way, you'll find that your honest emotional complaints will lead you very quickly into the root of your problems — just as they do in the communication workflow meetings I wrote about earlier in this chapter. Writing down your emotions and observing the gifts and skills that are available to you (see the emotion charts on pages 36–44) can help you understand and address your problems. These problems will now be in your conscious awareness, and you'll have the support and intelligence of your emotions to rely on. From that place of awareness, you'll have new options and ideas. This may sound contradictory, but you just can't be happy, and you can't access the gifts in all of your emotions, unless you can complain (consciously) when you truly need to.

Consciously complaining by yourself is an excellent way to develop your emotional vocabulary and become aware of the issues you face, but you can also use this practice with a partner. If you have supportive relationships at work and your colleagues would like to learn a healthy new way to share problems, this next practice can relieve and reduce yours and your colleagues' unpaid Peacemaking, Agitating, emotion work, and empathy work.

Conscious Complaining with a Partner [5]

In many workplaces (and everywhere else, really), people complain to each other unconsciously. They gripe, speak sarcastically, sigh loudly, or roll their eyes to let their colleagues know that they're unhappy. This is normal; people need to share what's going on for them. However, this unconscious and non-reciprocal form of complaining doesn't often make room for the fact that listeners may have their own backlog of troubles, or that they're struggling under a load of unsupported emotional labor, emotion work, or empathy work of their own. Emotion workers and empathy workers may also find that they're the go-to people for everyone else's complaints, and while their Peacemaking skills may give them a certain amount of pride and status, it can be seriously draining to be a living complaints department.[6] This following partner practice reduces that drain and builds equality and healthy relatedness into our natural need to complain.

Conscious Complaining with a Partner creates clear boundaries around complaining and *requires* reciprocity; people take turns so that no one has to do non-reciprocal empathy work. There are a few rules about time limits and acceptable complaining subjects so that people won't overburden or injure each other — but once these conditions are met, this practice is very simple.

How to Consciously Complain with a Partner

In Conscious Complaining with a Partner, each partner gets 3 minutes to complain while their listener supports them, *but doesn't try to solve anything*. This is important; there's a different communication practice to use when people need input or advice (see the Ethical Empathic Gossip practice on page 165). This partner complaining practice helps people clear the air while they keep each other company, but no one has to do any emotional heavy lifting or solve any problems.

There's a very important rule to follow before you begin, which is that you can't complain about your listener (or about people in your listener's demographic, such as *all* men, supervisors, the British, etc.) because that wouldn't be fair or empathic. If someone is willing to listen and provide support for your complaining, then complaining about them (or people like them) would be like taking a hostage! Conscious Complaining with a Partner is for times when the problems are *outside* of your relationship with your partner (or people like your partner). In the workplace, you should also pay attention to hierarchy and dominance; if your workplace is segregated, you may need to choose partners from your own level. Dominance hierarchies and segregation may create unhealthy power differences, empathy inequalities, and transactional relationships, and you need to feel comfortable and safe with your partner.

Once you and your partner are ready, here's how it works: If you're the complainer, you start by acknowledging that the complaining needs to happen. You could say, "I don't need you to fix me. I just need to complain," or, "I need to complain consciously; do you have some time?" Then, you can bring up whatever's bothering you: "Things are just rotten, this situation is a mess, and things are too hard," and so forth. You can set a timer for your 3 minutes.

Your listener's job is to support your complaining with helpful and up-beat "yeahs!" and "uh huhs!" — no advice or suggestions, just enthusiastic support. Your listener should create a safe haven — a repair station — for your complaining, which will help make your complaining feel purposeful and acceptable (which, by the way, it is).

As you complain, you may want to use the Emotional Vocabulary List and write down the emotions you feel so you can look up their gifts and skills later. When your 3 minutes are up, or when you feel done, you should conclude in a clear way, such as: "Thanks — that's been bothering me," or, "I'm done, thanks!" Then, you trade positions — your partner now gets their 3 minutes of Conscious Complaining time while you listen and provide enthusiastic support. When both of you are done, this practice is complete.

If either of you have ideas or advice for each other, ask if the other person wants input. Input is intentionally left out of this practice because it helps you and your partner connect to *your own* emotions and responses instead of each other's, and it's meant to give each of you some blessed time off from unpaid Peacemaking, emotion work, or empathy work.

You'll be amazed at how productive (and funny) this partner complaining practice is. We're all taught to avoid complaining — especially in the workplace — which means that we have to repress most of our emotions. Sadly, this repression tends to clog us up with all of the things we're not allowed to say, notice, or feel — and that's draining. This partner practice helps you restore your emotional flow because it clears you out and brings back your perspective and your sense of humor. It also helps you understand what you're feeling and how your emotions are responding to the situations in your life so that you can rely on their genius to develop your own solutions — and that's nourishing!

When you can't be honest about what's bothering you, and you can't complain consciously, you may get stuck in moody states that just won't resolve themselves (because you're not working *with* your emotions, you're suppressing them). The individual Conscious Complaining practice helps you tell the truth and restore your emotional flow in privacy; it gives you the freedom you need to feel your way under the surface and identify deeper issues that you may have repressed or overlooked. However, when you can complain consciously with a partner, there's a special secondary benefit: You can both learn how to reach out and develop stronger and more equal relationships when you're in turmoil. Instead of isolating yourself and suffering alone — or complaining *unconsciously* and dumping all over people — you can normalize complaining and make it a part of your skill set (individually and in relationships) and your sense of relatedness and belonging.

Conscious Complaining with a Partner can also support formal communication processes in the workplace. Sometimes, people need to find clarity before they can create workable processes for the communication issues I listed at the beginning of this chapter. In meetings, especially all-staff meetings, people may need a clear chunk of time to talk things out informally and complain consciously until they can truly understand the scope of the issues, mistakes, or conflicts they need to address. This informal and emotionally honest process can make formal communication much easier, and it supports all nine aspects of emotionally well-regulated social structures and all three aspects of motivation.

Workers of the World member and workplace consultant Sheila Diggs learned in her coaching training that "an unexpressed expectation is resentment in waiting."[7] In most emotionally unregulated workplaces, people may have no way of communicating their expectations, and so resentment will only grow. These Conscious Complaining practices can help people learn how to listen to their emotions, speak honestly about their expectations (and resentments), and make room for others to speak honestly as well.

Your workplace as a whole may not be ready to institute emotionally well-regulated communication processes, but you and your colleagues can certainly use Conscious Complaining with a Partner among yourselves so that your emotional lives and empathic workloads can become more manageable and nourishing. My colleagues and I rely on both of these complaining practices, and they definitely contribute emotional regulation and healthy empathy to our work, our workplace, and our lives.

There's another powerful repair station (page 56) that I developed in the gossip networks I saw in all of my workplaces, and in response to troubling forms of gossip that my family engaged in. This repair station relies on the astonishing gifts and skills that live in a form of communication that most of us have been taught (wrongly) to despise: *gossip*.

The Magical Power of Ethical Empathic Gossip[8]

Gossip has a *terrible* reputation. In many listicles (articles made of lists) on how to run a successful business, shutting down workplace gossip is highlighted in bold, italicized, and followed by three or four exclamation points. Frustratingly, this idea could not be more wrong. Gossip is absolutely necessary in every social group, and the quality and quantity of each group's gossip can tell you everything about the social and emotional health of that group. If the gossip is toxic, it's a commentary on the toxicity of the social structure and the failure of the group's emotional skills, relationship skills, repair stations, and more — it's not the fault of gossip!

Gossip can tell you deep truths about a social structure (Mateo knew this instinctively) and shutting down gossip is not only an absurd and emotionally ignorant idea, it's impossible. Gossip is a required form of communication; you cannot shut it down and you should not shut it down. However, you *can* help to make gossip ethical and empathic so that this required form of communication will nourish and support people rather than drain and divide them.

Gossip is a vital form of communication that must and should exist in any relationship and any social group. Anthropologically and linguistically speaking, gossip is simply this: It's any communication that exists outside of the formal (or permitted) modes of communication. It's the whispered information, the warning looks, the open and friendly conversations about the status quo, the secret backstage data, the emotional truths, the gathering of allies, the entryway into social groups, and the sharing of our inner lives. Gossip exists in every culture, in all genders, and in all age groups; it's also central to all forms of Keystone work.

Gossip is crucial to the everyday functioning of work relationships, workflow, and the maintenance of rules, culture, and power structure. Mateo knew this, and he used the gossip network on the smoking balcony to position himself as a Connector in his formal and rigidly segregated organization. Natalie, however, had heard that gossip was toxic. She avoided it like the plague and created artificial separations between herself and her staff, and as a result, she lost her ability to relate to or understand her staff's serious difficulties.

I learned very early to enter into gossip networks so that I could understand social structures and relationships. I came from a big family, and there was always something that people were hiding from one another. Being at the center of my family's many gossip networks kept me connected to everyone, and it kept me safe in the midst of my family's dramas. Gossip is particularly important for people who don't have power or a voice — such as children, or anyone at the lower levels of any hierarchy. Gossip can help us understand the social structure in every part of our lives, but it's particularly important in workplaces where clear communication processes don't exist. When there are no formal processes for communication, informal processes such as gossip must arise.

Gossip can help you figure out the unspoken rules in the workplace, the power relationships that aren't written on the hierarchy charts, and the backstage information that's crucial to know but no one can mention out loud. Gossip can help you understand when your coworkers are not feeling well but can't take time off (so that you can figure out how to work around them until they recover). Gossip can help you talk about a secret relationship the boss is having with your manager (so you won't say something insensitive and jeopardize your position). Gossip can help you talk about the hushed-up possibility that your work group will be moved to another department or be disbanded altogether (so that you and your colleagues can plan ahead). Gossip equalizes relationships and gives people access to vital information that's not being shared formally. Gossip is necessary, and you can't navigate gracefully in any social structure if you don't have access to the informal rules and information that only gossip can provide.

Gossip is also a necessary survival tool for anyone in a non-dominant or marginalized position in social groups, because the dominant majority is likely unaware of the ways that their social structure is unwelcoming or even hazardous to outsiders. People in marginalized or disempowered positions must learn to use gossip networks strategically so that they can survive and thrive. Therefore, we will absolutely support and encourage gossip; it's necessary for all of us. But it doesn't have to be toxic or unethical.

I've noticed that gossip is only toxic if the social structure is toxic, or if people have never learned how to use the powerful tool of gossip ethically. Gossip is as natural as breathing, and anthropologists see gossip in humans as a basic tool of socialization and connection — almost like the grooming behaviors that many animals use to form bonds. Gossip is older than humankind, and it's indispensable. However, we've all been harmed by careless and unethical gossip, and most of us have been shamed about gossiping, so it's important to be honest about the downsides to gossip.

A massive problem with gossip is that it can train us to talk *about* people, rather than talking *to* them. When we gossip, we may also learn to disrespect and attack people rather than try to understand or empathize with them. Gossip can also lead us to invade the privacy of the people we gossip about and betray them as we broadcast their private behavior all over the place. If we go back to the person we gossiped about without addressing the issue more openly, there will always be this *thing* hanging out there — this disloyalty and betrayal that we hope never gets repeated. Although gossip is a necessary form of communication, it can create serious problems if we aren't conscientious and ethical about how we use it. Gossip is a powerful tool, and we need to learn how to wield it with skill instead of hurting people (or ourselves) with it.

It's very easy to understand why people would want to forbid toxic gossiping at work, but a far more intelligent approach is to help workers learn to use the vital tool of gossip with their ethics intact. Gossip is a repair station in and of itself, and it may be the only repair station in an uncomfortable or emotionally unregulated workplace (such as Natalie's spa, which offered no privacy, no downtime, and no real break room for its struggling empathy workers). Gossip is necessary.

Gossip also helps us access the gifts and skills in two marvelous emotions that most people have been taught to despise: *jealousy* and *envy*. Think about the purpose of gossip and what it helps you achieve, and then look at the gifts and skills connected to jealousy and envy.

Emotion	Questions	Gifts and Skills
JEALOUSY arises when people's connection to love, loyalty, or security in their relationships is challenged.	*What has been betrayed?* *What must be healed and restored?*	Commitment, security, love, connection, belonging, loyalty, and the ability to create and maintain healthy relationships.
ENVY arises when people's connection to material security, resources, or recognition is challenged.	*What has been betrayed?* *What must be made right?*	Fairness, security, access to resources, proper recognition, self-preservation, and the promotion of equality and justice.

I call jealousy and envy the "sociological emotions," because they focus on equality, loyalty, and fairness in our relationships and our social structures. Jealousy and envy focus their genius on our social world, and their job is to make sure that we're safe and well connected to sources of love, relatedness, attention, security, loyalty, equity, and material resources. Throughout my life, I've been fascinated to observe how we've been trained to hate these emotions when they're so crucial to our survival. Why would anyone hate them, especially here in the US, which is an aggressively materialistic and capitalist society? My thought is that this hatred comes from the top down and is a form of maintaining the status quo in an unequal, unjust, and hierarchical world where only people at the very top are allowed to have true power and (obscene) wealth. It's also telling that envy is one of the seven deadly sins in Catholicism, which is a rigid, formalized, and deeply hierarchical religion. When I see people disrespecting or hating jealousy or envy, I look for the social control, the baked-in inequality, and the hierarchy; it's always there.

So, the hatred of gossip makes sense because gossip challenges the status quo, it can be toxic in untrained hands, and it helps us connect to two powerful but despised emotions. Gossip is informed by your jealousy and envy; gossip contains your social, relational, and sociological genius, and it helps you see the truth even when people in power want you to remain ignorant. Gossip is a powerful communication tool that helps you position yourself skillfully in your social world and understand the lay of the land. Luckily, when you can harness the wide-ranging social and emotional information gossip provides, you can turn gossip into a tool that will support you and the people around you. You can retrieve the social and sociological genius of jealousy and envy, dust them off, love them up, and learn how to turn gossip into an *ethical* and *empathic* communication practice.

I developed Ethical Empathic Gossip (EEG) to help people detoxify gossip and use it to support and revitalize every aspect of their relationships at home, with their friends and family, and in their workplace. You can use EEG when you need support in a specific relationship, when you're dealing with inequality and injustice, and when you catch yourself gossiping (usually in unempathic or unethical ways) about someone. This practice helps you access the Keystone powers of jealousy, envy, and gossip without abusing those powers. But of course, when you first try EEG, you may have to move into Conscious Incompetence for a while, because most of us have no idea how to gossip in healthy or ethical ways.

The difference between EEG and Conscious Complaining with a Partner is related to the situation. When you feel cranky or sad or unsettled for some reason, you can use Conscious Complaining (with or without a partner) to discover what your emotional responses are trying to tell you. EEG, on the other hand, comes into play when your relationships have stalled, when you're out of options, or when you catch yourself gossiping in unempathic ways. This EEG practice is intended for situations where you need help unraveling all of the threads and issues that are involved in a troubled relationship (or relationships).

How to Practice Ethical Empathic Gossip
First, this gossip practice should be optional for everyone. Most people have been shamed about gossiping or hurt by unethical gossip, so it's okay if people don't feel able to access this process. Everyone needs to have freedom to abstain.

It's also important for people to feel safe, and to choose people they trust as their partners; this cannot be an enforced practice. What you're looking for in an EEG partner is someone you trust and admire who can keep your confidences, and who you think may have new and useful information for you.

Take care if you're in a hierarchical workplace, and be mindful about people who are in non-dominant or marginalized groups; the ability to speak freely and tell the truth isn't equally shared in hierarchical or emotionally unregulated social structures. In fact, the freedom to speak the truth can be an unconscious form of privilege for insiders and people in the dominant majority. This gossip practice, which can be so freeing for equals who trust each other, could be dangerously exposing when equality and trust are not present in your workplace. Be aware of the power of gossip and EEG and choose your partners with care.

In EEG, you will gossip while your listener pays attention, engages with you, asks questions, and learns the details of the entire situation. Each EEG session takes between 13 and 15 minutes because there's usually a lot of back-and-forth conversation as your listener gathers information about the situation. If you have enough time in one sitting, you can take turns with your partner. If you don't have time for both of you to trade places, make sure that you schedule another time when you can be the listener and offer 13 to 15 minutes of reciprocal support for your EEG partner.

Here are the guidelines for EEG with a supportive partner:

- Identify a person (or people) you gossip about consistently, and with whom your relationship has stalled.
- Open the gossip session by acknowledging your trouble in the relationship.
- Ask your partner for help in dealing with your troubled relationship. Ask for opinions, ideas, techniques, and skills that will help you re-enter the relationship in a different way.
- Go for it — just gossip.
- Your partner should feel free to ask for clarification and backstory if needed.
- When your partner understands enough and gives you feedback, *pay attention*. Take notes if you need to.
- Close your EEG session with thanks, and then go back to the damaged relationship with your new skills and insights — or modify the relationship if it's too damaged to survive as is. *Don't go back in the same old way* — because that's what led to the need for gossip in the first place.

Tips for the EEG listener: Unlike Conscious Complaining with a Partner, you have an active role in EEG. Your job is to find out as much as you can about the situation, because you need to see the big picture. Let your gossiper talk and try not to give any advice until you've heard the entire story. A very good question to ask before you give advice is "What have you tried?" You can save a lot of time and refine your input if you don't just start throwing out ideas based on what *you* would have done (this isn't about you). Let your partner talk and let the genius of their jealousy and envy paint you a picture of the entire situation.

Here are some emotionally respectful questions that can help your partner access the far-reaching wisdom of jealousy and envy:

- What feels like a betrayal?
- What needs to be made right?
- What would be fair for everyone?
- How could everyone feel heard and respected?
- What would be the best outcome for everyone?

Remember that jealousy and envy, when they're allowed to bring their gifts and skills forward, are not focused on me, me, me. The particular genius of these two emotions is focused on fairness, equity, relatedness, and loyalty in relationships and social structures. When people fall into toxic gossip, they're nearly always reacting to the loss of these things and to inequality in their important relationships. Asking about the needs of *everyone* in the situation leans into jealousy and envy's skill set; both emotions keep their eye on balance and fairness in the social structure as a whole.

What's amazing in this practice is that when gossip is made conscious, you can clearly see what a stupendous information-gathering tool it is. When people are given the freedom to share all of the intricate social information their jealousy and envy have gathered, they can access the deep, socially aware, and emotionally rich undercurrents that exist in gossip, and in gossip networks. Gossip helps us connect with others, understand human behavior, recognize or change our social position, and support (or modify) rules and set them for others. Gossip also relieves tension — because it allows us to share the private information we've learned about others but are not allowed to mention in public. Gossip is a very powerful thing!

Using Ethical Empathic Gossip in a group: I have presented EEG to work groups who immediately wanted to gossip about a shared group concern. It actually works great, as long as the entire team understands the ethical and empathic parameters of EEG. In fact, there are some situations that *require* the social and emotional intelligence of an entire group because each group member sees things differently and may have information that others don't.

Setting the container of ethics and empathy is important for group EEG sessions, as is asking the questions (above) to help the group access the genius in their jealousy and envy. The purpose of EEG is to help people work through a difficult relationship or situation in an empathic repair station so that they can discover new ideas and skills. With those parameters in mind, EEG in groups can be amazingly helpful. In fact, most of the meetings in our DEI community include at least one group EEG session; it's a wonderful way for people to develop and sustain their social and emotional competence, Perspective Taking skills, empathy, relatedness, and sense of belonging.

Whether you use it in a duo or a group, this EEG practice can help you learn to ask for — and receive — help in dealing with difficult emotions, troubling situations, and challenging people. When you've hit a wall, this practice can help you reach out for the emotional and empathic assistance of others instead of isolating yourself. No one knows how to deal with all emotions, situations, or relationships — because we simply weren't taught how. For goodness sake, most of us weren't even taught how to listen to our own emotions! We can all use some assistance, and we all need to stick together and support each other as we become more aware of our emotions and more skillful in the social world.

Gossip is a vital and irreplaceable communication and connection tool that can help you tell the truth and understand exactly what's occurring in your workplace. As you learn how to gossip ethically, you'll become more informed and empathic about yourself and others, more skilled and emotionally agile in your relationships, and more comfortable in your social world. Gossip is a truly brilliant tool — as long as it's *ethical* and *empathic* gossip.*

---

*An important HR and workplace safety note about EEG: In emotionally unregulated workplaces, the unfairness and inequalities that EEG can surface may relate to workplace abuse or bullying. If so, these situations need to be communicated upward immediately — to HR, a supervisor, or the local labor board or labor commissioner. This is not something that colleagues should handle on their own; workplace abuse is a crime. No one should have to work in an abusive environment, and there are labor regulations that protect workers from toxic workplaces (see the Workplace Bullying Resources on page 253).

This is one of the reasons why it's so important for every workplace to have reliable and accessible processes for communicating about problems, dealing with conflicts and challenges, and communicating problems upward without danger. If workers don't have these processes to rely on, the workplace will be inefficient at best and endangering at worst. Abuse and bullying are unacceptable, but they're much more likely to occur in emotionally unregulated workplaces where people cannot tell the truth.

These Conscious Complaining and Ethical Empathic Gossip practices are personal and interpersonal repair stations, and every social group should have access to something like them. Every workplace should also develop reliable and shared ways to deal with everyday communication difficulties their workers face. We all need a full tool kit of communication skills and repair stations so that our workplaces will function smoothly, and so that we won't need to do empathic heavy lifting just to ask a question or learn how to unload the dishwasher.

However, repair stations should also be physical; there should be many ways for people to access comfort, privacy, rest, and quiet when they need to. Thankfully, providing these comfortable spaces doesn't need to be expensive; with some emotional and empathic ingenuity, you can create an environment that's physically *and* emotionally well regulated.

6

Good Fences, Clear Boundaries, and Repair Stations

Privacy, rest, comfort, and quiet are essential for social and emotional health, cognitive dexterity, learning and memory, and social harmony. A healthy and emotionally well-regulated workplace will incorporate clear boundaries and thresholds, welcoming and useful break areas, and an environment that supports human bodies and human needs.

Sadly, in many modern workplaces — especially ones with profoundly unworkable open-plan office environments — neither privacy, nor rest, nor quiet, nor true comfort are available to anyone. Boundaries don't exist, break areas are overstuffed, tragic, or absent, there are no thresholds between frontstage work and backstage repair stations, and human needs are not on the agenda. Let me give you just a few real-life examples of the uncomfortable and deeply unwelcoming state of the modern workplace:

- Workers of the World (WoW) member Jennifer Asdorian worked as a speech-language pathologist at a large metropolitan hospital where there were no staff break rooms at all. If she needed privacy, or if she needed to down-regulate after a particularly difficult session, she had to lock herself in a bathroom.
- WoW member Jennifer Nate worked at a large craft supply store chain where no one had their own private space; everyone was meant to be on the sales floor throughout their workday. The break room was scattered, messy, and stacked with boxes of extra merchandise.

The lunch tables were dirty, the chairs were the cheap fold-up variety, and the walls were plastered with garish corporate cheerleading posters that were entirely work related and focused on endless productivity and sales goals.

- WoW member Jeanette Brynn worked as one of fifteen hairdressers at a swanky high-end salon where the staff break and lunch area consisted of a small bench that could fit four people if they huddled together. This is not unusual; the beauty and personal care industry as a whole tends to have few welcoming break areas, often because many workers ignore breaks and lunches so that they can see more clients. Most personal care workers are contractors rather than employees (employee breaks are mandated, but contractors' health and well-being is left to them), and in many salons and spas, their avoidance of rest, nutrition, hydration, and self-care is tolerated or even encouraged by an industry where the needs of the clients come first.

- WoW member Andrea Watkins taught at a massage school where students and instructors shared the break room; the instructors were expected to answer questions and be available to students all day, even during their breaks.

- WoW member Tino Plank's office received regular bimonthly visits from the Employee Assistance Program (EAP) counselor before the pandemic sent everyone home, but there was no private room for her to meet with workers, and no time had been set aside in the work schedule for people to see her. During this pandemic, there has been an upside to working from home; now, workers are able to consult privately with the EAP counselor by phone or Webex.

- WoW member Bobbi McIntyre is a retired US Navy captain who worked at the Department of Defense, where everyone had free access to an EAP counselor. However, workers could lose their security clearances if they were known to be struggling psychologically, so very few people felt safe enough to visit the counselor.

- In response to workers spending more time in the bathroom (which may be the only private space available to them), organizations are not only *not* providing appropriate break areas, they're investing in atrocious slanted toilets that make sitting uncomfortable so that workers will be forced back to their work stations.[1]

- Workers in open-plan office environments deal with incessant interruptions, especially when their colleagues need to take calls. Instead of providing better soundproofing and privacy, many open-plan offices are now purchasing expensive glass phone booths so that people can finally make their normal daily calls without disturbing everyone.[2] Notice, however, that glass phone booths offer no privacy.

- A friend of mine came to work one Monday to discover that his office was being torn apart to create an open floorplan "based on employee feedback." Everyone was horrified and tried to remember what they had written on a workplace survey a few months earlier. They realized that they had agreed to a statement about enjoying "a light-filled environment," and their feedback was used as an excuse to tear down walls and cram more workers from other floors into their office space.

Our physical environment has a powerful effect on our behavior, yet many workplace environments create cognitive overload, emotional strain, and social turmoil all by themselves. Most workplaces seem to be designed for budgetary reasons first, executives and owners second, clients and customers third, and workers maybe not at all.

In Natalie's spa, for instance, the lack of repair stations or break areas in that swanky resort destabilized her entire staff and required an Agitator, constant conflict, a sudden firing, and then a fierce gossip network before Natalie could identify the problem. At Mateo's organization, the smoking balcony acted as a repair station, a gossip network, and a place for everyone to develop useful information about their rigid, segregated, and hierarchical organization — because nothing else besides a big noisy cafeteria was made available to them.

All workers require repair-and-rejuvenation stations where they can step away and take some downtime, especially if they're performing emotional labor or working in high-empathy-demand professions. These repair stations don't have to be elaborate; for instance, there can be a comfortable chair somewhere quiet, a room with a door, an invitation to walk outside — anything that offers privacy, rest, and a break from focus and intensity. Conscious Complaining and Ethical Empathic Gossip can also be social repair stations, as can developing communication processes for the everyday conflicts we explored in chapter 5. Providing repair stations and comfortable, restful places for workers is not difficult, but sadly, repair stations are often not even on the agenda — especially in many high-empathy-demand workplaces where repair stations should be mandatory.

As I observe our workplace-wide inability to create humane and comfortable environments, I see a deep connection between kicking the emotions out of the workplace and becoming woefully ignorant about the physical needs of actual human beings. A *child* could see that tiny, dirty break rooms (or no break rooms) tell workers that no one cares about them. And that same child could see that noisy, exposed, and uncomfortable open-plan office environments are absurdly nonfunctional. But we adults suffer through these pathetic circumstances as if we have no voice and no choice (of course, many of us don't have a voice, as the examples at the beginning of this chapter confirm). This blatant disregard for basic human needs feels very connected to the Theory X belief that people must be forced to work. You can see the thought process: "If we give workers restful spaces or comfortable toilets, they'll stop working, the lazy brutes." This idea is grotesque, but we see it absolutely everywhere, from the cheapest retail hellscapes and insecure gig jobs to the swankiest spas and sprawling hospitals; the social, emotional, and physical needs of workers are not even considered.

This is unacceptable. Workers must have free access to comfort, peace, rest, quiet, and privacy in order to do their best work and maintain their mental and emotional health. Sadly, many workers have to carve out repair stations for themselves, especially now that so many people are in open-plan environments that interfere with cognition, comfort, privacy, emotional health, and people's ability to focus and get their work done.

During this pandemic many people from open-plan offices are now working from home. Either that, or their offices have been retrofitted with plexiglass walls (or their desks have been separated to account for social distancing). These changes may address the public health risks that these offices create, but once people are back at work, the many social, emotional, and productivity harms these floorplans cause will continue unchanged.

The Open-Plan Office Is the Devil's Floorplan

I call the open-plan office the Devil's Floorplan because it creates a wildly inefficient, uncomfortable, and disharmonious working environment. When I was working in other people's businesses back in the day, I had to work in sad cubicle farms, but at least I had some form of a wall. Today, cubicle walls are mostly gone, and offices consist of long flat desks shared by as many as ten people who have no privacy. These offices are often dotted with glass-walled meeting rooms (that also offer no privacy), and distractions are a regular part of every hour and every day. Sound pollution and visual distractions are a constant issue, and if anyone gets sick, the entire office will be exposed to whatever's going around. In a pandemic, open-plan offices are not just inefficient and annoying; they're a serious public health hazard.[3]

I first discovered problems with the open-plan office in a different open-plan environment while doing research for my master's thesis on autism, empathy, and special education programs.[4] Most special education programs are located in a single classroom where students from many grade levels work with their aides at different tables. I found these classrooms noisy, confusing, and exhausting, and I wondered why the most vulnerable students were being taught in such inadequate classrooms (budget) and whether the confusion and noise in these open-plan classrooms disrupted learning (yes). These noisy and distracting classrooms definitely disrupt learning, and this is something that school systems have known about for nearly half a century.

In the 1960s and 1970s, the open-plan classroom movement hit the US and many other countries, and many school districts spent hundreds of thousands of dollars to tear down walls between classrooms. They created sprawling open-office-type environments with no privacy and large shared tables with multi-grade students working on different projects in a single room. Idealism was high, and educators thought that removing walls and boundaries would open up learning, increase collaboration and communication between students, and lead to the land of milk and honey.

None of that happened.

Later, testing showed that children in open-plan classrooms struggled and fell behind, specifically in the language arts: reading, speaking, and writing. Researchers discovered why; the visual distractions, multiple sounds and conversations, and lack of privacy in these open-plan classrooms created constant interruptions to children's attention.[5] And there was no way to fix this problem while maintaining the open plan. These attentional issues are a normal feature of human hearing and vision. We're habituated to pay attention to human speech, even if it's not directed at us, and we're habituated to focus on movement in our visual field (especially the movement of living things). We're particularly distracted by what researches call "irrelevant meaningful speech," which is conversation that does not involve or concern us, but is meaningful to the person speaking (such as someone talking on the phone near us).[6] This irrelevant speech was found to be particularly distracting, and far more distracting than other noises at similar volumes (such as creaking furniture or bird songs). Human hearing is strongly focused on speech, and we'll naturally shift our attention when we hear irrelevant meaningful speech. Children in these open-plan classrooms were dealing with the equivalent of someone poking them in the arm and repeating "hey listen, listen, listen" hundreds of times each day as they struggled (and failed) to learn.

Once educators understood their mistake, more money was spent to put walls back up and separate the grades again (at least, in schools that could afford it; sadly, in some poorer districts, open-plan classrooms persist to this day with all of their damaging effects intact). Many educators learned their lesson, but the open plan did not die; it remained untouched in poorer districts and special education classrooms, and then it moved into the workplace, where once again, schoolroom and Theory X ideas about enforcing structure on workers invaded the workplace.

Open-plan workplaces were already the norm for lower-level workers such as secretaries, stenographers, store clerks, or factory workers — usually so that managers and executives could keep a watchful eye on everyone. These workplaces treated workers as replaceable (and untrustworthy) cogs in a noisy and dehumanizing machine. But in the 1990s, open-plan offices became a hot fad for upper-level workers, especially in the tech world. Many unwitting executives and managers believed that these offices would promote Theory Y values; they would flatten their hierarchies, increase collaboration and creativity, and lead to the land of milk and honey. But none of that happened, and it's still not happening.

The research on open offices is very clear and scathing; there is no support for any of those positive claims. Open-plan offices reduce productivity, increase absenteeism, and interfere with collaboration because people can't focus. One study found that face-to-face interactions decreased by 70%(!) when people transitioned to open offices — many workers now used text and email to communicate, even though they could see each other.[7] The constant visual and auditory interruptions make multitasking (which most people can't do no matter how much they think they can) very difficult, and the visual distractions reduce short-term and long-term memory. Open-plan offices are complete failures.[8] And considering that it can take people between 10 and 20 minutes to return fully to a task once they've been interrupted, the loss in productivity created by these floorplans is overwhelming in scope.

Open-plan offices do one thing very well, however; they allow organizations to cram more people into their square footage. There is no other reason or purpose for the Devil's Floorplan; it's a sign of cheapness and an inability to Google "problems with the open-plan office." Sadly, as it is with all cheap fixes, the open-plan office ends up costing businesses far more than they ever saved by shoving too many people into one distracting and boundaryless space.

If you're working in the Devil's Floorplan or — heaven help you — if you've recently created one, you'll need to take a serious look at the situation with the help of everyone in your workplace. Yes, workers can learn how to focus and work in these places — I did, and most of us have done so, but so what? The drain on cognitive capacity and attention, the public health risks, and the strain on relationships and motivation are not worth the trouble; these floorplans need to get gone, or at the very least, get fixed. Luckily, because these rotten workspaces are still being created today, people who want to fix their open offices can find bargains on mountains of discarded individual desks and soundproofed cubicle walls at every used office furniture store in the land. All is not lost.

Empathic Healing Solutions for the Devil's Floorplan

The best solution, of course, is not to have an open-plan office, but if you're saddled with one, there are many things you can do to reduce their devilry. If you can cut down on visual distractions and people's awareness of movement, that's a great first step (you can wall off people's desk areas with cardboard if you don't have money to fix the problem). If people want to get anything done, noise-cancelling headphones and headsets for anyone on the phone are also necessary, as are clear, reliable, and shared processes for requesting attention from a busy person (see chapter 5 for ideas). That's crucial.

If you've got those glassed-in meeting fishbowls in your open office, install blinds or curtains so that meetings won't add yet another visual distraction to the workspace. And notice how much time people spend on bathroom breaks. Don't purchase creepy slanting toilets; the bathroom may be the only private space available to your workers, so take the hint and create something appropriate for them. Get everyone together and create a break room or private area so that workers will have self-created access to comfortable spaces where quiet, privacy, and rest are available. These things are not negotiable; quiet, privacy, and rest are *required* for cognitive dexterity, memory, learning, task completion, productivity, social and emotional health, and motivation.

Break rooms, rest areas, and/or physical repair stations should be provided by each organization, but in order to preserve and support the motivating factors of competence, autonomy, and relatedness, they should be planned and created by the people who will use them. Workers are adults, and they need to be able to develop their large-group social skills *as* adults, and not as voiceless worker-children.

Redesigning or reimagining your workspace with a focus on quiet, privacy, comfort, and cognitive rest may require time and attention if your workplace was designed without any of these things in mind. However, the input of your entire community and a willingness to engage in the *empathic design* process will help you create something that meets the true needs of your unique workplace. Here are some simple ideas to get you started.

EMPATHIC DESIGN

A design process that focuses on end users' needs and emotions, and employs multiple tryouts and redesigns until the end product meets those needs.

Empathic Design of Repair Stations

When I worked behind the scenes with Natalie to solve the troubles at her spa, one of the first things we tackled was the lack of a useful break room or *repair station*. Natalie had to work some of her magic in the areas of scheduling and process improvement to make a better break room possible, but when she created the new room, she invited her staff to tell her what the room should contain. This was both empathic and strategic; her staff deserved respect and they needed to have a voice, but they also needed to rediscover their competence, autonomy, and relatedness so that their emotional atmosphere could settle and they could find their internal motivation once again. Also, it was *their* room and it needed to meet *their* needs.

REPAIR STATIONS

Sociologist Erving Goffman's concept of protected backstage areas where people can be real and honest about what they're facing, or where they can rest and get away from the frontstage demands of their lives or their jobs. Repair stations in the workplace can be physical spaces such as break rooms or smoking balconies, or they can be social spaces such as intentional communication practices or trusting relationships.

Every worker-created break room or repair station will be entirely unique, but here are three simple guidelines to help teams create or redesign these areas of their workplace:

- **Set good thresholds and boundaries.** A break room or repair station needs to be separated from work and the workspace. Break rooms filled with overstock don't count, and break areas in full view of the workspace don't count either. But you don't need a door or a wall if those aren't available in your workplace. A couch or a row of tall chairs facing away from the workspace and toward a window can help; people need mental, visual, and auditory breaks on a regular basis (see the next section for the neuroscience of intentional breaks). You can also set aside a quiet area outside in good weather. Any place where people can disengage intentionally is important to ensure that their anger doesn't have to set boundaries constantly and their confusion and apathy don't have to enforce cognitive breaks. You want to create these spaces consciously so that people can consciously disengage their focus and reset their boundaries throughout the day; if you don't, people will have to perform these important mental health functions unconsciously or secretly.

- **Workers should design their own break rooms and repair stations.** Management should provide the space for break rooms and repair stations, but workers need to decide what they'll contain. Many workplaces with semi-decent break rooms or employee lounges look to me like someone has bought a bunch of gifts for a teenager they don't know very well: pool tables, motivational posters, coffee machines, aromatherapy, books no one reads, soft pillows, games, beanbag chairs . . . it's a hodgepodge, and only some of this stuff ever gets used. Some break rooms try too hard to say, "We're a fun workplace," *not* by changing the nature of the work itself or by creating a humane environment, but by throwing toys and bribes at workers.

    It's a tremendous waste of money, space, and time to design something for people without consulting them about it, and it's also not empathic. Only the workers know what kinds of repair stations they need; management can't know unless they're working alongside them, doing their jobs, and doing the precise emotional labor, emotion work, and empathic work they do.

It's important to invite workers to gather as many ideas as they can at the beginning of this design process. If your workers come up with too many good ideas (congratulations!) and they can't decide on the best ones, there's a useful voting process called N/3 (N over 3) that can help groups make democratic decisions.[9] You take the number of options (N), such as 12 suggestions for what the break room should contain, and divide that N by 3 to determine how many votes each person will get: 12/3 = 4. So in this example, every person will have four votes, but they can only vote once for each option. This will help the group see which options are the most interesting and valuable to their community, and their empathic design process will be off to a good start.

- **Make changes if the first design doesn't work as you thought it would.** Empathic design is a humanizing process that ensures users remain more important than the design. If the user isn't being served, then the design has to change. Expect that this break room will have to change as well. Most workers haven't experienced healthy or functional break areas, so they'll likely design their repair stations from the incompetent side of their learning process. This is fine; this is how we learn. Be flexible and follow the emotions as people engage with their new break area. Trust the innate intelligence of the workers and their emotional responses; they'll figure it out.

Additionally, Conscious Complaining and Ethical Empathic Gossip can act as social repair stations, because sharing difficulties with a confidante — and knowing that reliable, trustworthy communication is freely available — has measurable stress-reducing and community-building effects.

A key to the empathic design of repair stations (and to the workplace in general) is to continually ask yourself: "Are workers being treated as intelligent, respected, and internally motivated adults?" If so, carry on.

If not — if schoolyard or authoritarian teacher- or principal-like behaviors arise — stop and regroup. Return to Conscious Incompetence, refocus yourselves, and take an intentional break!

Fika, Banana Time, and the Science of Intentional Breaks

As you and your colleagues work to create your own break rooms and repair stations, it may help to understand why and how breaks and rest periods contribute to health, well-being, and productivity. This understanding may give your workplace community clearer ideas for what their break rooms and repair stations should contain.

Research over the past half century has helped us understand how important breaks, rest, and sleep are to memory, cognitive dexterity, mental health, and health in general.[10] Breaks have also been found to be crucial for productivity, but most businesses haven't caught up with this research yet. Here in the US, paid break times are mandated for full-time hourly employees at 15 minutes every 4 hours plus a lunch break of 30 to 60 minutes. The enforcement of these break times is sometimes rigid and sometimes ignored altogether (or concealed in falsified timesheets).[11]

Some countries treat breaks with more skill and respect, such as countries with daily *siesta* traditions where midday rest is a cultural norm (though siestas are sadly being phased out in most metropolitan areas as hyper-productivity becomes the new norm).[12] Sweden, however, has an excellent break-time tradition called *fika* (loosely translated to: "to have coffee") that's being preserved even as the Swedish workplace becomes more productivity obsessed.

FIKA

The Swedish tradition of friendly and relaxing coffee (or tea) breaks
that involve sweets and socialization (or sweets and private time).

Fika is not specifically a workplace break — it's a ritual that's shared at home, at school, at work, and throughout Swedish culture.[13] Fika refers to a coffee break that often includes pastries, such as cinnamon buns or cardamom buns, but a fika can also involve tea or water, and pastries aren't a requirement. What's required is to take a break from work and relax for 15 minutes or longer — either alone or in a casual, friendly group. In the workplace, fikas create a clear threshold between work time and casual time, and in many Swedish organizations, fikas may occur several times throughout the workday, or just once in the afternoon.

In the workplace, fika time is an unstructured break time where people can talk about work if they like, but they can also talk about their personal lives and interests. Fikas can help people develop large-group social skills as adults, and they can support relatedness, motivation, and creativity in ways that enforced team-building exercises can only dream of. If you want to address the many problems that rigid segregation and hierarchies create, cross-departmental fikas are a great way to begin; help people get to know each other as *people*, and you won't require so many Connectors and Peacemakers to act as go-betweens.

I've also seen fikas used to set auditory and attention-protecting boundaries in open-plan office environments: Everyone would work silently for a set period of time and then come together in a fika to talk and laugh in the kitchen or break room. At the agreed-upon time, someone would call out "fika!" and everyone would finish up their tasks and join the group; it was an effective thresholding approach to a troublesome auditory environment. Something to be aware of, however, is that fika breaks should be taken away from workspaces so that other workers' attention won't be pulled toward the irrelevant meaningful speech (and fun) of people sharing a fika.

In your workplace, people may have already developed some form of fika, and it's important to identify and protect these worker-created break times. Smokers create excellent communal break periods, which is why Mateo started smoking again when he arrived at his international aid organization. However, as smoking falls out of fashion (thankfully, for everyone's health), the non-smoking break becomes even more important. I refer to these causal and worker-created breaks as *banana time*.

BANANA TIME

Informal break-time rituals that are developed and led by workers themselves.

I learned about banana time in a 1959 workplace study by sociologist Donald Roy.[14] He worked for 2 months as a participant observer in a monotonous machinist's factory where low-wage workers were treated as cogs in a degrading Theory X machine. Roy studied the ways in which these dehumanized workers reasserted their humanity each day through a series of rituals, humorous attacks on each other, bantering, and unvarying fika-like breaks that revolved around sharing foods such as bananas, peaches, coffee, fish, and Coca Cola. The banana-time break, however, was startling to Roy at first, because it involved theft! One worker, Ike, would steal and eat the banana of another worker, Sammy, and a more senior worker, George, would roundly scold Ike. But every day, Sammy brought a banana in his lunch, and every day, Ike would loudly call out "banana time!" and eat Sammy's banana, without offering a bite to anyone else. Roy began to understand banana time as a way for these men to create their own schedules and routines, set boundaries, and develop a familiar absurdist humor in their monotonous and dehumanizing environment. These men were also inserting intentional breaks into their workdays, partly as a way to retrieve their sense of autonomy, competence, and relatedness, and partly (likely unbeknownst to them) to maintain their focus and productivity in a soul-killing and demotivating workplace.

We understand a lot more about the importance of breaks now than Ike, Sammy, or George could have in 1959, but their timing of breaks (roughly every hour or so for at least 10 minutes) is now understood to be a prime factor in healthy productivity that increases creativity and protects workers from mental and physical burnout.

In studies of workplace productivity, researchers observed the natural break-taking behaviors of productive workers and found that regular breaks are necessary.[15] In fact, it's important to take breaks every 50 to 90 minutes and get away from your work completely for 5 to 20 minutes. *Completely*. Checking emails, returning phone calls, and browsing on Facebook aren't breaks because you're still focusing and working. These breaks need to be real breaks, like fikas or banana time — a walk outside, a movement break, a rest, Conscious Complaining or Ethical Empathic Gossip, or an activity that opens your focus and helps you take a breather. Think about this as you develop your break rooms and repair stations. Can people take a *complete* break? If not, empathic design requires that your break areas undergo some modifications.

We also understand more about rest now, especially in connection with learning. Many research studies have found that resting or sleeping after you learn something new (or before a presentation or an exam) leads to deeper learning and better recall than cramming or long study sessions do.[16] Our brains are not idle when we take breaks, nor when we rest or sleep — they're deepening our learning, making connections, moving short-term learning into long-term memory, and organizing all of the data we take in. If we don't take regular breaks or rest periods, our learning will be shallow and uncreative, and our productivity will suffer. Breaks are not a waste of time — they're a way to make the most efficient and healing use of time.

I came across this research about the importance of well-paced breaks at a fortunate time; my normal way of writing has involved sitting at the computer for 4 to 6 hours in one stretch, burning myself out after a few weeks, and needing to take a few days off (my lower back has also called the labor commission to report me for creating a toxic workplace!). Getting up regularly and taking fikas, banana times, and Conscious Complaining strolls — or just lazing around on the couch with nothing on my mind — has completely revitalized my writing time and relieved the chronic pain I thought was normal. Thank you, research!

Many (most?) workplaces don't make space or time for the normal ways that learning, creativity, and productivity work. For instance, US labor laws mandate 15-minute breaks every 4 hours, but that timing isn't effective or helpful, and it's not how the brain works best. And, if you don't take well-paced breaks, your emotions will have to step in and create breaks for you. Recall that apathy and confusion bring you the gifts of a time-out when you need a break; both of these emotions will step in when you've pushed yourself past your optimal working intervals. As you learn how to take appropriate breaks, keep an eye on your apathy; if you lose your ability to care, it's time for a fika, banana time, a movement break, or a walk for 5 to 20 minutes. And notice how long you were working before you got bored; this can give you an idea about your optimal ratio of work-to-break time.

The same is true for your confusion; when you lose your focus and your ability to think, it's time for a break so that your brain can perform its important downtime activities. Take 5 to 20 minutes and come back to work when you feel refreshed. You'll have new ideas, more energy, and a higher level of productivity than people who power through for hours on end and don't take care of their brains, their bodies, or their healing social connections.

Fikas and banana times are great ways to bring people together across departments and levels of hierarchy, and they'll help you create a more flexible, connected, and democratic organization. Creating daily opportunities for workers to meet informally, laugh, rest, and hang out together is an excellent way to rejuvenate and rehumanize a rigid or overly segregated social structure. Fika breaks before or during meetings (especially all-staff meetings) can also support relatedness and large-group socials skills and make meetings less burdensome.

There's one type of workplace break, however, that may create problems of its own: Enforced mindfulness programs should be approached with care.

A Note About Enforced Workplace Mindfulness Programs

Meditation has become a huge workplace fad, and I've shared some of my concerns about it in the endnotes because I've noticed a troubling movement toward emotional repression in workplace (and school) mindfulness programs.[17] If you love to meditate and it really helps you, then by all means, use it as a break for yourself. But if meditation or mindfulness programs have been pushed onto you from above as a productivity booster or emotional management tool, be aware; sometimes, these programs can introduce a toxic positivity bias that may silence workers and lead to simmering conflicts that no one can address, except with more meditation.[18]

Also, many of these programs treat emotions as private events (or things to overcome) that must be managed internally; they don't treat emotions as brilliant aspects of cognition that help us become more aware and skillful. Though no one intends for this to happen, enforced workplace mindfulness programs can silence emotions rather than help people learn how to access them for the good of the community. Actually, any enforced program that mandates breaks, social skills, or emotional management techniques can cause trouble if it doesn't help people access their emotions in respectful ways, and if people aren't given a choice about learning them or using them.

As we saw clearly in the introduction, the workplace as an entity has a tragic record of failing to provide healthy social or emotional environments for workers. I don't mean to be cynical, but any program of workplace social and emotional management that becomes a fad (as corporate and school mindfulness trainings definitely have) raises my suspicions. I don't trust the intentions of the workplace as an entity. As a researcher, I'm also concerned about the promises that the multi-billion dollar mindfulness industry makes about research support that doesn't truly exist yet.[19] The cart is clearly leading the horse here, and underneath all of the hype, corporate mindfulness trainings seem to carry an unrecognized Theory X belief that workers and their emotions need to be managed and controlled rather than listened to and supported.

Again, meditation can be great if people choose it for themselves, but when it's sold as a productivity generator and mandated from the top down, it not only demeans the tradition of meditation, but it raises many ethical concerns about the true intentions behind it. The workplace as an appallingly failed entity hasn't earned the right to enforce emotion-management practices on a captive audience. All workers deserve to be treated with respect and dignity, and they need to have a choice and a voice in everything they do — especially in regard to their own internal emotional functioning.

In an emotionally well-regulated social structure, the structure itself can create an environment of healthy and noncoercive emotional regulation for everyone. Respectful break rooms and repair stations can set good thresholds and boundaries between work and rest, and they can give workers many ways to increase their autonomy, competence, and relatedness. Good repair stations can also help workers naturally regulate their emotions, because breaks give people the downtime they need to think their own thoughts, digest their experiences, and imagine new and creative ways to address projects, difficulties, and conflicts. The repair stations of Conscious Complaining and Ethical Empathic Gossip also give people ways to access the genius in their emotional responses and reach out for social and emotional support when they need it.

Learning how to transition between work and rest, times of focus and times of freedom, and solitary work and social engagement can help people develop deeper emotional and empathic capacities and stronger large-group social skills. The workplace as an entity can support these qualities by providing healthy communication processes and comfortable physical spaces, and by supporting workers' needs for cognitive rest and emotional self-determination. People also need to learn how to listen to and work with their emotions in a community; they shouldn't isolate themselves with the often emotion-silencing mindfulness practices that are being sold to workplaces. We need our emotional freedom, and we need each other.

Workplace communities should also develop emotionally respectful and agile processes for transitions, because the way changes and transitions are managed can make or break a social structure.

Emotionally Agile Transitions

When I go into businesses to consult, I often sense a haunted *something* in the air — grief, sadness, anger, anxiety, and sometimes panic — some unfinished difficulty that creates a chill, but that people try to conceal or ignore. In nearly all cases, this chill relates to a badly handled transition of some kind. Bad hiring decisions, poorly handled or secret firings, or poorly managed workplace changes and conflicts can create lasting damage. For instance, changing office spaces or redefining people's duties and projects without including them is deeply destabilizing, as is moving people into new roles without any onboarding processes. And people's emotions will take notice.

Mateo's gradual distancing as he transitioned into his directorship engaged anger, envy, jealousy, fear, anxiety, and some panic in the women who had been his smoking buddies (as it should have). And when Natalie fired her Agitator, she handled this abrupt transition in a way that seemed powerful and decisive to her, but engaged extensive grief, envy, jealousy, anger, and rage in her surviving workers (as it definitely should have).

In workplaces with poor or nonexistent onboarding processes for new employees, unpaid Ambassadors may need to arise or workers may have to take additional unpaid time out of their schedules to train the new person. The entire workplace community will have to make up for a lack of basic leadership — and anger, envy, jealousy, sadness, and depression may be required.

My friend whose office walls were shockingly torn down ("based on your suggestions") told me that anger, envy, jealousy, anxiety, panic, and hatred arose — and that his colleagues' trust in management was completely gone after that. Of course it was! People *live* at work, and this company essentially came into their workers' home and tore down their walls without warning. Of course their trust was gone.

If people aren't notified of transitions in their working lives, if proper support or reliable change processes don't exist, and if they have no say in situations that directly affect them, a pall may settle over the workplace and cement itself into the gossip networks. And it *should* because these actions signal that workers are seen as child-cogs in an authoritarian and uncaring machine. Any changes that follow these badly handled transitions will rightfully be met with suspicion or distrust, and the workplace culture may never truly recover from this breach of ethics and accountability.

Changes and transitions introduce novelty into the system, and people will always notice them. Changes and transitions will usually activate the gifts of fear, anxiety, anger, sadness, and grief; these emotional responses are normal and expected (except in emotionally unregulated workplaces, where they're ignored, suppressed, or jollied away). These emotions are also vital to any successful change process: Fear tells us when change, novelty, and possible hazards are present; anxiety helps us gather our resources and focus on what we need to do next; anger helps us identify what we value so that we can protect what's important to us; sadness helps us let go of things that aren't working; and grief helps us mourn and honor what's gone. Shame may also be necessary because it's a central part of the learning stage of Conscious Incompetence (for example, if a person in the middle of a changing situation can say to themselves: "Look, I don't know what I'm doing yet," they're working well with shame, which helps them focus on integrity, behavioral change, self-respect, and the quality of their work).

Emotions are a vital part of everything we do, and when changes and transitions are managed skillfully in an emotionally well-regulated workplace, our emotions can help us flow through shifts and novel situations with grace and humor. In an emotionally *unregulated* workplace, however, changes and transitions will likely be managed very badly or not at all, and workers will have to do emotional heavy lifting and extensive Keystone work just to get through each day. But in a workplace where workers and their emotions are respected, changes and transitions can be opportunities for deeper connections, welcoming social rituals, and humane and healing approaches to necessary workplace changes.

Let's observe some everyday workplace transitions and discover ways to make them easier and smoother for everyone. I'll list some ideas in the context of an emotionally well-regulated social structure, but of course, you and your workplace community should develop suggestions that make sense for your own unique needs.

Hiring people: Empathically speaking, hiring should be a community activity. The HR department or a supervisor (if you have them) can initiate the process and attend to the legal aspects when a new person is chosen, but the community should have a chance to meet with and get a feel for applicants who meet the initial requirements. This doesn't have to be a stress-inducing interview for the applicant; it can simply be an invitation to a fika and a chance to hang out. Humanizing the hiring process can help a workplace become an intentional community and pave the way for the relatedness and sense of belonging that new employees will require in order to do their best work.

Onboarding new workers: Beyond learning the nuts and bolts of their jobs, new workers need to understand the social structure, the communication processes their new colleagues have developed, and the different kinds of fikas, banana times, repair stations, and break areas that are available to them. You can also welcome them into the informal social structure and give them a sense of competence, autonomy, and relatedness by asking about their favorite break-time activities or whether they have any new ideas for the break area (you've got one, right?). If you've identified an unpaid Ambassador, it's a good idea to pay them to create a social and emotional onboarding manual or tour for new workers — and make sure that it includes an open invitation to the normal mistakes, confusions, and f*ckups that are a necessary part of learning and growth (it can help to share the consciousness and competence model too).

Transferring within the organization: When people leave their work group or take on a new position, they may feel fear, anxiety, and sadness along with happiness and excitement. Their surviving coworkers may feel sadness, grief, jealousy, or envy, and the workers in their new area may feel fear, anxiety, jealousy, envy, or anger. *It's a lot!* You'd think it wouldn't be; you'd think it would be simple to move from place to place or from position to position. But remember the crucial motivating aspect of relatedness, and the fact that no aspect of Maslow's hierarchy can function without closeness and belonging. People will be losing reliability in the relationships they developed in their previous position, and they'll have to build new relationships to support their new role. A farewell ritual or party in the person's original work group can help with the sense of loss, and a welcoming ritual or party in the next group can help everyone settle the worker into their new position.

Performance appraisals (avoid, avoid!): In many workplaces, performance appraisals are used to transition people into or out of positions, or to decide whether they deserve a raise. And though they're an accepted part of (unhealthy) workplaces, there's very little research to support their use. I am not a fan of performance appraisals, and I'm not alone.[20]

Research and common sense show that grading, reviewing, and critiquing people or making them set goals through coercive or authoritarian methods engages anger, jealousy, envy, depression, and even hatred. And it doesn't matter if it's self-appraisal, 360-degree appraisal, peer appraisal, upward appraisal, critical-incident appraisal, cost-accounting appraisal, behavioral appraisal, goal-setting or management-by-objectives appraisals, continuous feedback, ranking, or qualitative and quantitative evaluation. Performance reviews and appraisals interfere with people's sense of competence, autonomy, and relatedness; they're reliable motivation killers, and they're a huge factor in workplace misery.

If performance reviews are connected to pay or promotions, they can also select for competitive, unempathic, and narcissistic traits — and they often inject unconscious bias, racism, sexism, and ableism into the promotions process. Additionally, grading and critiquing workers brings the schoolyard into the workplace and creates an authoritarian Theory X hierarchy that doesn't belong in a healthy or democratic organization. These appraisals also give some people power over others that no one should have in adult relationships, and they often replace healthy communication and healthy relationships. There's really no argument for performance appraisals, and hundreds of strong, research-backed arguments against them. They're garbage, and our emotions have always seen right through them.

There's an excellent book by HR consultant Mary Jenkins and the late labor attorney Tom Coens called *Abolishing Performance Appraisals: Why They Backfire and What to Do Instead* that can help you and your colleagues find more intelligent, humanizing, and inclusive ways to support each other's learning and performance at work. There are dozens of healthy and respectful alternatives for every task that performance reviews and appraisals allegedly accomplish. One excellent and community-building alternative is to ask workers for regular informal input on the organization, its support structure and communication processes, its wins and losses, its culture and repair stations, and how their jobs could be expanded or modified to meet changing workflows and the needs of the community. Another world-changing alternative is to develop and nourish close relationships in an emotionally well-regulated social structure that treats workers as equals and fellow professionals.

Pregnancy and childbirth or adoption: Beyond giving an expectant parent a congratulatory party, many workplace communities lose their connection to workers who go on maternity or paternity leave, and this loss can engage sadness and grief in the workplace. The worker on leave may be completely consumed with the needs of the new child, but they may also feel sadness and grief about the loss of their previous position and relationships. If the new parent agrees, it can be supportive to invite them to fikas and banana times — with the child or without — and to keep them in the gossip, Conscious Complaining, and Ethical Empathic Gossip networks if they like.

Illness or trauma: In an emotionally well-regulated workplace where closeness and relatedness are encouraged, people become family. Any injuries or illnesses within the workplace need to be acknowledged (if the worker wants people to know), and so should the shock, fear, anxiety, sadness, and grief that people will feel. I've been in workplaces where ill workers simply disappeared, and no one was ever told what happened. The hole in our hearts took a long time to heal because we had no support whatsoever. People need to know what's happening to their friends and colleagues (again, if the colleague agrees), and they need time and space to feel their normal and necessary emotions.

The death of a worker or family member: Death and loss affect everyone in a social group, and the rituals of grief are required. Some sort of wake or tribute should occur in the workplace, and it can be helpful to create a memorial wall or area where people can remember the lost person and share their necessary and healing grief with each other.

When workers choose to leave the organization: This is a serious loss to the community that will engage grief, even if the worker is going someplace wonderful (which may engage jealousy and envy in the workers who are staying behind) — and even if people are glad that the worker is leaving (which may engage happiness and joy). The departing worker will likely be feeling fear, anxiety, sadness, grief, and perhaps panic alongside happiness, joy, and contentment, so it's a big emotional extravaganza for everyone. The HR department should handle the legal and logistical aspects of the transition, but the community will need their own transition process as well. Creating a farewell party or ritual can help the community mark the change and loss, and it can help the departing worker achieve a clear and intentional sense of closure with their former colleagues. In workplaces with high employee turnover (which likely means they're emotionally unregulated or even abusive), the constant unrecognized loss of colleagues and friends has a devastating effect on relatedness and motivation, which leads to increased turnover. These transitions must be recognized, and people must be allowed to feel and express their necessary emotions about loss and change.

Financial losses and reorganization: Workers need to know about these changes as soon as possible; everyone needs to have the dignity of foreknowledge and the opportunity to brainstorm or prepare for changes. The emotions of anxiety, fear, panic, sadness, grief, and anger will be necessary, and will help the community make these often-painful transitions. Farewell parties or rituals, and some form of a memorial or wake can help people let go of the old situation and reorient and restabilize themselves in the new one.

Opening or closing a workspace: Our physical environment has powerful effects on our mental health and our social well-being, so we naturally become attached to our workspaces (even if they're cruddy) and feel anxiety about new workspaces (even if they'll be much nicer). Workers of the World member Jennifer Asdorian recently opened a new office with several other clinicians, and they found that there was a kind of Maslow's pyramid of comfort that had to be established in a certain order. First, their physical surroundings had to be just right (colors, furnishings, heating and cooling), then their financial obligations had to be organized fairly, and *then* they could all settle into their working relationships. The physical stage had to be set properly first.

Introducing workers to new workspaces and giving them a say in the design and layout can help ease this transition, as can creating a farewell party or ritual for an old workspace (see the case study on page 197); people *live* at work, and they need to have a say in what happens in their workplace homes.

Transitioning to online and telecommuting work: During the pandemic, many people transitioned from communal workspaces to telecommuting and webinar meetings, and the change was a rough one. "Zoom fatigue" became a reality, and many people struggled to do their work and maintain their sense of community. People have stabilized somewhat, but I want to share some tips from our DEI community, which is a close-knit international community that has been meeting online for 6 years.

We learned early on that intentions were important for online meetings: *Why* were we meeting? *What* did we want to achieve? *How long* would we need? *Who* needed to be there? Of course, you should ask these questions about all meetings, but for online meetings that can be cognitively taxing in much the same way the Devil's Floorplan is, your intentions can help reduce fatigue and cognitive overload.

Last year, one of our DEI students (and now licensed DEI Trainer) Dariusz Klupi from Poland, suggested that we create a kind of fika in our online meetings. In longer online retreats, we introduced relaxed community mealtimes and informal sessions on Zoom, where we could all chat and hang out with each other in the way you can at an in-person retreat. These informal hangouts really helped us deepen our relationships. I think that a lot of Zoom fatigue may come from too much formality and focus; when people can't hang out aimlessly and have fika or banana time together, they can lose their sense of connection.

We also have many online repair stations in our DEI community: a private Facebook group, book clubs, brainstorming meetings, and regular access to Conscious Complaining and Ethical Empathic Gossip (EEG). It's normal for people in our DEI community to text each other and jump on Zoom for a quick EEG. We also do a lot of Conscious Complaining and EEG in our Facebook group, and that's nourishing and connecting for all of us.

There's an excellent book by meeting expert Priya Parker called *The Art of Gathering: How We Meet and Why It Matters.* If you run any gatherings or meetings, this book will help you bring a grounded sense of meaning, purpose, and true community into every gathering; it's a real game-changer (and it's now a required text in our DEI licensing programs).

Layoffs: These shocking business failures should never come as a surprise to workers; layoffs need to be handled with deep empathy and masterful emotional awareness. The normal and necessary emotional responses to these business failures are fear, panic, anger, anxiety, jealousy, envy, depression, hatred . . . basically every emotion will need to bring its genius to this catastrophic situation. Layoffs are uncontrollable losses, unwanted transitions, and shocks all rolled up into one situation, and workers will need support, the opportunity to grieve and be angry, and many ways to restabilize themselves after the shock subsides. All of the suggestions for helping people transition when a worker chooses to leave the organization should be followed; people will need to mark this transition as a community and create farewell rituals and grief rituals for this painful loss.

Firing people: Firing people should be the last possible option, because the losses can be extensive. Certainly, the fired employee will lose their income, their position, their security, the relatedness and love of their working community, and their future plans — but the business will incur losses as well. The workplace community will lose a group member, and depending on the employee, the financial losses to the business can range from $10,000 to $100,000 or more per fired worker. See the case study on the next page for an excellent examples of a well-handled and grief-mediated layoff of an entire division.

Hiring and training a worker is very expensive, and firing a worker should be a last option. If you've exhausted all of your options (mediation is extremely valuable if you can access it) and you must let someone go, there are legal and ethical issues to consider; for instance, HR should handle all of the legal and logistical aspects of the termination. Ethically speaking, you can and should share information about why the person was fired, but you should protect the terminated worker's privacy and dignity and provide a clear reason for letting them go. Firings may engage fear, anxiety, and panic in your community because everything has changed and workers will rightly feel destabilized and even unsafe. Your workers may also feel grief at the loss of their colleague, and anger, jealousy, and envy if they feel that the firing was unfair. You may need to bring the entire community together for a group EEG so that everyone can share their extensive social intelligence and organize their thinking about the termination. Some workers may also want to create a farewell ritual or memorial to mark this loss.

In many organizations, firings are done secretly and suddenly and usually on a Friday afternoon so that the fired worker can't speak to their colleagues. Sometimes, this harsh and dehumanizing approach is necessary if the terminated worker is abusive, but this shocking situation can frighten, anger, and confuse the surviving community. Don't keep terminations a secret from your workers; speak with ethics and empathy about what happened to their community, treat people as intelligent adults, and let them know what happened and why.

Disbanding your organization: During the pandemic, we're seeing many businesses falling by the wayside. In my small Northern California town, I'm seeing more empty buildings every time I go downtown. This is a deeply uncertain time and we're all dealing with multiple shocks and traumas because our leaders failed us with their chaotic and deadly approach to Covid-19. Though many people are settling into apathy and depression and going numb, it could help to set aside some focused time to say goodbye to businesses and organizations that have gone under.

If you need to disband your business, take some time to say goodbye, and to feel sadness, grief, anger, shame, hatred, jealousy, envy, and any other emotion you need to feel. Invite your colleagues to a farewell party or ritual so that they can feel their own emotions in a welcoming and nourishing community.

I'd like to share a real-life example of an extensive series of workplace transitions and losses that were handled with empathy, intelligence, and love.

Case Study: Closing an Entire Warehouse Division with Love and Empathy

My publisher, Sounds True, recently went through a difficult and complex transition away from running their own warehousing, distribution, and shipping divisions. This transition was handled with such grace and empathy that I asked if I could share their story. This story was told to me by Wendy Pardo, vice president of operations at Sounds True in Colorado.

Sounds True was one of the last publishers in the mind/body/spirit space to maintain their own self-distribution division, because their five longtime warehouse workers were so efficient that most people would have guessed that the warehouse employed at least thirty people. This warehouse was next door to the main building and the Sounds True team had a fond attachment to it as the place where all of their books and audio learning programs on healing had been housed and shipped across the world for decades.

The operations team had financially evaluated the self-distribution versus outsource model every 3 years for over 15 years, and they finally knew that partnering with a larger distributor and closing down the warehouse was the right move logistically and financially. However, everyone felt a great deal of sadness and anxiety about the decision because the warehouse staff were family, and no one wanted to lose them. It took Wendy and the team over 6 months to make the final decision, and Wendy felt sad the entire time because she and everyone else loved the warehouse crew.

An important decisive piece for Wendy was that she needed to see the working conditions of their future distribution partner. She flew out to Virginia to spend a day in the partner's warehouse and was able to meet all of the workers and see that they were being treated with respect. She heard their concerns and their pride in their work, and she saw that they were a dedicated team. And as she watched this Virginia crew smiling and working happily together, she was able to settle into the decision, because these people felt like an extension of Sounds True's home office. She knew that things were going to be okay.

Once they knew that the transition was going to happen, Wendy and the leadership team gave their warehouse crew 10 months' notice, even though there was a danger that the crew would leave before the transition occurred. Wendy and the warehouse manager took all five members of the team out to a 3-hour lunch to tell them, and of course, there were tears, sadness, grief, shock, anxiety, anger — everything you would expect to see when people face not only the loss of their jobs, but of their close relationships with their coworkers as well.

Wendy gave them the rest of the day off and a generous offer of severance if they would stay throughout the transition. All five of them stayed.

The logistical transition for the warehouse team included job shadowing in the main building for people who wanted retraining, tuition contributions for people who wanted to go back to school, support with resumes and with posting them to LinkedIn, mock interviews with HR, personal references, and time off for interviews.

The social and emotional support for the warehouse team — and for the entire Sounds True team who loved them — started in an all-staff meeting where the CEO, the vice president of sales, and Wendy announced the change. Wendy said: "When we announced this decision, there was so much grief and love it filled the entire office. I cried in front of everyone as I complimented each person on the warehouse team while they stood crying in the back row. They came up and hugged me, and we all felt grief, but it was a supportive grief where the whole company was sad but so grateful that we were showing the team the respect they deserved."

During their final 10 months, Wendy made sure that the team knew they were loved: "We had monthly celebrations with lunches and plenty of weekly snacks (we also filled their fridge with fun snacks that they loved). We had foosball tournaments. I sponsored many off-site happy hours. The warehouse team also started coming over to our main office to simply talk with people. We took it day by day and enjoyed our time together. The warehouse manager and I would listen when team members were stressed, and laugh when they were joking around; we offered support in whatever unique ways each person needed — especially as we got closer to the transition and their stress about the unknown increased. Something that really helped was that I've been laid off twice already, so I could share my experiences with them so they wouldn't feel alone. We also had a huge warehouse pizza party once we had cleaned out the warehouse."

The warehouse team was grateful for this caring and empathic transition, but so were all of the other workers. Losing the warehouse and the tiny, mighty warehouse team was a shocking experience full of so many necessary emotional responses, and Wendy and Sounds True managed it with humanity, intelligence, and love.

Contrast Sounds True's masterful transition with the experience of a client of mine who was laid off on a Friday afternoon with no notice after 6 years on the job. He was not allowed to tell anyone that he was leaving, and he had to box up all his belongings after the others had left. By Monday afternoon the next week, his coworkers were texting him frantically, and their understandable fear, panic, anger, anxiety, and grief were not addressed in any way; they were told to get back to work. As you can imagine, the workers felt betrayed and endangered, because if this well-respected worker was discarded in this way, they had no reason to believe that they wouldn't be thrown out too. They lost their trust and respect for the company, and within 6 months, 8 of the remaining 15 staff members had left.

Handling a transition badly is not just unprofessional and unempathic, it's bad for business, because losing trained workers can cost organizations up to hundreds of thousands of dollars per person (depending on their salary, length of service, and expertise), and it can shatter relationships and trust between workers and management. There is no upside to bad transitions; they're bad for everyone.

Creating Healthy Transitions by Respecting the Emotions

All changes require the gifts and skills of fear and anxiety, and all transitions require the gifts and skills of sadness and grief. Depending on the situation, many other emotions will bring their unique genius to bear, and in an emotionally well-regulated workplace, all will be welcome. With the help of the emotions, organizations can intelligently prepare and support workers as they acclimate to new or shifting surroundings, situations, colleagues, positions, responsibilities, and losses.

It is my hope that you can use the approaches and processes in this chapter (and in this entire book) to create a healthy and emotionally well-regulated workplace where respect, empathy, adult relationships, internal motivation, love, and the needs of all workers are valued and supported. Not just in the mission statement, but in the everyday world of all workers' lives.

7

When Emotions Are Your Vital
Professional Tools

A
s I've studied emotional labor, emotion work, and empathy work, I've noticed that many occupations rely on one or more emotions to the exclusion of others. I began to call the workers in these occupations *Emotion Professionals*: Anxiety Professionals, Grief Professionals, and so forth. These are workers who rely on the gifts and skills of one (or a few) emotions as tools to get their work done.

EMOTION PROFESSIONALS

People whose work depends primarily on the gifts and skills in one or more emotions, such as grief for hospice workers, or focused anxiety for air traffic controllers.

These people are not doing emotional labor in the precise way that Arlie Hochschild described it — such as flight attendants who have to display happiness and friendliness (and suppress almost everything else), or bill collectors who have to display anger and distrust (and suppress almost everything else). These Hochschildian forms of emotional labor require workers to display and suppress specific emotions (depending on the occupation), but Emotion Professionals are working with emotions in a different way. These workers (usually unknowingly) rely heavily on the gifts and skills in specific emotions such as anxiety, anger, or grief in order to get their work done. This is a more advanced topic, but I want to introduce it here because it's yet another problem to be aware of in emotionally *unregulated* workplaces.

The difficulties and conflicts that can arise for Emotion Professionals are unique because these workers are relying on one or more emotions to the exclusion of all the others. As we've all experienced in our personal lives, too much of any one emotion (such as anger or anxiety) can overload or destabilize us; we need *all* of our emotions to be available to us. However, in many occupations, too much of one emotion is a job requirement!

How to Identify Different Types of Emotion Professionals

Each occupation is unique, and so are individual workers; however, we can observe different occupations in regard to the central emotions that might be required.

For instance, workers who set boundaries, expect specific behaviors, and maintain enduring values, such as accountants, police officers, human resources administrators, or quality control specialists, may be *Anger Professionals*. Workers who help others let go of unnecessary things like clutter or physical tension (such as home organizers, housecleaners, landscapers, or massage therapists) may be *Sadness Professionals*. Workers who hold others accountable for their behavior and expect them to make amends (such as addiction counselors, bill collectors, judges, or parole officers) may be *Shame Professionals*. And workers who help people find exactly what they're looking for (such as real estate agents, personal shoppers, salespeople, or headhunters) may be *Envy Professionals*.

You may also see entire departments working with one or more emotions to the exclusion of others, such as the payroll department (anger), the custodial staff (sadness), the marketing department (envy and jealousy), or the acquisitions department (anxiety and happiness). These are just suggestions, of course. You and your colleagues will have a clearer idea about what your work entails, whether any of you are Emotion Professionals, and which specific emotions your work requires.

This understanding is important in every workplace, because unsupported emotion work and empathy work will lead to fatigue, conflict, overwhelm, depression, or even burnout. We know that already. But if we don't know that our work requires over-reliance on one or more emotions, we can become destabilized, *not* because the work is hard or emotions are a problem, but because we lose access to the richness and diversity of our entire emotional ecosystem. Our emotions exist in an interconnected realm of skills and intelligence that work best when we're free to respond without unhealthy repression or overexpression. If we don't realize that we're Emotion Professionals, and no one else in our organization does either, we may suffer needlessly, and our colleagues may make things worse because they don't understand the work we're doing. Emotion Professionals need specific forms of support so that they won't become overextended or overwhelmed.

I'll share two in-depth examples of work that requires heavy reliance on one emotion, and we'll explore ways to build an environment of support around these Emotion Professionals.

Case Study: How Heavy Drinking Uncovered Anxiety Professionals

In my 2020 book, *Embracing Anxiety*, I devoted a chapter to Anxiety Professionals, or people whose jobs require them to live and work in the future. We all rely on the gifts and skills of anxiety to help us plan ahead and organize our workflows, but the workers I'm calling Anxiety Professionals essentially *live* in the future.

I first became aware of the concept of Emotion Professionals when I consulted with a construction management group in a large city. These weren't construction workers who worked with power tools and machinery — these were project engineers and managers who were overseeing massive, multi-million-dollar projects with numerous shifting and interconnecting parts. The scope of their work was stunning in its complexity, but I didn't know that until I began to wonder about the heavy drinking I witnessed in this group.

I visited this group in person a number of times, and was often taken out to dinner while I was with them. The first time I went, I watched people drink very expensive drinks with fancy names; it seemed to be a competition, and I thought I was seeing an unusual party behavior. But each time I went back, I saw this kind of drinking and heard stories about hangovers, which suggested that heavy drinking was a community norm. I was surprised, because another norm in the group was competitive wellness and exercise (competition, as you may guess, was also a norm there). I don't drink at all (this is unusual, I know), but I couldn't truly understand the need for so much alcohol in this health-conscious, highly educated, environmentally conscious, supportive, and well-paid group of workers.

On my third visit, I asked them to walk me through just one of their projects (they usually had three to five projects running at any given time), and I learned that from beginning to end, each large construction project could take as long as 5 to 8 years. During this time, city governments could change, tax rates could change, the economy could change, construction rates could change, land prices could change, the desirability of their city as a corporate headquarters could change — anything and everything could change, but these project managers had to keep their eye on the final product and work toward it no matter what. The organizational and planning skills they had developed were all-encompassing, and their ability to work toward a distant and uncertain future with clarity and certainty was masterful — and all of these skills live in *anxiety*.

As you know, anxiety can be a highly activating emotion. Its job is to help us organize ourselves and arrive in the future prepared and on task. Anxiety helps us complete our work and meet our deadlines, and in the workplace, we could say that we're all Anxiety Professionals to one extent or another. We all have tasks to complete and deadlines to meet, and we all need to organize ourselves, gather our tools, and get the job done. We all work with anxiety every day. But this group's work reached very far out into the future, and the number of tasks, deadlines, and moving pieces that they had to manage was enormous and continually shifting. They needed to access their anxiety skills all day, every day, with no time to let down their guard or relax. They had developed a couple of different forms of fika and banana time breaks, but these necessary breaks were not built into their schedule. Many of these workers told me that they woke up in the middle of the night thinking about a missed phone call, a looming deadline, or a nagging problem. Their anxiety was on the job constantly, and this unbalanced emotional load was interfering with their peace of mind, their sleep, and their health.

There was another issue, which is that their supervisor loved to try out new management ideas and approaches on them. Whatever fad was going around was eventually going to make its way to this group, and their supervisor regularly introduced ever-changing approaches to management, communication processes, workflows, financial projections, conflict management, team-building, office layouts, and more. Though this supervisor's intentions were good, the effect of this perpetually shifting workplace environment was to add more stress and anxiety to the group. They had no stability, and they had to waste important working hours learning whatever new management fad their excitable supervisor brought in every few months.[1] Their work required continually activated anxiety, but because of their supervisor's mistaken focus on constant change and novelty, this group's workplace *environment* required a regular activation of fear and anxiety as well. Thresholds, privacy, and repair stations were not stable or even available sometimes, and there was no restful groundedness anywhere.

Now that I understood their work as Anxiety Professionals, their heavy drinking made so much sense. Their overwhelmed emotional systems needed complete relaxation, and their overworked minds needed some serious time off. They needed to feel silly and carefree and oblivious, and they needed a way to down-regulate from all of the activation and focus they maintained constantly. They all needed a break, but because there was no understanding of the emotional heavy lifting they were doing, the only thing they could think of was to drink alcohol — *a lot* of alcohol. This was entirely understandable, but I was concerned about the toll the alcohol would take. Also, the alcohol didn't solve any of the issues in their anxiety-requiring workplace, so their need for the alcohol would only increase over time while the unbalanced emotional conditions of their workplace remained completely unaddressed.

With the group's input, I developed the following list of supportive practices for Anxiety Professionals — and note that I included drinking alcohol as one of the practices. These workers didn't need to be shamed or treated like misbehaving children; their drinking was an excellent unconscious fix for a completely unconscious problem. Now that the problem was brought out into the light of day, they were able to find many ways to address it consciously, competently, and intentionally.

Workday Practices for Anxiety Professionals[2]
- Listening to your emotions
- Paying attention to any emotions that arise alongside your anxiety; they may be offering support
- Paying attention to the emotions of others
- Developing shared emotional skills and communication practices with your colleagues
- Identifying any other emotional labor, emotion work, or empathy work that you and your colleagues are doing, and then supporting each other
- Using a project management tool to download all of your ideas, deadlines, and tasks in one place so that you can take a mental break
- Creating order and managing small problems in a regular rhythm
- Sighing and breathing downward
- Taking relaxing and unfocused breaks throughout the day, every 50 to 90 minutes for at least 5 to 20 minutes
- Taking banana times and fikas with supportive and relaxing colleagues
- Reducing caffeine, or stopping intake by 2 p.m. so that you can clear the caffeine and relax before bedtime (fikas after 2 p.m. should be caffeine-free)
- Using Conscious Complaining (with or without a partner) to allow all of your emotions to have a voice
- Using Ethical Empathic Gossip to find (and offer) support for complex social situations
- Asking for help
- Laughing out loud and being silly

Management Support Practices for Anxiety Professionals
- Providing a stable and calm working environment with as little unnecessary change as possible
- Maintaining clear boundaries and easy access to privacy
- Providing many opportunities for quiet time and downtime throughout the day
- Fixing the Devil's Floorplan if they're trapped in one
- Providing space and support for communally designed break rooms and repair stations
- Encouraging informal fikas or banana times (*enforcing* breaks defeats the purpose of breaks)

Home Practices for Anxiety Professionals
- Lazing around with no purpose
- Being with supportive friends and family
- Being in nature
- Listening to your emotions
- Paying attention to any emotions that arise alongside your anxiety; they may be offering support
- Laughing out loud and being silly
- Playing with animals
- Asking for help
- Being listened to
- Making art or engaging with music, art, drama, dance, or design
- Crying when you need to
- Meditating (be aware that some forms of meditation and deep breathing may worsen your anxiety; if they do, move on to another form ASAP)
- Getting heated up (sweating is important)
    - » Sweat-producing exercise
    - » Awesome sex or masturbation
    - » Sauna, hot tub, or hot bath until you're utterly relaxed
- Using alcohol or marijuana if they don't impair you the next day
- Using anti-anxiety medications or beta blockers if you need them
- Developing good, healthy sleep patterns[3]

As you scan through these suggestions for Anxiety Professionals, notice that they don't try to shut anxiety down or turn it into another emotion. They do list many relaxation activities that bring in the soothing influence of sadness, and they add meandering breaks that bring in the soothing influence of confusion and apathy, but these aren't meant to silence or erase anxiety. Instead, these soothing emotions can help these professionals create balance in their heavily anxiety-focused work lives. These suggestions take the need for anxiety seriously, and work to surround Anxiety Professionals with support, community, and intentional downtime so that they can do their work efficiently without being overtaxed, and also enjoy their lives outside of work.

This group began to develop better emotion regulation with each other, and they now had ways to create more stability in their working relationships. Because they could identify themselves as Anxiety Professionals who dealt with constant focus and activation, they learned to check in with each other carefully instead of inadvertently increasing each other's anxiety. They also spent a lot of time designing the simple workplace process flows we explored in chapter 5, especially around interrupting busy people and reporting mistakes and problems. Though their work continued to require lots of anxiety, they now had many ideas and options besides heavy drinking to support themselves and each other, to bring balance to their social and emotional lives, and to do their best work.

Case Study: Grief Professionals and Hospice Kibble

My husband, Tino, is a hospice nurse educator who worked as a hospice bereavement counselor before he became a nurse; he has dedicated his working life to end-of-life care, and he is a Grief Professional. Tino and his hospice colleagues work with death and loss every day, but instead of avoiding grief or putting a happy face on the realities of death (as many of us do), they walk directly into situations where death and loss will certainly and inevitably occur.

Hospice work does not hasten death, in fact, the focus of hospice is to make each person's final days as comfortable and fulfilling as possible. Many people who transition early enough into hospice from regular medical care improve greatly and live far longer lives than they would have with care that was focused on trying to cure them instead of accepting that they were dying.[4] Hospice is a remarkable service and hospice workers are skilled empathy workers and Grief Professionals; however, just as it is with Anxiety Professionals, too much focus on only one emotion can take its toll.

The work of grief is to mourn what was lost and let go completely when you have no other choice. Many people mistake sadness and grief for each other, but the work of these two emotions is very different. Sadness helps you let go of things that aren't working any longer: an idea, a possession, a relationship, a job . . . and with sadness, you have a choice. But grief helps you mourn when the loss is completely out of your control: the death happens, the job is taken away, the relationship is gone, the item is destroyed, or the future is lost. Grief comes to help you in situations of serious loss that you have no choice about.

Grief Professionals are letting go continually, creating space and time for the emotions of others, and working with the fact that they have no power to change the inevitable — though they can offer presence, kindness, empathy, and care. Unlike Anxiety Professionals who are energized and future focused, always working and moving ahead (and feeling that they have control), Grief Professionals are making regular everyday preparations for irretrievable losses that they can prepare for, but cannot control.

As healthcare workers, hospice Grief Professionals also perform heavy and non-reciprocal empathy work; they must be fully present and meet the needs of dying patients and their families, but there's no formal process for their patients to reciprocate that empathy or care (nor should they — they're dying and may not have the energy to do so). As such, these professionals require a lot of support, repair stations, comfort, privacy, peace, and quiet that are usually nowhere to be found in their workplaces.

The healthcare profession is deeply troubled, emotionally unregulated, and often abusive. Even in the best hospitals and hospice agencies, social and emotional support is often lacking, and suitable repair stations (or private spaces) are rare. This lack of basic workplace support for empathy workers is also rampant in assisted living and skilled nursing facilities, medical clinics, childcare centers, and schools. The problems caused by a lack of emotional regulation and humane practices in our modern workplaces affect all of us, but these problems land particularly hard on empathy workers. Healthcare work can be intensely draining, yet very few healthcare workplaces even think to nourish or provide appropriate care and support for these essential workers.

I began to understand this lack of nourishment in regard to something Tino joked about: *Hospice Kibble.* The communal kitchens and break rooms in hospices and care facilities are often filled with sweets, candies, pastries, and chips. These simple carbohydrates aren't toxic, but the people eating these mostly empty calories are healthcare professionals who understand the value of eating complex carbohydrates for sustained energy and blood sugar control. Tino and I don't eat a lot of sweets, so whenever we were gifted with cookies or candies, Tino would put them out in the break room. We joked about the interval between Tino placing the treats on the counter and their total disappearance a few moments later; people would *pounce* on them even though there were already many treats in the break room. We began to call all sweet treats and candies Hospice Kibble, because sweets were a staple for many hospice workers (and many other healthcare workers) who didn't seem to be able to manage their intake of these delicious but empty foods.

I felt into this behavior with my own emotions and identified something fascinating in the sweets: the presence of happiness and joy, certainly, but also of jealousy and envy. Most of us associate sweet treats with happiness, joy, and celebration, but the way that hospice workers would dive onto new and homemade treats displayed a profound sense of desire and longing. Desire, longing, wanting, and taking are aspects of both jealousy and envy, and I saw how important these actions were for Grief Professionals who spent their workdays preparing for uncontrollable loss and death, and whose empathy work was draining, non-reciprocal, and almost entirely unsupported. So much was flowing out and away from these Grief Professionals, but very little was flowing back toward them. Grabbing these sweets and devouring them was a way to bring some sense of control and balance to their draining, non-reciprocal, and hyper-empathic working lives.

I felt into the ways that these sweets were feeding and nourishing these people emotionally; they were bringing sweetness and joy into their drained bodies and helping them reach out and grab what they wanted even though (and perhaps *because*) they weren't "supposed to." Their treat-taking was a clear attempt to nourish themselves, experience sweetness, perform self-care, make emotional choices in the face of powerlessness, assert their autonomy, and take what they wanted — and it all made a deep kind of sense. I wondered: "Would any other kind of treat provide all of these things as effectively?"

I haven't worked with Grief Professionals yet (other than Tino), but I developed a list of suggestions to help support and stabilize the emotional and empathic workloads of these essential workers. Of course, I wouldn't implement any of these changes in any workplace without the agreement of the workers; I would always defer to the greater wisdom and wishes of the workers themselves.

The ideas and practices below share many features with the suggestions I developed with the Anxiety Professionals, because most of these suggestions help create emotionally well-regulated social structures for every type of Emotion Professional (and every type of worker). Every worker needs a basic foundation of emotional, empathic, relational, and physical support in order to do their best work.

Workday Practices for Grief Professionals

- Listening to your emotions
- Paying attention to any emotions that arise alongside your grief; they may be offering support
- Developing shared emotional skills and communication practices with your colleagues
- Identifying any other emotional labor, emotion work, or empathy work that you and your colleagues are doing, and finding support for this work
- Taking fikas and banana times with your colleagues so that you can fill up on nourishing relatedness *as well as* sweet treats

- Ensuring that physical boundaries and privacy are available for everyone
- Taking intentional breaks between every patient contact (for at least 10 to 20 minutes) to care for yourself and rest
- Critiquing and redesigning your break areas (or creating them from scratch if there are none)
- Using Conscious Complaining (with or without a partner) to allow all of your emotions to have a voice
- Using Ethical Empathic Gossip to find (and offer) support for complex social situations
- Asking for help
- Taking what you want
- Being with supportive and relaxing colleagues
- Welcoming sarcasm and gallows humor
- Laughing out loud and being silly and snarky

Management Support Practices for Grief Professionals
- Providing a stable and comfortable working environment where workers have control over their surroundings
- Providing easy access to quiet and privacy
- Providing opportunities for quiet time and downtime throughout the day
- Providing adequate turnarounds (at least 10 to 20 minutes) between patient contacts
- Fixing the Devil's Floorplan if they're trapped in one
- Providing space and support for communally designed break rooms and repair stations
- Encouraging informal fikas or banana times where the focus is on relatedness and camaraderie *as well as* sweets

Home Practices for Grief Professionals
- Being around growing things and new life; gardening, being with young animals and babies

- Doing long-term planning for things you enjoy, places you want to go, and things you want to experience, grab, take in, and have
- Taking time to be alone and do whatever you want
- Being selfish whenever you feel like it
- Being with supportive friends and family
- Being in nature and watching the cycles of life
- Listening to your emotions
- Paying attention to any emotions that arise alongside your grief; they may be offering support
- Laughing out loud and being silly
- Being cranky and stubborn when you feel like it
- Being sarcastic when you feel like it
- Asking for help
- Being listened to
- Using Conscious Complaining and Ethical Empathic Gossip
- Finding nourishing friendships and/or intimate relationships
- Making art or engaging with nourishing music, art, drama, dance, or design
- Developing nourishing and healthy sleep patterns[5]

As it was with Anxiety Professionals, these suggestions for Grief Professionals don't try to shut down the grief; instead, they work to build a world of support around these professionals and recruit the gifts and skills of specific emotions such as anger, happiness, joy, jealousy, and envy to help bring balance to their lives.

Professional Care for Emotion Professionals

I want to point out that all of these suggestions are simple; none of them are complex, expensive, or hard to implement. Providing healthy and humane environments is simple once you understand the intelligence inside emotions, how to treat adults with respect and empathy, how to support internal motivation and healthy productivity, and how to identify and support your emotional laborers, emotion workers, empathy workers, and Emotion Professionals.

Pay attention to the ways that people cope with their emotional labor, emotion work, empathy work, or Emotion Professional status: How are they balancing themselves? Is their emotion work nourishing or draining (see chapter 4 to find out)? How are they managing the emotional and empathic demands of their work, and does their workplace environment support them — or are they surrounded by noise, unaddressed conflict, poor or nonexistent communication workflows, uncomfortable spaces, unhappy coworkers, and badly handled transitions that make their lives and their jobs harder?

If workers are not properly supported, you'll see all kinds of compensating behaviors bubble up: squabbling, goofing off, disengagement, conflict, unethical gossip, addictive behaviors, emotional destabilization, or even mutinies and rebellions. And if you feel into these behaviors empathically, you may discover the balancing emotional and empathic genius inside them. The solution to all of these behaviors is not to obsess over individuals or try to punish, fix, coach, or control your colleagues as if they were schoolchildren; the solution is to use your emotional and empathic skills (and the emotional genius that lives in your workplace) to build and nourish an emotionally well-regulated social space where equality-based adult relationships, competence, autonomy, relatedness, emotional awareness, empathy, internal motivation, and the development of large-group social skills are supported. That's what's missing in the workplace, and that's what's required in the workplace (and everywhere else).

If you learn how to listen to emotions — yours and your colleagues — they'll help you achieve and sustain all of these things. That's the power of emotions at work.

8

Nurturing Your Emotionally
Well-Regulated Organization

uilding a just, inclusive, naturally motivating, democratic, and emotionally well-regulated organization is a journey that continues for a lifetime. Of course, conflicts and upheavals will still occur, because they're necessary and expected parts of doing business. But when you and your colleagues share reliable social and emotional skills, workable communication processes, a supportive physical environment, a humane workload, and healthy transition processes, you'll be able to weather conflicts and upheavals and learn from them. And when you understand the specific emotional and empathic workloads that you and your colleagues face, you'll be able to develop ingenious support structures and create a truly intentional community.

As I did the research for this book, I combed through studies on high-performing workplaces where people did excellent work in difficult and stress-inducing situations. Sadly, I didn't find many examples, but I did find a 2014 organizational study that explored the emotional and social features of successful high-intensity workplaces. This study looked at what the authors called "high-reliability organizing" in fast-paced workplaces such as aircraft carrier flight decks and nuclear power control rooms, where unreported or unaddressed problems can literally kill people.[1]

The researchers described what they found in academic terms, such as *affective foundations* (emotional skills), *prosocial other-focus* (empathy), and *emotional ambivalence* (the ability to work with more than one emotion at the same time), but what they actually discovered in these successful high-intensity workplaces were empathic, emotionally well-regulated social structures where workers trusted each other and communicated skillfully — especially about problems. These workers had developed many ways to quickly report problems upward, look for trouble and inefficiencies, watch out for each other, take each other's perspectives, and maintain their camaraderie, emotional skills, empathy, and sense of humor even in their high-intensity environments.

So, it can be done. Creating a humane, emotionally well-regulated, and empathic environment for high-performing workers is doable, and each of us can create and nurture these environments — even in occupations where mistakes and communication breakdowns won't lead to fiery deaths or nuclear winter.

I sought out research on high-intensity workplaces because I wanted to challenge the ridiculous idea that emotional skills are soft skills, best left to kindergarten teachers and massage therapists (who, we can now see, are masterful, kickass empathy workers). We've all seen the workplace-wide carnage that occurs every day because emotions were kicked out of the workplace, and we've all worked in monotonous or gruesome workplaces where emotional skills were required, *stat*. Emotions, emotional skills, and empathy are crucial tools no matter what kind of work we do; they're also the beating heart of every workplace culture, and of all cultures.

Emotions never left the workplace and they never will, so learning how to work with them is not only necessary and protective for everyone, but it can lead to high-reliability work teams who can land jets on tiny platforms in the middle of the rough ocean, or skillfully manage nuclear fission. Emotional skills and empathic skills lead to flexible, brilliant, connected, strong, and effective individuals, teams, and communities who then radiate emotional skills and empathy to their clients and customers; to their neighborhoods, towns, and cities; to each worker's extended family; and to our waiting world.

Emotions are crucial to everything we think, everything we do, every idea we have, and every dream we envision; emotions are everything. And learning how to work with them empathically can change our work and personal lives — and our entire world — for the better.

Remembering Consciousness and Competence

As you continue onward with your emotional explorations and your empathic workplace design process, remember the interplay between consciousness and competence (see page 73); this interplay is a vital part of all learning.

After reading this book, you're no longer unconscious about the need for emotional skills and awareness at work, and you're building competence with them. Soon enough, your ability to work with emotions may move fully to the right side of the model, and you'll be in *Unconscious Competence* — you'll have reliable, everyday emotional skills that you won't have to think about. However, as you move forward, you'll discover new areas where you and your colleagues may have been unconscious or incompetent for years, and my hope is that after the first necessary pangs of fear, shame, anxiety, sadness, or depression, you'll be able to share a fika, banana time, Conscious Complaining, or Ethical Empathic Gossip session so that you and your colleagues can share the process of real learning and growth together. Learning is clumsy and messy sometimes, and it's always helpful to reach out for camaraderie and support. In an emotionally well-regulated workplace, you'll have that support.

I often print out the consciousness and competence flowchart when I work with groups, and have people identify where they are as we work through processes or learn new skills. Of course, most people want to avoid the incompetent side of the model at first, but after a while, people will claim it with laughter and relief. Knowing that we're all incompetent and unconscious connects us; it becomes a community-building "problem time" or F*ckup Night where people can relax and be real with each other; it's very healing.

This model can also help you and your colleagues identify incompetence in your workplace skills that you don't actually *want* to change. That's perfectly acceptable. For instance, if Natalie had known about the empathic heavy lifting she'd have to do with her spa workers before she took that job, she could have claimed her incompetence openly and found something more suitable for her natural talents. In my businesses, I once tried to learn and do every conceivable job, including coding my own websites!

Consciously claiming my incompetence and paying for someone else's competent coding skills has freed me to focus on what I can do, and do well. Incompetence is normal, and we don't have to become competent at every possible job and task; that's what community is for.

In the introduction, I explored the Unconscious *Emotional* Incompetence that has plagued the workplace for hundreds of years. The structure of the workplace itself has been trapped in unconsciousness and incompetence because the emotions — those irreplaceable aspects of our cognition, social skills, and understanding of large-group behaviors — were banished (or we thought they were).

As you work to bring your social structure out of its zombie-like state, know that you'll regularly find places where the structure *itself* is incompetent or unconscious. Your Keystones will pinpoint many of these troubled places, and so will the work you do to develop reliable communication processes for the everyday conflicts we explored in chapter 5. As you and your colleagues gather to address structures and processes that have operated unconsciously and incompetently, your emotions will arise to tell all of you exactly what has been happening, and exactly what to do about it. As the poet Rumi wrote about emotions more than 800 years ago, " . . . meet them at the door laughing, and invite them in. Be grateful for whoever comes, because each has been sent as a guide from beyond."

Trusting the Emotions, Always

As a newly initiated member of the emotional OSHA team, I welcome you into this work and thank you for your willingness to see what others have been forced to ignore and hear what others have been trained to tune out. When you can observe emotions in yourself and others, you'll have access to stores of wisdom and energy that are magnificent in scope. Observe them, respect them, and trust them; emotions know what they're doing, and they always have.

As you go through your day, ask yourself: "Are workers being treated as intelligent and internally motivated adults? Are our Keystones being identified and supported? Is there nourishing support and plenty of repair stations for emotional laborers, emotion workers, and empathy workers? Do we have processes to identify and address bias, exclusion, prejudice, and the unconscious emotional and empathic incompetence of dominant people and groups? Are there enough ways for people to find peace, quiet, and privacy whenever they need it? Are there easy ways for people to get together informally in fikas and banana times? Are we managing our communication processes and transitions intelligently and democratically? Are all emotions welcome?" If so, carry on. If not — stop and regroup, return to Conscious Incompetence, and refocus yourselves. This is a lifelong learning process.

Thank you for the work you do to create and nurture emotionally well-regulated social structures so that people can do their best work in welcoming, just, inclusive, and nourishing communities. Thank you for bringing more emotional awareness and more healthy empathy into the workplace, and into a struggling world that needs both of these things right now.

Emotional and empathic Workers of the World, I salute you!

ACKNOWLEDGMENTS

T hough I truly love to write, writing this book was hard, *hard* work, and not just because of the pandemic. I always knew that the workplace was a deeply troubled place, but running my own businesses and having complete freedom to develop healthy social structures for more than two decades separated me from the daily grind that most workers endure. Reading book after book about the workplace and doing research for this project dropped me into a series of deep emotional valleys because I hadn't been close to the problems in the workplace for decades — and now I was; I became overwhelmed by the destructive yet casual inhumanity of the workplace.

Even being with my beloved Workers of the World (WoW) colleagues didn't help, because I would bring my ideas to them in hopes of finding stories about wonderful workplaces that I could write about, but we could only think of a few tiny instances. In many cases, we all felt depression and grief as we realized that emotionally well-regulated workplaces basically didn't exist unless we built them ourselves.

As I did my research for this book, I questioned myself constantly and gave up more than once; I thought I was being an ungrounded utopian thinker, even though I've created many emotionally well-regulated social structures and helped others build them as well. Luckily, I understand my emotions as aspects of genius, so I listened to them — the grief and depression, the anger and hatred, the anxiety and panic, the envy and jealousy, and the deep despair — and each time, I found ways to do solitary Conscious Complaining or talk with my husband, Tino Plank, who has been my rock and business partner for 27 years. Or, I'd have an Ethical Empathic Gossip (EEG) session with my right-hand colleague, Amanda Ball, whose fierce determination and emotional genius helped me create Dynamic Emotional Integration (DEI for short) as a licensing program. Tino and Amanda listened to my Conscious Complaining, my rage, my despair, my EEGs, and my hopes, and they created an emotionally well-regulated environment in which I could finally kick my way out of the hellscape of the modern workplace and say exactly what I came to say. I am grateful to them.

    I give many thanks to all the individuals and work groups I consulted with — for inviting me into their worlds and trusting me with their struggles, their communities, and their dreams for the future. I thank the many people whose stories combined to create Natalie and Mateo, and the many organizations I combined into the stories I tell throughout this book.

    I'm also grateful to the WoW members and our DEI community. Our meetings, I now see, were perfect in their sadness, grief, anger, hatred, sarcasm, and bitter tears, because these people and their emotions were telling me the truth and showing me the truth. Our WoW meetings helped to make this book deeper, more pointed, and more real. These licensed DEI professionals are (in alphabetical order): Jennifer Asdorian from Washington, D.C.; Pia Ault from Dubai, U.A.E.; Amanda Ball from California and Massachusetts; Annemiek Berkel from the Netherlands; Jeanette Brynn from Washington; Sheila Diggs from Maryland; Camilla Jørgensen from Copenhagen, Denmark; Marion Langford from Ontario, Canada; Bobbi McIntyre from South Carolina; Jennifer Nate from Alberta, Canada; Michael Perez from Florida; Tino Plank from California; and Andrea Watkins from Colorado.

    My editor at Sounds True, Haven Iverson, has been with me for four books now, and I truly enjoy writing with her as my first reader. Her feel for the written word is so empathic, precise, and funny that even in the midst of the struggles I had with this book, knowing that she would read these words made all the difference. Thank you, Haven. Thanks also for telling me the story of the closing of the warehouse, and for having Wendy Pardo fill me in on the details. Thanks, Wendy!

    Thanks also to the team at Sounds True for seeing the value in this book and supporting its production process: Tami Simon, Jaime Schwalb, and the acquisitions team; designers Jennifer Miles, Linsey Dodaro, and the art department; Leslie Brown, Evie Carrick, and the proofreading and indexing teams; production editor Jade Lascelles; Kira Roark and Wendy Gardner in marketing and publicity; and the dogs in the office (and at home during the pandemic) for keeping everyone properly herded.

Thanks to the researchers, educators, philosophers, sociologists, anthropologists, and social psychologists who studied the workplace and continually pointed to better and more humane ways to build and support democratic and naturally motivated working groups. Thanks to Alfie Kohn and Mary Jenkins for their valuable input on performance appraisals and bias, and thanks especially to the magnificent Arlie Hochschild for critiquing my explanations of her work and my own conceptualization of *empathy work*.

I'm also grateful to you for reading this book and joining me in envisioning ways to protect ourselves from the five-alarm fire of failure that the modern workplace has become. Thank you for feeling alongside me, for being willing to confront the problems and failures of our modern workplace, for envisioning a healthier future, and for making a welcoming space for the power and genius of emotions at work. Here's to the adventure of rebuilding our workplaces so that they *work* — for us, for our colleagues, for our customers and clients, for our communities, and for our entire struggling world. Thank you.

Take care and be well.

APPENDIX

The Emotional Vocabulary List[1]

I developed this vocabulary list to help people build strong and supple emotional vocabularies, not just for each emotion, but also for the differing levels of intensity in each emotion. Developing Empathic Accuracy with your emotions can help you increase your Emotion Regulation skills because you'll know what and how you're feeling.

When you know what you feel, you'll be able to access the gifts and skills that your emotions bring to you. And if you can identify the emotions of others with skill and empathy (always deferring to their own emotional autonomy and competence, of course), you can develop more robust empathic skills and deeper relationships. It all starts with your emotional vocabulary. Of course, there are many more words for emotional states than what I have here, but this is a great start.

Anger, Apathy, and Hatred
Soft Anger and Apathy
Annoyed ~ Apathetic ~ Bored ~ Certain ~ Cold ~ Crabby ~ Cranky ~ Critical ~ Cross ~ Detached ~ Displeased ~ Frustrated ~ Impatient ~ Indifferent ~ Irritated ~ Peeved ~ Rankled

Medium Anger
Affronted ~ Aggravated ~ Angry ~ Antagonized ~ Arrogant ~ Bristling ~ Exasperated ~ Incensed ~ Indignant ~ Inflamed ~ Mad ~ Offended ~ Resentful ~ Riled up ~ Sarcastic

Intense Anger and Hatred
Aggressive ~ Appalled ~ Belligerent ~ Bitter ~ Contemptuous ~ Disgusted ~ Furious ~ Hateful ~ Hostile ~ Irate ~ Livid ~ Menacing ~ Outraged ~ Ranting ~ Raving ~ Seething ~ Spiteful ~ Vengeful ~ Vicious ~ Vindictive ~ Violent

Shame and Guilt
Soft Shame and Guilt
Abashed ~ Awkward ~ Discomfited ~ Flushed ~ Flustered ~ Hesitant ~ Humble ~ Reticent ~ Self-Conscious ~ Speechless ~ Withdrawn

Medium Shame and Guilt
Ashamed ~ Chagrined ~ Contrite ~ Culpable ~ Embarrassed ~ Guilty ~ Humbled ~ Intimidated ~ Penitent ~ Regretful ~ Remorseful ~ Reproachful ~ Rueful ~ Sheepish

Intense Shame and Guilt
Belittled ~ Degraded ~ Demeaned ~ Disgraced ~ Guilt-Ridden ~ Guilt-Stricken ~ Humiliated ~ Mortified ~ Ostracized ~ Self-Condemning ~ Self-Flagellating ~ Shamefaced ~ Stigmatized

Fear, Anxiety, and Panic
Soft Fear and Anxiety
Alert ~ Apprehensive ~ Cautious ~ Concerned ~ Confused ~ Curious ~ Disconcerted ~ Disoriented ~ Disquieted ~ Doubtful ~ Edgy ~ Fidgety ~ Hesitant ~ Indecisive ~ Insecure ~ Instinctive ~ Intuitive ~ Leery ~ Pensive ~ Shy ~ Timid ~ Uneasy ~ Watchful

Medium Fear, Anxiety, and Panic
Afraid ~ Alarmed ~ Anxious ~ Aversive ~ Distrustful ~ Fearful ~ Jumpy ~ Nervous ~ Perturbed ~ Rattled ~ Shaky ~ Startled ~ Suspicious ~ Unnerved ~ Unsettled ~ Wary ~ Worried

Intense Fear and Panic
Filled with Dread ~ Horrified ~ Panicked ~ Paralyzed ~ Petrified ~ Phobic ~ Shocked ~ Terrorized

Jealousy and Envy
Soft Jealousy and Envy
Disbelieving ~ Distrustful ~ Insecure ~ Protective ~ Suspicious ~ Vulnerable

Medium Jealousy and Envy
Covetous ~ Demanding ~ Desirous ~ Envious ~ Jealous ~ Threatened

Intense Jealousy and Envy
Avaricious ~ Gluttonous ~ Grasping ~ Greedy ~ Green with Envy ~ Persistently Jealous ~ Possessive ~ Resentful

Happiness, Contentment, and Joy
Soft Happiness
Amused ~ Calm ~ Encouraged ~ Friendly ~ Hopeful ~ Inspired ~ Jovial ~ Open ~ Peaceful ~ Smiling ~ Upbeat

Medium Happiness and Contentment
Cheerful ~ Contented ~ Delighted ~ Excited ~ Fulfilled ~ Glad ~ Gleeful ~ Gratified ~ Happy ~ Healthy Self-Esteem ~ Joyful ~ Lively ~ Merry ~ Optimistic ~ Playful ~ Pleased ~ Proud ~ Rejuvenated ~ Satisfied

Intense Happiness, Contentment, and Joy
Awe-Filled ~ Blissful ~ Ecstatic ~ Egocentric ~ Elated ~ Enthralled ~ Euphoric ~ Exhilarated ~ Giddy ~ Jubilant ~ Manic ~ Overconfident ~ Overjoyed ~ Radiant ~ Rapturous ~ Self-Aggrandized ~ Thrilled

Sadness, Grief, and Depression
Soft Sadness
Contemplative ~ Disappointed ~ Disconnected ~ Distracted ~ Grounded ~ Listless ~ Low ~ Regretful ~ Steady ~ Wistful

Medium Sadness, Grief, and Depression

Dejected ~ Discouraged ~ Dispirited ~ Down ~ Downtrodden ~ Drained ~ Forlorn ~ Gloomy ~ Grieving ~ Heavy-Hearted ~ Melancholy ~ Mournful ~ Sad ~ Sorrowful ~ Weepy ~ World-Weary

Intense Sadness, Grief, and Depression

Anguished ~ Bereaved ~ Bleak ~ Depressed ~ Despairing ~ Despondent ~ Grief-Stricken ~ Heartbroken ~ Hopeless ~ Inconsolable ~ Morose

Depression and Suicidal Urges

Soft Depression and Suicidal Urges

Apathetic ~ Constantly Irritated, Angry, or Enraged (see the anger list above) ~ Depressed ~ Discouraged ~ Disinterested ~ Dispirited ~ Feeling Worthless ~ Flat ~ Helpless ~ Humorless ~ Impulsive ~ Indifferent ~ Isolated ~ Lethargic ~ Listless ~ Melancholy ~ Pessimistic ~ Purposeless ~ Withdrawn ~ World-Weary

Medium Depression and Suicidal Urges

Bereft ~ Crushed ~ Desolate ~ Despairing ~ Desperate ~ Drained ~ Empty ~ Fatalistic ~ Hopeless ~ Joyless ~ Miserable ~ Morbid ~ Overwhelmed ~ Passionless ~ Pleasureless ~ Sullen

Intense Suicidal Urges

Agonized ~ Anguished ~ Bleak ~ Death-Seeking ~ Devastated ~ Doomed ~ Gutted ~ Nihilistic ~ Numbed ~ Reckless ~ Self-Destructive ~ Suicidal ~ Tormented ~ Tortured

Note: If you're having any thoughts of suicide, don't feel as if you have to wait until you're in the throes of torment to reach out for help. If you can learn to catch your suicidal urges when they're in the soft stage, you can often stop yourself from falling into the pit of anguish. In the territory of the suicidal urge, your capacity for emotional awareness and sensitivity can literally save your life!

If you or anyone you know is feeling suicidal, free and confidential help is available. In the US, you can call the National Suicide Prevention Lifeline (NSPL) at 1-800-273-TALK (8255). For people living in other countries, the International Association for Suicide Prevention has a list of crisis and suicide prevention centers throughout the world. In Canada, see the Canadian Association for Suicide Prevention.

How to Be Helpful to Someone Who Is Threatening Suicide (from the NSPL website)

- Be direct. Talk openly and matter-of-factly about suicide.
- Be willing to listen. Allow expressions of feelings. Accept the feelings.
- Be non-judgmental.
- Don't debate whether suicide is right or wrong, or whether feelings are good or bad.
- Don't lecture on the value of life.
- Get involved. Become available. Show interest and support.
- Don't dare them to do it.
- Don't act shocked. This will put distance between you.
- Don't be sworn to secrecy. Seek support.
- Offer hope that alternatives are available but do not offer glib reassurance.
- Take action. Remove means, such as guns or stockpiled pills.
- Get help from people or agencies specializing in crisis intervention and suicide prevention.

Thank you for your concern and your willingness to reach out.

An Alternative Emotional Vocabulary List: Weasel Words!

If people don't seem able to identify or admit to their own emotions (or if they're bothered by the true names for emotions), you can use soft emotional vocabulary words from the Emotional Vocabulary List above, or you can use these Weasel Words below to gently bring awareness to the emotions.

Of course, you should frame your observations as questions (or use the phrase: "It seems that you might be feeling . . . ") in order to respect people's dignity, competence, and autonomy, but opening the conversation can help both of you develop better Emotion Recognition, Empathic Accuracy, relatedness, and emotional vocabulary.

This list starts with soft emotion words and then transitions into what I jokingly call the Weasels, then the Wonder Weasels (bad, stressed, unhappy) and Lesser Weasels (hurt, upset) if they're appropriate to each emotion. Also note the teen weasel word: *Whatever*!

Anger: Affronted, Agitated, Annoyed, Disappointed, Displeased, Frustrated, Peeved, Tense, Vexed, Whatever, Bad, Hurt, Stressed, Unhappy, Upset

Apathy and Boredom: Detached, Disinterested, Indifferent, Whatever, Unhappy

Shame and Guilt: Awkward, Bad, Demeaned, Exposed, Flustered, Humiliated, Hurt, Stressed, Unhappy, Upset

Sadness: Blue, Bummed, Disappointed, Discouraged, Down, Low, Whatever, Bad, Hurt, Stressed, Unhappy, Upset

Grief: Blue, Down in the Dumps, Lost, Low, Whatever, Bad, Hurt, Stressed, Unhappy, Upset

Depression: Blue, Detached, Disinterested, Low, Whatever, Bad, Hurt, Stressed, Unhappy, Upset

Fear: Cautious, Curious, Jumpy, Off, Uneasy, Unsettled, Stressed, Upset

Anxiety: Agitated, Bothered, Concerned, Jumpy, Off, Tense, Unsettled, Bad, Stressed, Unhappy, Upset

Jealousy: Insecure, Sensing Disloyalty, Stressed, Bad, Hurt, Unhappy, Upset

Envy: Insecure, Sensing Unfairness, Bad, Hurt, Stressed, Unhappy, Upset

Panic: Bothered, Cautious, Nervous, Uneasy, Stressed, Upset

Contentment: Fine, Good, Happy, Pleased, Proud, Satisfied

Notice that I don't include happiness or joy in this Weasel Words list because most people are fine saying those words outright. As you go through this list, however, notice how the five weaselly words (bad, hurt, stressed, unhappy, and upset) can describe pretty much every emotion except happiness, contentment, and joy. That's stunning, but it explains why so many of us struggle to develop our vocabularies or the empathic aspects of Emotion Recognition, Empathic Accuracy, and Emotion Regulation — because all of these skills are linked to a strong emotional vocabulary!

NOTES

Preface

1. "1918 Pandemic (H1N1 virus)." Centers for Disease Control and Prevention. From cdc.gov/flu/pandemic-resources/1918-pandemic-h1n1.html.

2. "Triangle Shirtwaist Factory fire." Wikipedia. From wikipedia.org/wiki/Triangle_Shirtwaist_Factory_fire.

   This clear retelling of the story explores the tragedy with dignity and a lack of sensationalism, and it includes the workplace protections that were developed in the aftermath of this deadly catastrophe.

3. "About One-in-Four US Hispanics Have Heard of Latinx, but Just 3% Use It" (August 11, 2020). Luis Noe-Bustamante, Lauren Mora, et al. Pew Research Center. From pewresearch.org/hispanic/2020/08/11/about-one-in-four-u-s-hispanics-have-heard-of-latinx-but-just-3-use-it.

   I'm using the term *Hispanic/Latinx* in this book with some reservations, because I know that the new term *Latinx* is gaining popularity. However, this term is not accepted within the community itself yet. In fact, many in the community prefer the descriptor Hispanic over Latino/Latina/Latinx, and many prefer to refer to themselves in relation to their or their families' countries of origin (i.e. Mexican, Cuban, San Salvadoran, Chilean). In a Pew Research Center study from 2020, only 24% of the community knew what the term Latinx referred to, while only 3% used Latinx to refer to themselves.

4. "Nurses say Kaiser not taking sufficient precautions with coronavirus" (March 19, 2020). John Fitzgerald Rodriguez. *San Francisco Examiner*. From sfexaminer.com/news-columnists/nurses-say-kaiser-not-taking-sufficient-precautions-with-coronavirus.

   "Coronavirus Pandemic: Bay Area Kaiser nurses protest lack of masks, medical supplies" (March 24, 2020). Kate Larsen. ABC 7 News. From abc7news.com/coronavirus-in-bay-area-cases-corona-virus-california/6044429.

   "This anesthesiologist was told to not wear a face mask amid COVID-19 crisis" (March 27, 2020). Ashley Hiruko. NPR's KUOW.org. From kuow.org/stories/swedish-caregivers-concerned-over-scarce-masks-leads-to.

"Amid medical protective gear shortage, nurses are suspended for refusing coronavirus care without N95 masks" (April 16, 2020). Martha Mendoza, Kimberlee Kruesi, and The Associated Press. Fortune. From fortune.com /2020/04/16/protective-gear-shortage-nurses-suspended-coronavirus -n95-masks.

5. I know this because I am an In-Home Supportive Services worker for a disabled family member.

6. "COVID-19 Crisis Presents Especially Tough Challenges for Home Care Workers" (March 31, 2020). David Myles. AFSCME. From afscme.org/blog /covid-19-crisis-presents-especially-tough-challenges-for-home-care-workers.

"San Diego home care providers are fighting for personal protective equipment" (April 23, 2020). Abbie Alford. CBS KFMB 8. From cbs8.com /article/news/local/san-diego-home-care-providers-are-fighting-for-personal -protective-equipment/509-2294db63-1c95-4970-a7dd-32ec4614188f.

7. "Mandates of the Special Rapporteur on contemporary forms of racism, racial discrimination, xenophobia and related intolerance" (August 12, 2020). Palais Des Nations. From spcommreports.ohchr.org/TMResultsBase /DownLoadPublicCommunicationFile?gId=25476.

Introduction: The Great Migration

1. "Mind the Workplace" (2017). M. Hellebuyck, T. Nguyen, et al. Mental Health America & Faas Foundation. From mhanational.org/sites/default/files /Mind%20the%20Workplace%20-%20MHA%20Workplace%20Health%20 Survey%202017%20FINAL%209.13.pdf.

2. "An Exploratory Study of Employee Silence: Issues that Employees Don't Communicate Upward and Why" (2003). F. J. Milliken, E. W. Morrison, et al. *Journal of Management Studies*, 40(6), 1453–1476. From onlinelibrary.wiley .com/doi/abs/10.1111/1467-6486.00387.

3. "2021 WBI U.S. Workplace Bullying Survey." From workplacebullying .org/2021-wbi-survey/.

4. "State of the Global Workplace" (2017). Gallup. From gallup.com /workplace/238079/state-global-workplace-2017.aspx.

5. "State of the Global Workplace" (2017). Gallup. From gallup.com /workplace/238079/state-global-workplace-2017.aspx.

Gallup estimated in 2017 that in the US alone, the financial losses caused by miserable workplaces ranged from $483 billion to $605 billion per year. Gallup explains this differently than I do—they identify disengaged employees as the source of the losses instead of locating the losses properly in the miserable and inhospitable workplaces that cause disengagement.

6. "The US ranks worse than these major economies for systematic violation of workers' rights, according to a new report" (June 18, 2020). Anagha Srikanth. The Hill. From thehill.com/changing-america/respect/equality/503472-the-us -ranks-worse-than-these-major-economies-for-workers.

Developing humane and emotionally well-regulated workplaces is especially crucial for US workers; this 2020 study ranked the US as one of the worst countries in the world for worker protections and labor rights.

7. My four businesses: I began my career as a professional writer in 1985; I started my publishing company, Laughing Tree Press, in 1997; I founded Emotion Dynamics LLC in 2014; and I created the online learning community empathyacademy.org in 2015. My colleagues and I teach courses about emotions and empathy, and we administer a 14-month online licensing program in my applied work, Dynamic Emotional Integration.

8. I grew up in the working class and had no financial support, so starting my own businesses often meant being poor while I poured everything into them. It also meant that I did not receive benefits, health insurance, or contributions into retirement or Social Security. Life would have been much easier and more financially stable for me if I had ever found a workplace that was worth my time or energy.

9. "The impact of work environment on mood disorders and suicide: Evidence and implications" (2008). Jong-Min Woo, Teodor T. Postolache. *International Journal on Disability and Human Development*, IJDHD 7(2), 185. From ncbi. nlm.nih.gov/pmc/articles/PMC2559945.

10. "The Relationship Between Workplace Stressors and Mortality and Health Costs in the US" (2016). J. Goh, J. Pfeffer, et al. *Management Science*, 62(2), 608–628. From gsb.stanford.edu/faculty-research/publications/relationship -between-workplace-stressors-mortality-health-costs-united.

This 2016 Stanford University study focuses on common workplace stressors, including lack of health insurance, job insecurity, work-family conflict, low job control, high job demands, low social support at work, and low organizational justice. It finds that more than 120,000 deaths per year and approximately 5% to 8% of annual healthcare costs may be attributable to how US companies mismanage their workforce. These results suggest that management practices are important (and detrimental) contributors to morbidity and mortality in the US.

11. *The Corporate Culture Survival Guide* (1999). Edgar Schein. San Francisco, CA: Jossey-Bass.

Chapter 1: Five Foundational Models to Help You Access the Power of Emotions

1. *How Emotions Are Made: The Secret Life of the Brain* (2017). Lisa Feldman Barrett. Boston, MA: Houghton Mifflin Harcourt.

2. "Unpacking Emotion Differentiation: Transforming Unpleasant Experience by Perceiving Distinctions in Negativity" (2015). T. B. Kashdan, L. Feldman Barrett, et al. *Current Directions in Psychological Science*, 24(1), 10–16. From journals.sagepub.com/doi/abs/10.1177/0963721414550708.

   How Emotions Are Made: The Secret Life of the Brain (2017). Lisa Feldman Barrett. Boston, MA: Houghton Mifflin Harcourt.

3. *Born for Love: Why Empathy Is Essential — and Endangered* (2010). Bruce Perry and Maia Szalavitz. New York: William Morrow.

   Bruce Perry's groundbreaking work with traumatized children has helped him understand how vital warm connections are to human development, and how even in the most traumatizing situations, warm and caring connections can help traumatized children survive and thrive.

4. "The Bonus Effect: One Kind of Interest that Rewards Don't Kill" (September 27, 2016). Alfie Kohn. From alfiekohn.org/blogs/bonus.

5. "Self-determination theory and the facilitation of intrinsic motivation, social development, and well-being" (2000). R.M. Ryan and E. L. Deci. *American Psychologist*, 55(1), 68. From psycnet.apa.org/record/2000-13324-007.

   Thanks to WoW member Camilla Jørgensen (from the relative worker's paradise of Denmark) for reminding me about Deci and Ryan!

6. "Understanding contemporary forms of exploitation: Attributions of passion serve to legitimize the poor treatment of workers" (2019). J. Y. Kim, T. H.

Campbell, et al. *Journal of Personality and Social Psychology*, 118(1), 121–148. From psycnet.apa.org/record/2019-21488-001.

Exploiting passionate workers is a mirror image of discarding disengaged workers; both are signs of a lack of human regard in emotionally unregulated environments..

7. *No Contest: The Case Against Competition* (1992). Alfie Kohn. Boston, MA: Houghton Mifflin Harcourt.

Punished by Rewards: The Trouble with Gold Stars, Incentive Plans, A's, Praise, and Other Bribes (1999). Alfie Kohn. Boston, MA: Mariner Books.

8. *Abolishing Performance Appraisals: Why They Backfire and What to Do Instead* (2002). Mary Jenkins, Tom Coens. San Francisco, CA: Berrett-Koehler Publishers.

This book offers an in-depth exploration of why performance appraisals are time-wasting, demotivating failures, and what smart organizations are doing instead.

9. "Standardized Testing and Its Victims" (September 27, 2000). Alfie Kohn. From alfiekohn.org/article/standardized-testing-victims.

10. "Narcissistic Personality Disorder" (May 16, 2018). Sheenie Ambardar. Medscape. From emedicine.medscape.com/article/1519417-overview#a5.

Narcissistic people tend to do well in hierarchies and competitions—employee of the month, best this or that—where superiority and winning are the focus. Competitive workplaces, hierarchies, bureaucracies, ladders of success, contests, grades, and performance appraisals often (inadvertently) create an atmosphere that selects for and rewards narcissism. It's why you find narcissistic people at the head of divisions or organizations—the competitive atmosphere creates a world in which they flourish. Because of the way we've set things up, the top is a healing place for them; you'll find narcissistic people at the top in many places. Narcissistic personality disorder (NPD) is found in less than 1% of the population, but in 20% of military personnel, and 17% of first-year med students. Some people suggest 50% of CEOs have narcissistic tendencies or even NPD. Extreme hierarchies and competition attract, reward, and preferentially select for narcissistic behavior and NPD because superiority requires inferiors and a lack of healthy relatedness.

11. "Relationships between medical student burnout, empathy, and professionalism climate" (2010). C. M. Brazeau, R. Schroeder, et al. *Academic Medicine*, 85(10), S33–S36. From pubmed.ncbi.nlm.nih.gov/20881699.

    "Empathic Communication as a 'Risky Strength' for Health During the COVID-19 Pandemic: The Case of Frontline Italian Healthcare Workers" (2020). Serena Barello, Lorenzo Palamenghi, et al. *Patient Education and Counseling*. From ncbi.nlm.nih.gov/pmc/articles/PMC7313503.

12. "1 in 4 First Year Residents May Meet Criteria for Clinical Depression" (August 12, 2016). Kara Gavin. Univeristy of Michigan Health Lab. From labblog .uofmhealth.org/med-u/1-4-first-year-residents-may-meet-criteria-for-clinical -depression.

    "Residency Program Factors Associated with Depressive Symptoms in Internal Medicine Interns: A Prospective Cohort Study" (June 2019). Karina Pereira-Lima, Rahael R. Gupta, et al. *Academic Medicine*, 94(6): 869–875. From ncbi.nlm.nih.gov/pmc/articles/PMC6538448.

    "Suicide among physicians and healthcare workers: A systematic review and meta-analysis" (December 12, 2019). Frédéric Dutheil, Claire Aubert, et al. *PLoS One*, 14(12), e0226361. From ncbi.nlm.nih.gov/pmc/articles/PMC6907772.

13. Because empathy is an emotional skill, any situation that impacts a child's ability to identify or understand emotions will also impact their empathy development; however, everyone is empathic, and emotional and empathic skills can be developed and honed at any stage of life.

Chapter 2: Five Models and Two Studies: The Power of Emotions at Work

1. *The Managed Heart: Commercialization of Human Feeling* (updated, 2012). Arlie Hochschild. Berkeley, CA: University of California Press.

2. *Stigma: Notes on the Management of Spoiled Identity* (reissue ed., 1986). Erving Goffman. New York, NY: Simon and Schuster.

3. *Born for Love: Why Empathy Is Essential—and Endangered* (reprint ed., 2011). Bruce D. Perry, Maia Szalavitz. New York, NY: HarperCollins.

    The Boy Who Was Raised As a Dog: And Other Stories from a Child Psychiatrist's Notebook—What Traumatized Children Can Teach Us About Loss, Love, and Healing (3rd ed., 2017). Bruce D. Perry, Maia Szalavitz. New York, NY: Basic Books.

These books by child development psychiatrist Perry (with Szalavitz) offer excellent discussions of how children develop empathy, and what can be done when empathy has been impeded.

4. DEI professional and Workers of the World member Marion Langford is a workplace consultant who introduces the idea of the "non-smoking smoke break" in her workshops on self-care. She wrote: "If I have smokers in the room, it's helpful, because they will talk about what it means to go outside and just chat about anything with another smoker. Smokers do not spend their break on their phones or at their desks. They change their environment. Often there is an exchange of important and helpful gossip about work and/or their lives. There is a strong bond that develops with smokers, and they are often better informed about what's happening in other places in the workplace. So, I say to people, take your smoke breaks! This usually gets them nodding and grinning, and now that we know about the concept of the fika break [see chapter 6], there's a healthy option for smokers and non-smokers."

5. "Narcissistic Personality Disorder" (May 16, 2018). Sheenie Ambardar. Medscape. From emedicine.medscape.com/article/1519417-overview#a5.

6. "Rethinking Hierarchy in the Workplace" (September 5, 2017). Dylan Walsh. Stanford Graduate School of Business. From gsb.stanford.edu/insights /rethinking-hierarchy-workplace.

   Also, see Edgar Schein's books in the recommended resources section, especially *Humble Leadership*.

7. "Employee Tenure Summary" (2020). U.S. Bureau of Labor Statistics. From bls .gov/news.release/tenure.nr0.htm.

8. "Managing Without Managers" (September-October, 1989). Ricardo Semler. *Harvard Business Review*. From hbr.org/1989/09/managing-without-managers.

   "Innovation Democracy: W.L. Gore's Original Management Model" (September 23, 2010). Management Innovation eXchange. From managementexchange.com /story/innovation-democracy-wl-gores-original-management-model.

   It's important to note that both Semler and Gore created their respect-based and humanitarian workplaces themselves, based on what their workers and their unique organizations required. These weren't things they learned about in MBA programs; these are examples of truly empathic workplace design.

9. See educator Alfie Kohn's books in the recommended resources section.

10. People who grow up in churches may have a clearer idea about how to work in large-group environments, and they may have seen adults work together effectively toward a common goal. Unless, of course, those church groups are based on a hierarchical, top-down model of obedience.

11. "Teaching For Learning" (February 20, 1969). Martin M. Broadwell. *The Gospel Guardian*. From wordsfitlyspoken.org/gospel_guardian/v20/v20n41p1-3a.html.

    "Four stages of competence" Wikipedia. From en.wikipedia.org/wiki/Four _stages_of_competence.

    This consciousness and competence model was first mentioned by educator Martin M. Broadwell in 1969 where he applied the model to the competence level of teachers. Later, in the 1970s, Noel Burch at Gordon Training International further developed the concept and applied it to learners.

Chapter 3: Identifying Emotional Labor and Empathic Workloads

1. Thanks to DEI student Catherine Wohlin for connecting me to the excellent Workplace Bullying Resources in the recommended resources section.

2. "The Concept Creep of 'Emotional Labor'" (November 26, 2018). Julie Beck. *The Atlantic*. From theatlantic.com/family/archive/2018/11/arlie-hochschild -housework-isnt-emotional-labor/576637.

    Arlie Hochschild has been concerned about the "concept creep" that has occurred in regard to emotional labor, where people are calling family activities such as making school lunches for their children "emotional labor." This interview clarifies her terms, and Hochschild warns about this loss of specificity and clarity, because the burden of housework that falls primarily on women may be a sign of systemic issues of economic and sexual inequality rather than solely a situation of unequal emotional labor.

3. Having my own business gives me a kind of freedom, but it's also very precarious. Failure is common (the US Bureau of Labor Statistics reports that 66% of small businesses fail within the first 10 years), and self-employed people aren't protected, insured, or supported by anyone but themselves. I'm glad I have my own businesses, but being self-employed is not a walk in the park. For instance, I rely on my husband Tino's corporate job for my health insurance because the insurance rates for self-employed people are astronomical.

4. For simplicity's sake, non-dominant groups in the US (and elsewhere) are any groups that are not White, able-bodied, Christian, heterosexual males. This is clearly too simplistic, because even these men can be unwanted and non-dominant outsiders depending on the social context. However, if you look at which groups are usually excluded or treated as outsiders, this definition of dominance holds true. And while no individual male has created these systems of racism, ableism, religious intolerance, sexism, heterocentrism, and dominance, their very dominance gives them a voice and a level of power that can cause suffering if they are unaware. On the other hand, if they *are* aware, they can use their power to dismantle these systems of dominance, prejudice, and exclusion. May we all use whatever power, dominance, or privilege we have for the good of all.

5. "The Development of a Community and Its Culture" (January, 2005). Jim Sinclair. Autism Network International. From autreat.com/History_of_ANI.html.

   A note about using the word *Autistic* to describe Jim (this is Jim's preference): In many areas of the Autistic and neurodiversity communities, identity-first language is preferred over person-first language (*Autistic person* instead of "person with autism"). Person-first language is avoided by many disabled people. See this interview with Jim for a deeper understanding of the troubling implications of person-first language: "Interview with Jim Sinclair." Michael Ellermann. The Autism and Asperger Association. From autism.se/RFA/uploads/nedladningsbara%20filer/Interview_with_Jim_Sinclair.pdf.

6. *The Color of Law: A Forgotten History of How Our Government Segregated America* (2017). Richard Rothstein. New York, NY: Liveright Publishing Corporation.

   For instance, Richard Rothstein uncovers decades of legal statutes and actions that impede or stop African Americans from obtaining jobs, bank accounts, mortgages, and the right to purchase or keep their homes in the US. These exclusionary practices have been used against many other groups throughout US history.

7. "How to Be a Privilege Traitor." Karla McLaren. From karlamclaren.com/how-to-be-a-privilege-traitor.

   "How to Support Antiracism in Yourself and the World." Karla McLaren. From karlamclaren.com/how-to-support-antiracism-in-yourself-and-the-world.

Chapter 4: Is Your Emotion Work Nourishing or Draining?

1. "Why Shrinks Have Problems" (1997, reviewed on June 9, 2016). Robert Epstein. Psychology Today. From psychologytoday.com/us/articles/199707 /why-shrinks-have-problems.

"Suicide Risk in Nurses Higher Than General Population" (July 12, 2019). Shannon Firth. MedPage Today. From medpagetoday.com/nursing/nursing/81003.

"Suicide among physicians and healthcare workers: A systematic review and meta-analysis" (December 12, 2019). Frédéric Dutheil, Claire Aubert, et al. *PLoS One*, 14(12), e0226361. From ncbi.nlm.nih.gov/pmc/articles/PMC6907772.

Chapter 5: Creating Communication Workflows for Everyday Emotional Issues

1. "Privacy, Please: Open Office Plans Are Terrible for Workers, So Why Do They Persist?" (January 21, 2019). Alison Green. Slate. From slate.com/human -interest/2019/01/jobs-workplace-privacy-open-offices-cubicles.html.
2. Thanks to licensed DEI trainer Dariusz Klupi from Poland for telling me about The Failure Institute.
3. "An Exploratory Study of Employee Silence: Issues that Employees Don't Communicate Upward and Why" (2003). F. J. Milliken, E. W. Morrison, et al. *Journal of Management Studies*, 40(6), 1453–1476. From onlinelibrary.wiley .com/doi/abs/10.1111/1467-6486.00387.

As a reminder, 85% of workers have avoided communicating serious problems upward, partly due to toxic positivity biases, and partly due to a lack of social or emotional awareness in their workplaces.
4. *The Language of Emotions: What Your Feelings Are Trying to Tell You* (2010). Karla McLaren. Boulder, CO: Sounds True.
5. *The Art of Empathy: A Complete Guide to Life's Most Essential Skill* (2013). Karla McLaren. Boulder, CO: Sounds True.
6. "When You're the Person Your Colleagues Always Vent To" (November 30, 2016). Sandra L. Robinson and Kira Schabram. *Harvard Business Review*. From hbr.org/2016/11/when-youre-the-person-your-colleagues-always-vent-to.

Robinson and Schabram have found that being the go-to person for everyone else's complaints can cause psychological and physical pain and distress.

7. Sheila Diggs learned from her teacher Julio Olalla from the Newfield Network that people often confuse an expectation with a commitment. She notes: "If someone doesn't fulfill an articulated and agreed-upon commitment, we have the right to complain that they have broken their promise. An unexpressed expectation is not a request and no commitment has been made . . . it is just something in our head that we want but haven't articulated. We often become disappointed if the expectation isn't met, yet we haven't actually made a request of another person about what is wanted, nor has anyone agreed to commit to our request. We make ourselves more powerful by stating a request openly rather than leaving it in the form of an unarticulated expectation."

8. *The Art of Empathy: A Complete Guide to Life's Most Essential Skill* (2013). Karla McLaren. Boulder, CO: Sounds True.

Chapter 6: Good Fences, Clear Boundaries, and Repair Stations

1. "Slanted Toilets Are the Logical Extreme of Hyperproductivity" (December 19, 2019). Joe Pinsker. *The Atlantic*. From theatlantic.com/health/archive/2019/12/slanted-toilet-standardtoilet-productivity/603898.

2. "Can 'phone booths' solve the problem of open-plan offices?" (August 9, 2019). Jessica Gross. BBC. From bbc.com/worklife/article/20190802-can-phone-booths-solve-privacy-issues-in-open-plan-offices.

3. "Even the Pandemic Can't Kill the Open-Plan Office" (May 14, 2020). Sarah Holder. Bloomberg CityLab. From citylab.com/life/2020/05/open-office-design-coronavirus-risk-safe-workplace-health/611299.

4. "Interrogating Normal: Autism Social Skills Training at the Margins of a Social Fiction" (2014). Karla McLaren. Sonoma State University. From sonoma-dspace.calstate.edu/bitstream/handle/10211.3/138418/McLarenK_Thesis.pdf.

5. "The Open Classroom" (updated July 6, 2006). Education Next. From educationnext.org/theopenclassroom.

6. "Noise in open plan classrooms in primary schools: A review" (2010). Bridget Shield, Emma Greenland, et al. *Noise and Health*, 12(49), 225–234. From noiseandhealth.org/article.asp?issn=1463-1741;year=2010;volume=12;issue=49;spage=225;epage=234;aulast=Shield.

7. "The impact of the 'open' workspace on human collaboration" (July 2, 2018). Ethan S. Bernstein, Stephen Turban. *The Royal Society Publishing*. From doi .org/10.1098/rstb.2017.0239.

8. "Why open offices are bad for us" (January 11, 2017). Bryan Borzykowski. BBC. From bbc.com/worklife/article/20170105-open-offices-are-damaging -our-memories.

9. Thanks to the late Jon Magoon, who taught this N/3 process in his excellent course on meeting management at Santa Rosa Junior College.

10. "How Do Work Breaks Help Your Brain? 5 Surprising Answers" (April 18, 2017). Meg Selig. Psychology Today. From psychologytoday.com/us/blog /changepower/201704/how-do-work-breaks-help-your-brain-5-surprising-answers.

11. *On the Clock: What Low-Wage Work Did to Me and How It Drives America Insane* (2019). Emily Guendelsberger. New York, NY: Little, Brown and Company.

    For a wild ride through the hellscape of low-wage work in the US and its authoritarian adherence to break times, read this book by Guendelsberger, who worked at an Amazon shipping warehouse, a call center, and McDonald's as she researched her book. You will never treat any low-wage worker, essential worker, or customer service rep badly again, and you will likely never order anything from Amazon again either. This is essential reading for anyone interested in justice, equality, and human rights in the workplace.

12. "It's time to put the tired Spanish siesta stereotype to bed" (June 11, 2017). Jessica Jones. BBC. From bbc.com/worklife/article/20170609-its-time-to-put -the-tired-spanish-siesta-stereotype-to-bed.

13. There's a marvelous short video series about fika online at tohave.coffee.

14. "'Banana time': Job satisfaction and informal interaction" (1959). Donald Roy. *Human Organization*, 18(4), 158–168. From doi.org/10.17730humo.18.4 .07j88hr1p4074605.

15. "There's an optimal way to structure your day—and it's not the 8-hour workday" (March 4, 2019). Travis Bradberry. Quartz. From qz.com /work/1561830/why-the-eight-hour-workday-doesnt-work.

16. "How Resting More Can Boost Your Productivity" (May 11, 2017). Alex Soojung-Kim Pang. *Greater Good Magazine*. From greatergood.berkeley.edu /article/item/how_resting_more_can_boost_your_productivity.

17. *McMindfulness: How Mindfulness Became the New Capitalist Spirituality* (2019). Ronald Purser. London, England: Repeater.

I've been concerned about the ways that mindfulness has inserted itself into our schools and our workplaces, because many forms of meditation have a troubling and controlling relationship to emotions. I've also been wary because meditation can produce powerful effects (for good and bad), and I don't like to see it being enforced from the top down—especially in captive audiences of school children and workers. Mindfulness can be helpful, but people need to choose it freely rather than have it forced on them as a workplace practice.

The powerful book by Purser, a Buddhist teacher, critiques the commercialization of stripped-down mindfulness as a way to teach children and workers to control their normal emotional responses and calm themselves rather than learn how to listen to and heed the genius in their emotional responses. In a very real way, this commercialized mindfulness training transfers the responsibility for dealing with workplace or schoolday suffering onto the people with the least power so that no one will be able to question why the suffering exists (and why it's allowed to go unchallenged). If corporate mindfulness programs are used to enforce an artificial calm and a toxic positivity bias, it will likely silence workers and send their necessary emotions into the shadows.

Again, if you love to meditate and it really helps you, then by all means use it as a break for yourself. But if meditation or mindfulness are being enforced from above, you may be in an emotionally unregulated social structure that's controlling its workers' emotions rather than learning how to listen to and support them.

18. "Is modern mindfulness a corporate scam? This management professor thinks so" (August 22, 2019). Rina Raphael. Fast Company. From fastcompany.com/90392141/is-modern-mindfulness-a-corporate-scam-a-critique-of-meditation-culture.

19. "Mind the Hype: A Critical Evaluation and Prescriptive Agenda for Research on Mindfulness and Meditation" (January, 2018). Nicholas T. Van Dam, Marieke K. van Vugt, et al. *Perspectives on Psychological Science*, 13(1), 36–61. From pubmed.ncbi.nlm.nih.gov/29016274.

This 2018 study critiques the hyped-up research basis for many of the claims of the corporate mindfulness industry.

20. "Why performance appraisals need to be scrapped" (February 22, 2014). Ray Williams. Financial Post. From financialpost.com/executive/careers/why -performance-appraisals-need-to-be-scrapped.

Chapter 7: When Emotions Are Your Vital Professional Tools

1. Sadly, my consultation process was treated as one of these fads, and I learned a lot about how much abuse workers undergo when they're used as guinea pigs in shiny new workplace processes dreamed up by outsiders. My empathic workplace consultation processes don't enforce change from the outside or from the top down, but this group couldn't have known that. A lot of the preparatory work I did with them involved establishing trust that had been broken by a previous workplace consultant. This consultant had forced two group members to expose their interpersonal conflicts in a public meeting with the group, and they were counseled, Dr. Phil-style, in front of everyone. This kind of abusive consulting story is not unusual; workplace consulting is a completely unregulated, Wild West kind of world where anything goes. I hesitated to add more processes to their working lives, because I knew that I was just one person in an ever-revolving series of outsiders who would be brought in to manhandle this group. I worked with them very gingerly and carefully and hoped with all my heart that the tools I brought to them might help, and might last for more than a few months.

2. *Embracing Anxiety: How to Access the Genius of This Vital Emotion* (2020). Karla McLaren. Boulder, CO: Sounds True.

    This list is excerpted from pages 190–192.

3. *The Sleep Solution: Why Your Sleep is Broken and How to Fix It* (2017). W. Chris Winter. New York, NY: New American Library.

    This is an excellent and anxiety-supporting book by Winter, a sleep expert who won't scare you about your troubled sleep.

4. My mother went into hospice when she had 6 months left to live, and the shift to helping her deal appropriately with chronic pain (and her inability to eat or exercise because of it) improved her condition so much that she got kicked off

of hospice — twice! Returning to regular medical care reliably brought back her symptoms until she deteriorated and qualified for hospice again, but it was still worth the upheavals. By focusing on the reality of death and making my mom's life flow more smoothly, hospice gave her — and us — another 2 years of comfortable and meaningful end-of-life process.

5. *The Sleep Solution: Why Your Sleep is Broken and How to Fix It* (2017). W. Chris Winter. New York, NY: New American Library.

Chapter 8: Nurturing Your Emotionally Well-Regulated Organization

1. "The affective foundations of high-reliability organizing" (2014). T. J. Vogus, N.B. Rothman, et al. *Journal of Organizational Behavior*, 35(4), 592–596. From psycnet.apa.org/record/2014-14136-008.

Appendix

1. *The Art of Empathy: A Complete Guide to Life's Most Essential Skill* (2013). Karla McLaren. Boulder, CO: Sounds True.

   This list was developed for my website in 2010 and appeared in print in this book.

RECOMMENDED RESOURCES

On Emotional Awareness and Regulation

Embracing Anxiety: How to Access the Genius of This Vital Emotion (2020).
Karla McLaren. Boulder, CO: Sounds True.

Emotion: The Science of Sentiment (2002). Dylan Evans. New York, NY:
Oxford University Press.

Emotional Flow Online Course (2012). Karla McLaren. Boulder, CO:
Sounds True.

Happiness: The Science behind Your Smile (2006). Daniel Nettle. New
York, NY: Oxford University Press.

How Emotions Are Made: The Secret Life of the Brain (2017). Lisa
Feldman Barrett. New York, NY: Houghton Mifflin Harcourt.

*Meeting Your Shadow: The Hidden Power of the Dark Side of Human
Nature* (1991). Connie Zweig and Jeremiah Abrams (eds). New York,
NY: Tarcher Putnam.

The Dynamic Emotional Integration® Workbook (2018). Karla McLaren.
Windsor, CA: Laughing Tree Press.

The Gift of Fear: Survival Signals that Protect Us from Violence (1997).
Gavin deBecker. Boston, MA: Little, Brown and Company.

The Happiness Myth: The Historical Antidote to What Isn't Working Today
(2007). Jennifer Michael Hecht. New York, NY: HarperOne.

The Language of Emotions: What Your Feelings Are Trying to Tell You
(2010). Karla McLaren. Boulder, CO: Sounds True.

The Scapegoat Complex: Toward a Mythology of Shadow and Guilt (1983).
Sylvia Brinton Perera. Toronto, Ontario: Inner City Books.

The Sleep Solution: Why Your Sleep is Broken and How to Fix It (2017). W. Chris Winter. New York, NY: New American Library.

What Motivates Getting Things Done: Procrastination, Emotions, and Success (2017). Mary Lamia. Lanham, MD: Rowman & Littlefield.

On Communication

Taking the War Out of Our Words: The Art of Powerful Non-Defensive Communication (2008). Sharon Ellison. Deadwood, OR: Wyatt-McKenzie Publishing.

Talk to Me: What Educators (and Others) Can Learn About De-Escalation from Hostage Negotiators (2019). Emma Van Der Klift. Victoria, BC: Tellwell.

The Art of Empathy: A Complete Guide to Life's Most Essential Skill (2013). Karla McLaren. Boulder, CO: Sounds True.

The Art of Gathering: How We Meet and Why It Matters (2018). Priya Parker. New York, NY: Penguin Random House.

Why Won't You Apologize? Healing Big Betrayals and Everyday Hurts (2017). Harriet Lerner. New York, NY: Gallery Books.

Wishcraft: How to Get What you Really Want (1997). Barbara Sher with Annie Gottlieb. New York, NY: Ballantine.

On Empathy and Emotional Labor

Born for Love: Why Empathy Is Essential — and Endangered (2010). Bruce Perry and Maia Szalavitz. New York, NY: William Morrow.

The Art of Empathy: A Complete Guide to Life's Most Essential Skill (2013). Karla McLaren. Boulder, CO: Sounds True.

The Managed Heart: Commercialization of Human Feeling, Twentieth Anniversary Edition (2003). Arlie Russell Hochschild. Berkeley, CA: University of California Press.

On Equality, Justice, and Antiracism

An Indigenous Peoples' History of the US (2015). Roxanne Dunbar-Ortiz. Boston, MA: Beacon Press.

Emergent Strategy: Shaping Change, Changing Worlds (2017). Adrienne Maree Brown. Edinburgh, Scotland: AK Press.

Erasing Institutional Bias: How to Create Systemic Change for Organizational Inclusion (2018). Tiffany Jana and Ashely Diaz Mejias. Oakland, CA: Berrett-Koehler Publishers.

How to Be an Antiracist (2019). Ibram X. Kendi. New York, NY: One World.

My Grandmother's Hands: Racialized Trauma and the Pathway to Mending Our Hearts and Bodies (2017). Resmaa Menakem. Las Vegas, NV: Central Recovery Press.

Nickel and Dimed: On (Not) Getting by in America (2001). Barbara Ehrenreich. New York, NY: Henry Holt and Company.

No Contest: The Case Against Competition (Why We Lose in Our Race to Win) (1992). Alfie Kohn. 20th Anniversary Edition. New York, NY: Houghton Mifflin.

On the Clock: What Low-Wage Work Did to Me and How It Drives America Insane (2019). Emily Guendelsberger. New York, NY: Little, Brown and Company.

Reel Bad Arabs: How Hollywood Vilifies a People (2001). Jack G. Shaheen. Northampton, MA: Interlink Publishing Group.

So You Want to Talk About Race (2018). Ijeoma Oluo. New York, NY: Seal Press.

Stamped from the Beginning: The Definitive History of Racist Ideas in America (2016). Ibram X. Kendi. New York, NY: Bold Type Press.

Subtle Acts of Exclusion: How to Understand, Identify, and Stop Microaggressions (2020). Tiffany Jana and Michael Baran. Oakland, CA: Berrett-Koehler Publishers.

The Color of Law: A Forgotten History of How Our Government Segregated America (2017). Richard Rothstein. New York, NY: Liveright Publishing Corporation.

The Making of Asian America: A History (2016). Erika Lee. New York, NY: Simon and Schuster.

Winners Take All: The Elite Charade of Changing the World (2018). Anand Giridharadas. New York, NY: Alfred A. Knopf.

On the Workplace

Abolishing Performance Appraisals: Why They Backfire and What to Do Instead (2002). Tom Coens and Mary Jenkins. San Francisco, CA: Berrett-Koehler Publishers.

Coming Up Short: Working-Class Adulthood in an Age of Uncertainty (2013). Jennifer M. Silva. New York, NY: Oxford University Press.

Effective Behavior in Organizations: Cases, Concepts, and Student Experiences (2000). Allan R. Cohen. New York: McGraw-Hill Education.

Human Resource Management (2015). R. Wayne Dean Mondy and Joseph J. Martocchio. Upper Saddle River, NJ: Pearson Education.

Humble Consulting: How to Provide Real Help Faster (2016). Edgar H. Schein. Oakland, CA: Berrett-Koehler Publishers.

Humble Leadership: The Power of Relationships, Openness, and Trust (The Humble Leadership Series) (2018). Edgar H. Schein and Peter A. Schein. Oakland, CA: Berrett-Koehler Publishers.

McMindfulness: How Mindfulness Became the New Capitalist Spirituality (2019). Ronald E. Purser. London, UK: Repeater Books.

Nickel and Dimed: On (Not) Getting by in America (2001). Barbara Ehrenreich. New York, NY: Henry Holt and Company.

On the Clock: What Low-Wage Work Did to Me and How It Drives America Insane (2019). Emily Guendelsberger. New York, NY: Little, Brown and Company.

Organizational Culture and Leadership, 5th Edition (2017). Edgar Schein with Peter Schein. Hoboken, NJ: Wiley.

Parcival's Briefcase: Six Practices and a New Philosophy for Healthy Organizational Change (1993). Tony Smith. San Francisco, CA: Chronicle Books.

Productive Workplaces Revisited: Dignity, Meaning, and Community in the 21st Century (2004). Marvin R. Weisbord. Hoboken, NJ: Pfeiffer Publishing.

Punished by Rewards: The Trouble with Gold Stars, Incentive Plans, A's, Praise, and Other Bribes (2018). Alfie Kohn. 25th Anniversary Edition. Boston, MA: Mariner Books.

The Corporate Culture Survival Guide (2019). Edgar H. Schein and Peter A. Schein. Hoboken, NJ: Wiley.

The Cultural Study of Work (2003). Douglas Harper and Helene M. Lawson. Lanham, MD: Rowman & Littlefield Publishers.

Working: Sociological Perspectives (1998). Robert A. Rothman. Upper Saddle River, NJ: Pearson Education.

Workplace Bullying Resources

The Workplace Bullying Institute was founded by psychologists Ruth Namie and Gary Namie, and offers resources, research, support, and expert witnesses for victims of workplace bullying in the US. Online at workplacebullying.org.

The American Psychological Association has a resource page about bullying and workplace bullying. Online at apa.org/topics/bullying.

Minding the Workplace was founded by David Yamada, professor of law and director of the New Workplace Institute at Suffolk University Law School in Boston. This site contains support, resources, and information on legal remedies for workplace bullying. Online at newworkplace.wordpress.com.

INDEX

ABOUT THE AUTHOR

Karla McLaren, M.Ed., is an award-winning author, social science researcher, and empathy pioneer. Her lifelong work focuses on her grand unified theory of emotions and empathy, which revalues even the most "negative" emotions and opens startling new pathways into self-awareness and healthy empathy. She is the founder and CEO of Emotion Dynamics LLC and the creator of the online learning site EmpathyAcademy.org.

Her applied work, Dynamic Emotional Integration® (also known as DEI), is a groundbreaking approach to emotions and empathy that reveals the genius and healing power within the emotional realm. Since 2015, Karla has taught and licensed an international group of DEI professionals across the US, South America, Canada, the UK, and Europe.

Karla is a certified Human Resources Administrator and a certified Career Development Facilitator who helps people find their ideal professions and identify the emotional labor, emotion work, and empathy work they're expected to perform (or expect others to perform, often without realizing it). When these forms of labor are brought out into the open and managed skillfully, individuals and organizations can avoid unnecessary conflict, burnout, and loss of productivity — and they can build an emotionally well-regulated workplace together.

Karla consults with business owners, managers, and workers across the globe, and is the developer of the Emotional Dynamics at Work® consulting and training process, which helps individuals, teams, and organizations develop shared emotional skills, humane and emotionally well-regulated workplaces, and effective communication processes that help the workplace actually *work*.

She is also the codeveloper, with nurse-educator Tino Plank, MSN, RN, of the Healthy Empathy® consulting and training process for healthcare professionals. Healthy Empathy helps health and healing professionals develop sustainable empathy and compassion skills in their high-empathy-demand practices, in their workplaces, and in their lives.

Karla has also put all of this knowledge into practice; she runs four businesses and works with DEI licensees, contractors, and employees across the world. Together, this empathic community connects with each other; identifies and supports each other's emotional labor, emotion work, and empathy work; laughs uproariously; complains, argues, and commiserates with one another; and continually updates their communication and intercultural skills as they work to bring emotional skills and healthy empathy to everyone.

Karla is the author of *Embracing Anxiety: How to Access the Genius in This Vital Emotion* (2020), *The Dynamic Emotional Integration® Workbook* (2018), *The Art of Empathy: A Complete Guide to Life's Most Essential Skill* (2013), *The Language of Emotions: What Your Feelings are Trying to Tell You* (2010), and many online and multimedia courses at EmpathyAcademy.org.

Karla is also the coauthor (with cult expert Dr. Janja Lalich) of *Escaping Utopia: Growing Up in a Cult, Getting Out, and Starting Over* (2017). She lives in Northern California with her family and is online at karlamclaren.com.

ABOUT SOUNDS TRUE

Sounds True is a multimedia publisher whose mission is to inspire and support personal transformation and spiritual awakening. Founded in 1985 and located in Boulder, Colorado, we work with many of the leading spiritual teachers, thinkers, healers, and visionary artists of our time. We strive with every title to preserve the essential "living wisdom" of the author or artist. It is our goal to create products that not only provide information to a reader or listener but also embody the quality of a wisdom transmission.

For those seeking genuine transformation, Sounds True is your trusted partner. At SoundsTrue.com you will find a wealth of free resources to support your journey, including exclusive weekly audio interviews, free downloads, interactive learning tools, and other special savings on all our titles.

To learn more, please visit SoundsTrue.com/freegifts or call us toll-free at 800.333.9185.